THE UNIVERSITY OF
WINCHESTER

Martial Rose Library
Tel: **01962 827306**

Terr
tre. S
Univ
She

To be returned on or before the day marked above, subject to recall.

For my parents, Morris and Florence Stoller

TALES OF THE TRICYCLE THEATRE

TERRY STOLLER

Methuen Drama in association with
The Society for Theatre Research

B L O O M S B U R Y
LONDON • NEW DELHI • NEW YORK • SYDNEY

Bloomsbury Methuen Drama

An imprint of Bloomsbury Publishing Plc

50 Bedford Square	175 Fifth Avenue
London	New York
WC1B 3DP	NY 10010
UK	USA

www.bloomsbury.com

First published in Great Britain in 2013 by Methuen Drama in association with
The Society for Theatre Research

British Library Cataloguing-in-Publication Data
A catalogue record for this book is available from the British Library.

ISBN: HB: 978-1-4081-8315-1
PB: 978-1-4081-8380-9
ePub: 978-1-4081-8520-9

Library of Congress Cataloging-in-Publication Data
Stoller, Terry.
Tales of the Tricycle Theatre / Terry Stoller.
pages cm
"First published in Great Britain in 2013 by Methuen Drama in association
with The Society for Theatre Research"–T.p. verso.
Summary: "An inside look at London's Tricycle Theatre which with its
series of verbatim plays has made a significant contribution to
contemporary political theatre"– Provided by publisher.
Includes bibliographical references and index.
ISBN 978-1-4081-8315-1 (hardback) – ISBN 978-1-4081-8380-9 (paperback)
1. Tricycle Theatre–History. 2. Theaters–England–London. 3. Political plays,
English. 4. English drama–21st century. I. Title.
PN2596.L7T75 2013
792'.09421–dc23
2012049773

Typeset by Newgen Imaging Systems Pvt, Ltd, Chennai, India
Printed and bound in India

CONTENTS

FIGURES

ACKNOWLEDGEMENTS

My heartfelt thanks go to Nicolas Kent for trusting me to write about his extraordinary theatre and for opening doors so that I could accomplish that goal. And to Mary Lauder who extended her friendship and so graciously helped me every step of the way. Without the support of Nick and Mary, I could not have written this book. They let me look through their archives, made space for me in their already crowded offices, and allowed me to ask them hundreds of questions. I appreciate their generosity and the generosity of their staff – first and foremost, the incomparable Trish McElhill. She helped me immeasurably throughout the entire project. Many thanks also to Tricycle staff present and past, Shaz McGee, Zoe Ingenhaag, Holly Conneely, Gillian Christie, Lucy Freeman, Kate Walker and Sarah O'Hanlon. And thanks to Rod Rhule for his kindness during the time that he was the Tricycle's cinema manager and for his friendship ever since.

Oral history is the heart of this book, and I am indebted to the Tricycle's architect, and the actors, directors, designers, writers, board members, and staff, who all shared their stories with me. Their names and words appear throughout these pages.

I've found good friends while working on this project. Claudette Williams and Tariq Jordan made introductions for me and were fabulous companions during my visits to London. I was so lucky too that friends from New York were living in London. Jennifer Parker-Starbuck, Josh Abrams and Zeena Starbuck cheered me on and were always up for seeing the latest Tricycle production, even the Sunday marathons! Thanks to their friend Graham White for sharing his expertise, and to my friend Loren Edelson for her wise counsel. And a very special thanks to Elaine Yudkovitz.

A huge thank-you goes to Kate Dorney, curator of Modern & Contemporary Performance at the V&A. She fielded many questions and gave me invaluable advice. Thanks very much to the staff at the V&A Theatre and Performance archives who worked hard on my behalf. I also appreciate the assistance of Guy Baxter, formerly of the V&A, and Rosamund King at the Brent Archives.

I owe a great debt to Dr Marion O'Connor and Dr Trevor R. Griffiths of the Society for Theatre Research for their efforts on my behalf. They not only accepted my manuscript for publication and gave me terrific feedback, but also went out and found our wonderful copublisher.

Thank you so much to my editor Mark Dudgeon at Methuen Drama for his patience and excellent advice. And my thanks also to Emily Hockley.

I thank my friend and mentor Jonathan Kalb for his guidance and for allowing me to use portions of my articles from HotReview.org.

I'm exceedingly grateful to Michael Billington for contributing his exquisite foreword.

There are many people to thank for permission to use their photographs. First, there's Mike Thacker, who, without ever having met me, went to a great deal of trouble to take the beautiful photos of the Tricycle on the Kilburn High Road for the cover of the book. Thank you to John Haynes for allowing me to use his production photos, and thank you to Tristram Kenton for his production photo of *Tactical Questioning*. Thanks to Joy Richardson for her photo of the *Lonely Cowboy* rehearsal. It was Kate Dorney who told me about the Douglas H. Jeffery collection at the V&A, and I'm so happy to be able to include his photographs in this book. A very big thanks to Amy King at the V&A Theatre and Performance archives and Davina Cheung at V&A Images for locating the production photos I needed.

And finally I'd like to thank my sister Susan Stoller for the countless powwows and for her unwavering love and support.

FOREWORD

I've been going regularly to the Tricycle since it opened in 1980. What images and memories does it conjure up? The hazards of a slow, stop-start drive up Kilburn High Road, which seems to exist in a permanent state of disrepair. The pleasure of sitting in that plain, simple auditorium based, as theatre consultant Iain Mackintosh proudly told me, on the model of the Georgian courtyard theatre. Above all, the stimulus of knowing that I'd see something on stage that really mattered. I've had great, good, and sometimes so-so experiences at the Tricycle. I don't recall anything that seemed pointless or trivial.

If I focus on the Nicolas Kent years (1984–2012), it is because I'm not sure the extent of his achievement has even now been fully grasped. A lot has been written about the 'tribunal' plays that he, Richard Norton-Taylor, and, initially, John McGrath pioneered. But what they really signalled was a belief that theatre had the capacity to address the big issues of our time. G. K. Chesterton said of Bernard Shaw that 'he has introduced into the theatre the things that no one else had introduced into a theatre – the things in the street outside'.[1] By that Chesterton meant such subjects as arms manufacture, medical ethics, female liberation. Kent and his team have done precisely the same. They have taken subjects traditionally regarded as the province of the press or BBC's *Newsnight*, including illegal arms sales or institutionalised racism, and put them on stage. They have even, in the case of Gillian Slovo's remarkable *The Riots*, quite literally reflected what was happening on the streets outside.

There is a nonsensical belief in some quarters that big issues don't necessarily make for good theatre. The Tricycle has knocked that firmly on the head by staging work about Iraq (*Justifying War*), the use of security to excuse curtailment of liberty (*Guantanamo: 'Honor*

Bound to Defend Freedom'), the successive invasions of a particular country (*The Great Game: Afghanistan*), and reliance on the nuclear deterrent (*The Bomb – A Partial History*). And the Tricycle has not merely tackled big issues. It has consistently exposed the fault lines in British society. As David Hare wrote of *The Colour of Justice*, based on the Macpherson inquiry into the Metropolitan Police's handling of the Stephen Lawrence case: 'In that act of editing, he [Norton-Taylor] laid before a live audience all the subtleties and intricacies of British racism, all its forms and gradations, with a clarity which I had never seen emulated by television, documentary or newspaper.'[2]

This is the great lesson to be learned from Kent's Tricycle: that issues matter and that theatre, as a medium, can have an impact wholly disproportionate to its size. It is, I'm happy to say, a lesson that has been absorbed by other theatres. As I write this, I have lately seen on successive evenings a scientific lecture on the dangers of overpopulation, *Ten Billion*, at the Royal Court's Theatre Upstairs and a verbatim play about the Syrian civil war, *The Fear of Breathing*, at the Finborough Theatre. I was asked by highly intelligent American students at a summer school whether work on such momentous issues did not cry out to be seen in bigger spaces. My answer was that information and ideas have a habit of quickly spreading, and I cited the example of the Tricycle. What is impressive is the way work that originates in a 235-seat theatre in north London ignites a national debate, gets seen on television (*The Colour of Justice*), and, in the case of *The Great Game: Afghanistan*, is even given a special Washington performance for the benefit of the US Defense Department.

The Tricycle is rightly lauded for its political adventurousness. But it is also dedicated to the cause of good drama. One reason why *The Colour of Justice* was so effective was that it exposed the layers of deception within the Metropolitan Police with a Sophoclean irony. And over the years, Kent's Tricycle has realised that the best way to attract a diverse audience is to present fine plays from a wide variety of sources. August Wilson's monumental survey of black American experience has been assiduously charted, with *Joe Turner's Come and Gone* an outstanding highlight. Arthur Miller's *Broken Glass*, brilliantly revived by Iqbal Khan, offered a riveting portrait of the way American 1930s anti-Semitism led to a debilitating desire for assimilation. And Lynn Nottage's *Fabulation*, boasting a suitably fabulous performance by Jenny Jules, sharply satirised the social snobbery and inner vacancy of the new black bourgeoisie.

These are all American plays. But the Tricycle has also been home to generations of black British writers (as well as actors and directors) ranging from veterans such as Mustapha Matura and Alfred Fagon to younger figures like Roy Williams, Kwame Kwei-Armah and Bola Agbaje. Unsurprisingly, given Kilburn's rich ethnic mix, the Tricycle has also played host to some of the best Irish plays: the list is long and ranges from Brendan Behan's *The Hostage* and Mary O'Malley's *Once a Catholic* to Marie Jones's *Stones in His Pockets* and Frank McGuinness's *Greta Garbo Came to Donegal*. Although I'd like to have seen more Tom Murphy, who ranks with Brian Friel amongst the best living Irish dramatists, the Tricycle has long been conspicuous for its proud wearing of the green.

As Nicolas Kent departs and Indhu Rubasingham succeeds him, the Tricycle will inevitably change. But it's good to have the theatre's history recorded in hard covers. Over the course of three decades, it has done many remarkable things. It has been both defiantly local and proudly international, it has held a mirror up to British society, and, above all, it has proved that political engagement is not incompatible with the highest artistic standards. It has helped make my life as a critic worthwhile and has ensured that it is worth enduring the slow chug-chug up the Kilburn High Road for the riches that lie at one's destination.

Michael Billington
July 2012

Introduction

This book is indeed about a remarkable theatre, a theatre that reaches out to its multicultural community and takes its political and social responsibilities seriously. The Tricycle opened its doors in 1980 on a lively high street in Kilburn, a decidedly untheatrical neighborhood in northwest London. Nicolas Kent became its artistic director in 1984. Throughout his tenure, he guided that theatre with vision and a singular dedication. Six months after Kent took the job at the Tricycle, general manager Mary Lauder joined him there, and for almost three decades, Kent and Lauder together tended their theatre, creating what actor Kobna Holdbrook-Smith calls 'a national treasure'.

Although I'm based in New York City, I had heard about the Tricycle in the late nineties: a small London theatre was staging trial transcripts (actually an inquiry, I soon found out). But it wasn't until 2004 that I really got drawn in by the Tricycle when its verbatim play *Guantanamo: 'Honor Bound to Defend Freedom'* received international press coverage. I saw the play in the West End and again in New York City when it came to my hometown a couple of months later. Then I found out that the Tricycle has a true interest in its community and over the years has produced black plays, Irish plays, and Jewish plays. And that's when I decided to make my way to Kilburn for a firsthand look at this trailblazing theatre.

It's hard not to fall in love at first sight with the Tricycle. It's in an old-fashioned, funky building, which has a snazzy modern cinema extension that opens to the side road. At 269 Kilburn High Road, you enter the 1920s building onto aluminium checker-plate flooring. The narrowish entrance is partly framed by signs that announce the current production. When you venture inside the 'warren', as actress Pauline Black describes it, a clanging overhead moving sign illustrates the many offerings at the Tricycle: drama, comedy, film, artwork, food and drink. You continue down a long, mirrored corridor onto blue carpet imprinted with red tricycles, past the small box office. Along the way are production posters, glass cases with photographs, and the many articles about the latest production. Then four Ralph Steadman paintings lead the way into the auditorium. From the side road, Buckley Road, you enter the upstairs foyer of the swanky sunken cinema, all light and airy, with brightly coloured walls in its alcoves. And everywhere you look, in the old and the new space, there are skylights.

The Tricycle's admiration for African American playwrights James Baldwin and August Wilson is apparent in the rooms named for them. The James Baldwin Studio and the August Wilson Creative Space house education programmes, workshops for children of all ages, parties, and special programmes for the socially excluded. When the theatre was severely damaged in a fire in 1987, Baldwin showed his regard with a contribution to its appeal campaign: 'The Tricycle Theatre was a marvellous community reality and I was very happy that it housed my play *The Amen Corner* so generously. It has disappeared in fire but I believe those ashes are alive with challenge and promise.'[1]

The theatre reemerged after the fire even stronger, with improvements to the premises. In his 2007 article 'Stage right', Michael Billington rated the Tricycle as one of a small group of modern theatres in Britain that are 'totally successful'.[2] Kent says, it is an exciting building to watch a play in. He also says that 'it's a difficult building in many ways for an artistic director because of the restrictions – lack of wing space, lack of flexibility of the seating, and various other things like height restrictions that don't make life any easier. But in a way, those obstacles concentrate the mind.' Writer-actor Shane Connaughton is an enthusiast for the 235-seat theatre: 'It's one of those intimate theatres, yet with an epic feel to it. And there aren't many spaces in London like that, or anywhere for that matter.' (Sources for most of the interview material have not been added as notes. See Bibliography for details.)

In June 2006, I began to collect an oral history of the theatre in a series of interviews with people who have worked there: board members, staff, directors, playwrights, actors and designers. Granted I asked some leading questions, about the unique opportunities at the Tricycle and about what the theatre means to them, but I must report that I heard this refrain: that the Tricycle was welcoming, that artists could feel safe there, that they were taken care of by Nick Kent and Mary Lauder and everyone else on the staff. Actress Marion Bailey calls it 'one of the proper places in London, where you always feel you're going to be respected and looked after'. That's in contrast to other places, she says, where 'you really don't feel that. Some places you feel as an actor the whole building would run like clockwork if it only weren't for the actors getting in the way.' For actor Michael Cochrane, working at the Tricycle is much more than just a job because everyone there cares 'unaffectedly about the human condition'. Playwright Winsome Pinnock, who was a writer-in-residence and a member of the theatre's playwrights group, says the Tricycle is 'a place to belong as a writer, and where you feel you belong as a black woman'.

People get hooked on the Tricycle. Architect Tim Foster, a member of the board, began his relationship with the Tricycle in the late seventies, when cofounders Ken Chubb and Shirley Barrie asked him to build the theatre: 'It's become much more than a professional relationship. It's something that I've been involved with from the very beginning that I feel passionately about, and want to see it continue to flourish.' Writer Kerry Lee Crabbe, whose connection to the theatre started in the eighties, maintains an abiding affection for the Tricycle: 'What I'd kind of like – particularly when I think, Oh, God, how am I going to pay the rent? – I'd kind of like to move in there.

There's all sorts of stuff I miss, like stand-up comedy, jazz nights. I'd like just to be plugged in there. I often said to Nick in desperation: "I'd do anything. I'll sweep up, if you want me to. I'll work behind the bar.'"

And I know what he means. I'd sweep up too if that meant I could spend more time there. The Tricycle, nicknamed the Trike, is usually alive with activity. There are children's workshops, art exhibitions, play rehearsals, films in the cinema. During the week, you might see pensioners on their way to a drop-in advice session. Or school groups coming in for a weekday matinee. Or the youth theatre company off to rehearse its latest production. On Sunday, there might be a public event to support human rights.

Saturday at the Tricycle can be a standout experience. On a typical Saturday afternoon (before the main show's matinee and evening performances), kids are running up and down the foyer, skipping from the old building to the new one, while they wait for the theatre's doors to open and the children's play to begin. Some are carrying gifts upstairs to a preshow birthday party in the Baldwin Studio. Some are queueing with their parents in front of the auditorium so that they can rush in when it's time. Still others have been filing into the cinema to see a family film. And locals and visitors like me are hanging out in the bar area, perhaps having a cup of tea and a piece of cake or looking at the art in the gallery/café or meeting up with friends.

I have seen the word 'unfashionable' used by the press to describe the Tricycle's neighborhood. Kilburn, says actress Heather Tobias, was run down in the 1980s. But the area has been gentrifying somewhat. In the early 2000s when actor David Ganly first started working at the Tricycle, 'there were still a lot of little-old-man pubs in Kilburn'.

David Ganly: These pubs have now turned into gastropubs, and they're gone. And somehow or other, the Tricycle, in spite of its glitz and glamour, still has the capacity to be a wonderful meeting point and central point for communities – not just the Irish and not just the African Caribbean. The catchment is huge in that part of north London. It has a wonderful way of pulling people in. It knows what it's about.

Jenny Jules [actress and board member]: I know the make-up of the community is changing. It's not so black and Irish now. There are Brazilians, Somalians, a huge Asian community, Turkish. There are people from everywhere in Brent. But the Tricycle still feels to me a place where ethnic minorities can have a voice, where they can go and listen, where they can go and experience something, where they can tell their hidden history.

The tradition at Tricycle press nights for many years was to serve up curry delivered by the neighborhood's own Shamrat Tandoori Restaurant. Rick Warden's first contact with the Tricycle was in the late nineties working in a front-of-house job at the theatre for a few months in between acting gigs. That 'extraordinary' curry looms large in his mind. He says it is one of his 'lasting memories' from that period. 'The bar staff got to eat it when everyone had gone. So come one o'clock at night after press night, you'd find four or five bar staff devouring the rest of this curry.' When he returned to the Tricycle in 2009 to join the acting company of *The Great Game*, he found that it hadn't changed. 'It was the same curry, and it was still that good.'

The curry might have been the same, but the theatre is forward looking and ever expanding in its programming and ever changing (even physically). Running the Tricycle was a lot of work for Kent, Lauder, and their small staff – which included longtime members, administrative manager Trish McElhill, technical director Shaz McGee, and education director Gillian Christie, plus newer members of the team, associate producer Zoe Ingenhaag and marketing director Holly Conneely. From the first day that I paid them a visit, the staff welcomed me into the fold. It was a wonderful adventure getting to know all of them and learning about their very special theatre.

This book is a narrative interwoven with oral history. In the first chapter, I give an overview of the Tricycle's story. The chapters that follow focus on the three mainstays of the theatre's repertoire, from 1980 to 2012: black theatre, Irish theatre, and verbatim plays as well as the Tricycle's play cycles, *The Great Game: Afghanistan* and *The Bomb – A Partial History*. While I know the categories can be contested – especially the term 'black theatre' – I'm using them in an expansive manner to refer to the writers, plays, subject matter, and casts at the Tricycle, and I've chosen highlights from those productions as points of focus. The final chapter contains tales that take you into the Tricycle's dressing rooms, along with a variety of extra stories that I found irresistible.

1

A brief ride through the Tricycle's history

The early days

When Ken Chubb and Shirley Barrie arrived in London from Canada in the early seventies, the fringe-theatre movement was well under way. Alternative venues were opening up in London pubs and basements. Lunchtime theatre had caught on and was being offered by the likes of the Soho and the Basement. After a lunchtime-theatre group suddenly departed the Pindar of Wakefield pub near King's Cross, Chubb got permission from the publican to try his hand at producing theatre in the pub's back room. And so in 1972, he and Barrie founded a theatre company. They called themselves the Wakefield Tricycle Company (WTC), borrowing Wakefield from the pub's name and balancing the reference to the medieval mystery cycle with the playful twist of Tricycle.

The company did a season of lunchtime plays at the Pindar of Wakefield, premiering with Sam Shepard's *Red Cross* and presenting an array of international one acts from Ionesco's *The Lesson* and Jean Tardieu's *The Sonata and the Three Gentlemen* and *Mr. Me* to American playwright Tom Eyen's *The White Whore and the Bit Player*. They went on to produce lunchtime theatre (increasingly by

English writers, Barrie wrote)[1] at the King's Head (1973), the Soho Poly (1974), and the Africa Centre (1975). At first, Barrie and Chubb funded their plays themselves. 'We would share any proceeds with the people who worked on the show – if there were any', Barrie says. 'And sometimes there weren't, and sometimes people got enough for bus fare, and sometimes they got a little bit of money.'

Barrie was approached at the Pindar of Wakefield by Nicholas Barter, then Arts Council drama officer. He thought the company was doing good work and suggested that the group apply for funding. But the grants weren't generous, Barrie says. One of the goals of the Association of Lunchtime Theatres, organised in 1972 (the WTC was a member), was to get enough funding to pay actors at least £3 a week.

Nevertheless, the WTC attracted accomplished artists along with emerging talents.

Ken Chubb: The thing about London is that there are far more actors than there are jobs. We met a lot of actors through the Aba Daba Music Hall at the Pindar of Wakefield. They'd do 'turns' to keep their hand in when out of work. So it's a buyer's market in a sense. And when you approach somebody with a good part and give them a kind of spotlight, they're attracted to it.

He cast Frank Middlemass in the John Antrobus play *Why Bournemouth?* at the King's Head in 1973. 'John was already established as a playwright. And the King's Head was established as a venue', says Chubb. 'So people would do things for very little. I think Frank did get paid, but I think it was a very small amount of money.'

Lunchtime theatre was also a chance for young actors to get 'seen'. Anton Phillips, an actor-director who has had a long association with the Tricycle, remembers performing in one of the group's early productions at the King's Head (Colin Bennett's *Love Story*, 1973), which he calls a 'totally obscure play'. 'This is one of the things Ken and Shirley really liked', Phillips told me, 'very avant-garde plays'. In a stroke of good fortune for him, a casting director who came to see fellow actor John Duttine spotted Phillips and invited him to be in the TV series *Space: 1999*. 'I ended up doing the whole series', he says, 'from a little lunchtime play'.

The company also produced evening shows at the Bush, the Open Space, and the King's Head. Phillips played Francis of Assisi in the WTC's production of Arrabal's *Ceremony for a Murdered Black* (1973) at the Howff. What he recalls about that show is that a young Simon MacCorkindale, in his pre–TV star days, served as the 'body in a trunk'. During the seventies, the WTC roster also included actors Cheryl Campbell, John Castle, Paul Freeman and Dudley Sutton.[2]

It was in 1974 that Chubb and Barrie took to the road, touring the United Kingdom for the first couple of years with original, issue-oriented rock-musical revues. Chubb says this was partly a financial consideration.

Ken Chubb: There was a limit to the amount of revenue you could make at lunchtime, or that you could ask for in terms of grants. As soon as you said you'd take something outside of London, the grant structure went up considerably. And the sizes of audiences went up – not always, but sometimes. It depended what circuit you were on. The Arts Council was very interested in developing a circuit. There was a circuit of studio theatres at the universities, and that took in some things, but the council was interested in using community centres and other venues just to spread theatre around the country.

The list of venues that WTC played included working men's clubs.

Ken Chubb: I remember in one working men's club, we actually had to stop the play before the end of the first act because they had to have their bingo at nine o'clock whatever happened. And then after they'd done the bingo, we could resume. [Which they did.] There was still lots of the evening left, and we had another act to do. But I had no idea they were going to be so religious about it.

They just wanted to do the bingo during what they thought was the interval. But in fact it was locked in at nine o'clock. There were lots of things like that.

The company's revues had titles such as *A Roof Over Your Head* (by Derek Smith and Peter John) and *The Counter Inflation Christmas Show* (by Shirley Barrie and Eric Twiname). *The End of the World Show* (by Derek Smith), which stopped over at the Bush in 1975 during a tour, was described by *Stage and Television Today* as a 'science fiction rock musical with cheery political overtones'.[3]

> **Shirley Barrie:** We were also becoming caught up in that very political environment that was London theatre in the seventies. Everybody had a political angle, it seemed. I would go to meetings, and people would introduce themselves as Marxist Leninist or Maoist or a Trotskyite or from the Socialist Workers Party. And there were a lot of social issues that were bubbling away and burning away. And we got very involved with some of them, and that was reflected in the kind of work that we did about housing and multicultural casting and things like that.

By the late seventies, they were commissioning and producing new plays by writers Olwen Wymark (*Loved* at the Bush and on tour in 1978) and Adrian Mitchell (*Hoagy, Bix and Wolfgang Beethoven Bunkhaus* on tour and at the King's Head in 1979). And they were touring university theatres, Chubb says, which meant working in 300-seat black boxes. When they wanted to bring those shows into London, they would be 'stuck in a very small upstairs room of a pub', forcing them to cut pieces off their sets and spoiling the show. 'The smaller theatres were limited in terms of the number of audience you could get in, but also in terms of the size of the performance. You just couldn't have six or seven people on the stage of the King's Head. You could, but it was hopelessly cramped. The King's Head was a wonderful space, but it was very limiting, as was the Bush.' And, Barrie adds, when they played at those venues, the productions would be connected with the venue rather than with their company. Chubb and Barrie set out to get a theatre of their own in London.

Finding a home

Before fixing on Kilburn, the couple approached the borough of Kensington and Chelsea with the idea for a theatre under the arches of the motorway in Notting Hill. That borough wasn't prepared to come up with enough money, says Chubb. They turned to their home council of Brent instead. The Labour-controlled council liked the idea, in particular the chairman of the leisure services committee, Terry Hanafin. He was really enthusiastic about having a professional theatre in Brent, Barrie says. Hanafin told me that his committee had adopted a policy 'to improve arts and entertainments in the relatively deprived southern part of the borough of Brent'. When Chubb and Barrie approached the council, he says, 'we thought, that's great, we've got a match between our policy and their aims and skills'.

> **Terry Hanafin:** But we didn't know how good they were. We got our officers to find out from people like the Arts Council of Great Britain, who gave very positive reports. However, we wondered whether they had that magic that you experience from theatre at its best. So a number of Brent councillors went to see some of their productions. We went to see *Loved* by Olwen Wymark in October '78, *Zastrozzi* by George F. Walker in December '78, and *Hoagy, Bix and Wolfgang Beethoven Bunkhaus* by Adrian Mitchell in early '79 – three very different productions. And we were wowed.

Meanwhile, with the help of Ray Beswick, the council's arts and entertainments manager, the hunt for the building began.

In the 1970s, architect Tim Foster was working with Iain Mackintosh at Theatre Projects Consultants. Theatre Projects had been helping Chubb and Barrie devise the plans for Notting Hill. When Kensington and Chelsea turned them down, and the couple got Brent's support, Foster came on board for what would be his first theatre as an architect in his own right.

Tim Foster: I used to get called by Ken from time to time, saying they had found another building to look at. And I went with them and must have looked at half a dozen different buildings, from old, disused garages to all sorts of buildings.

Then they took a look at 269 Kilburn High Road. At the time it was occupied by Brent Community Relations Council, the Citizens Advice Bureau and some of the council's housing staff.

Tim Foster: It was the place where people who lived in social housing went to pay their rent and complain. So we went to see this building. It was originally a Foresters Hall built in the 1920s, I think really as a dance hall. But when we went into the building, you couldn't see the space at all because the council had divided up what is now the theatre into little cellular offices with cardboard partitions.

However over the tops of the cubicles, Chubb says, you could see the old proscenium arch. 'It was a big building, and you knew it was solid. And you knew that a theatre could be dropped in there.' The offices weren't eager to leave, says Hanafin, but the council persuaded them that they would be moved to better facilities. They vacated Foresters Hall, and Foster went to work. He had to figure out how to create a theatre on a very limited budget. 'It was at that point', he says, 'that I came up with the idea of the scaffolding theatre'.

The scaffolding theatre

Foster drew on a number of inspirations for the Tricycle: the scaffolding theatre from the Pittsburgh Public Theater in Pennsylvania and the idea for a freestanding structure in an old building from the Royal Exchange in Manchester, which had opened in 1976. The Tricycle's courtyard design was modelled on the Georgian playhouse in Richmond, Yorkshire (eighteenth-century theatre was a special interest of Mackintosh's). Foster says he was excited when he saw the playhouse and thought the simple, rectangular theatre space 'could be quite easily reproduced in scaffolding'. The Tricycle's design was based on a standard contractors' scaffolding system, he says, with almost everything coming 'straight out of the catalogue'.

Tim Foster: The company had taken over the building and had a little money to deal with the safety issues. They didn't have any money for the theatre. So we got a builder in, and we went ahead and did the work to the fabric of the building. Meanwhile they started trying to raise some funds. And I don't think it was until about April 1980 that they finally said, 'OK, I think we can just about raise the money. Let's go for it.' So between April and September, when the theatre opened, we built it. And of course with the scaffolding system, it was very easy to build. The other aspect of the design was that it should be possible for it to be built by the theatre's own staff. In other words, by theatre carpenters, not by building contractors.

We dealt with the fire escapes, and we put some ventilation into the roof. The structure of the theatre sat on old railway sleepers because it was cheaper than making foundations for it. It was built by theatre staff, me and some representatives from the scaffold company who'd never seen anything like this. They got quite excited about it. They used to come down on their weekends and help as well. And it was built in about three months.

Foster and company installed metal scaffolding (originally standard safety orange, later painted red) with blue 'canvas gallery fronts', Mackintosh wrote, 'inspired by the cockpit of ocean racing yachts'.[4] And in keeping with the theatre company's philosophy that the stage be brought out into the same space as the audience, Foster says, they pulled the whole stage 6 m in front of the old proscenium. The seating was fixed benches, which also had a political rationale.

Tim Foster: It was supposed to be a democratic theatre where people were pushed together and made to share a communal experience. And I still think bench seats are a wonderful way of achieving that sort of audience cohesion. We're creating something of the eighteenth-century atmosphere in the theatre. I think modern audiences want to sit in comfortable chairs, sit there and say, 'Entertain me'. So the seating was deliberately not terribly comfortable. And the other important aspect of it, which still causes arguments to this day, is that it wasn't numbered. You can't reserve a seat; you simply reserve a place. It's first come, first served as to where you sit. With modern audiences, that causes some problems. So they now have a system, where you can pay more money and reserve seats.

Tip-up benches have replaced a number of the fixed ones; there are individual seats on the sides of the stalls and the upper level, and generally the seating is more comfortable. And even though about 40 seats are allocated, much of the theatre is still unreserved (in spring 2012), so that when the house opens, there can be a raucous scrambling for seats as patrons seek out the 'perfect' one. Foster says the regulars have a system: 'They arrive, they go into the auditorium, they put their coat on their seat, and then they go to the bar.' In the auditorium, the benches still create the feel of community. On the tip-up benches, you have to coordinate with your neighbor sitting down and standing up. And as Kent once told a reporter: 'If you cross your legs, then the whole row has to cross their legs.'[5]

A theatre in Kilburn

Chubb and Barrie adopted an inclusive policy for the Tricycle.[6] (In deference to Brent Council, they dropped the Wakefield – 'a red herring' – from the name of the theatre.)

Shirley Barrie: That we were going to be a theatre in the community, and we were going to reflect the community that was around us – which included West Indian, Irish, South Asian – that we were going to have a youth programme and at the time, terribly ambitiously, we were going to continue our touring programme as well.

There were bumps along the road, though, before they opened the theatre: following the Conservative win in the May 1979 general election and the cuts instituted by Margaret Thatcher's government, there were councillors who spoke out against the borough's £50,000 grant for the Foresters Hall conversion and the £25,000 annual grant for the community programmes. (The building of the theatre was also funded by the Arts Council, the Greater London Council [GLC], and, among the donors, the Calouste Gulbenkian Foundation.) A campaign by Hanafin and Chubb secured the council's funding, and by September 1980, Kilburn had its own professional theatre, a 200-seat, two-level auditorium, along with a bar and a space for workshops.[7] On the event of the opening, Catherine Itzin, who chronicled alternative theatre, called the WTC's success in creating the 'innovative theatre space' a tribute to 'its tenacity and its track record'.[8]

Chubb asked artist Ralph Steadman if he would be willing to do something to help them raise money, and Steadman, who kept up a generous relationship with the theatre, donated to the Tricycle 'Seasoned First-Nighters and a First-Time Theatregoer', a cartoon of a full house, with interestingly expressive audience members at the front of the stalls: some perplexed, at least one outraged, one yawning – and some fast asleep. Thirty years later, you could still buy a poster or postcard version of the cartoon at the box office.

The opening of the theatre with *Samba* by Michael Abbensetts went very well, says Chubb. After the celebration, they began the work on developing an audience for the Tricycle. ('It took quite a number of years to build up to a consistent business', he says.) That first season included a Paines Plough production, *Rise of the Old Cloud* by Mike Dorrell, a play about Welsh miners; Snoo Wilson's *Space Ache*, involving cryogenics and a journey into outer space, with music by Nick Bicât (Frances Barber was in the cast); and a carnivalesque show about nuclear power by the provocatively named women's company Cunning Stunts, which ran during the Christmas holiday season – a great success, says Barrie.

In subsequent seasons under Chubb and Barrie, there were new plays; there were entertainments by humorist Ivor Cutler and a People Show Cabaret; and visiting companies like Hull Truck and Foco Novo; and productions by the National Theatre of Brent. The Tricycle presented a series of shows by women's groups in 1981 – the Women's Theatre Group, Bloomers, Monstrous Regiment, Bag and Baggage, Cunning Stunts, Lilith, and Sadista Sisters – part of their 'wide-ranging policy of inclusiveness', says Barrie. It 'was quite a conscious choice to do a season of plays by women, and we suffered for it . . . That was Maggie Thatcher time, and there were repercussions because we were having these radical feminist groups.'

Among the homegrown new plays, a favourite for director Chubb was *Jack Sheppard's Back* (1982–3), the Tricycle's version of the tale of the legendary eighteenth-century thief, penned by Barrie who also wrote the lyrics to Ian Barnett's music, and starring a young Neil Pearson in the title role.

For the community, the Tricycle offered children's programming – and free crèche services when parents attended shows. There were exhibitions of work by local artists, and a local playwrights' group was led by, among others, Anthony Minghella. And people came just to socialise. Chubb remembers the 'amazing atmosphere' of the place: 'Ken Livingstone used to meet people in there on a Saturday all the time before he became mayor of London, back in the days when he was a councillor, Red Ken.'

Funding troubles

Chubb credits the Tricycle's initial survival to support from 'all three levels of government': the borough, the GLC, and the Arts Council. But in the mid-eighties, that support was under threat. In 1984, the Arts Council's *The Glory of the Garden* policy proposed a greater investment for regional organisations while rolling back funding elsewhere, and the Tricycle wound up on a list of those slated to have their grants withdrawn.

There was some unpleasant feedback on the theatre's home turf. The Brent North Conservative MP Dr Rhodes Boyson was quoted in the local press as saying he welcomed the Arts Council decision to withdraw the Tricycle's funds, that he was 'informed' the theatre often produced plays 'aimed at the destruction of the social fabric of our society'. He recommended that arts monies go to amateur groups in his constituency instead.[9]

The attacks on the Tricycle felt very personal to Barrie.

Shirley Barrie: We had worked so hard to get the theatre together and . . . we lived in the borough where the theatre was. I remember going down to the door at home one day to get the mail, and there was a leaflet that they were circulating throughout the whole borough that said we've got to get rid of some of these money-eating things, and in the list was the Tricycle Theatre. It hit you where you lived and where you worked because you felt you had become a political football that was being tossed around as well.

Still 'the borough was strong through it', says Chubb, 'and that was very important because they did own the building . . . and it had been a serious conversion. It was a fair amount of money spent building the theatre.'

Chubb launched an effort to get the Arts Council money back. Andrée Molyneux, a Tricycle board member for almost 30 years, was at that time a director/producer for the BBC. She and other members of the board, including writer Mustapha Matura and chair Bernard Sandler, went with Chubb to make a personal appeal to the Arts Council.

Andrée Molyneux: None of us met beforehand, but we all went to the Arts Council, and because Ken had organised it so well, we all made our own contribution. I think each person only spoke once. And yet we all said exactly the right thing, and without saying anything prepared. Ken had just rung us up individually and asked us questions and said, Yes, it would be good if you emphasised that.

In early 1984, Chubb and Barrie had made the decision to return to Canada.

Ken Chubb: The frustration, I think, in leaving was that it had become more about running the place than about putting on the shows, and that is always a difficult balance. But at that point, I was looking to move on and to move into film and television, which I've been working in ever since.

A new artistic director

'It was the luck of the Irish', says Chubb, that Nicolas Kent's Oxford Playhouse production of *Playboy of the West Indies* by Mustapha Matura came to the Tricycle in February 1984 and did so well. (It had a second run in April.) Kent applied for the job of artistic director, and he was chosen, Molyneux says, because of his record and because of his ideals, which were in accord with those of the board. The main thing, she says, was his interest 'in providing a theatre for the area'. That summer the new artistic director shared his plans with the local press: to build on the programming for the 'working class and ethnic groups in the area' and to continue with plays from regional theatres but to extend the runs of the productions so that the Tricycle would be the place in London to see those shows. He intended to expand the Tricycle's role as 'a community resource' with a greater range of workshops and increased hours for food service – with an eye on people 'coming and going in the building'.[10] By autumn, the foyer, bar, and gallery restaurant had been refurbished. And in January 1985, Mary Lauder became administrator (later called general manager) of the Tricycle, which fitted her, she says, 'in terms of what I thought theatre was about'.

The Tricycle had got back its Arts Council grant at the end of July 1984, read a programme note that September: 'Over 4,000 wrote to the Chairman of the Arts Council on our behalf.'[11] But there were more money problems to come, including the abolition of the GLC.

Nicolas Kent: When I took over, we'd lost the Arts Council grant, so we had to get it back. And then the GLC went down, and then Brent threatened to take their grant away. Every major funder started taking its grant away at one time or other.

The GLC was shut down on 31 March 1986, just a few months after a triumph for the Tricycle: Howard Sackler's *The Great White Hope*, a play based on the first black world heavyweight boxing champion. The production had a big cast and live music. Kent deliberately chose a play of this scale as a strategy to deal with the funding crises the Tricycle faced.

Nicolas Kent: *Great White Hope* in a way owed something to *Nicholas Nickleby*. Trevor Nunn put the RSC on the map in London with that. I realised when the GLC was going down, we were going to be without a grant. I thought we've got to establish ourselves. We've got to do something so big. So we published this souvenir programme which said, the next time you come to this theatre, we won't be here.

Kent told this story about the last of the monies the Trike received from the GLC.

Nicolas Kent: Just after we'd done [*The Great White Hope*], I had various meetings with [GLC leader] Ken Livingstone when Margaret Thatcher was abolishing the GLC. I said, we've done this show, and we're now bankrupt. I need you to underwrite it. A lot of MPs came to see the show. It was a huge success at the time. And [the GLC] wrote us a cheque in the last two days. They wrote us two cheques. One for a photocopy machine, which cost the earth in those days, and we really needed it. And the other was for a grant for £88,000, something around that area. They were just writing cheques to organisations. They had money left over, and it was going to get lost, and we were all lobbying to get the money out. You went to these committee hearings and you stood there and persuaded them, but when the money was voted for you, the problem was getting the cheque because it was so chaotic. It was like the fall of Saigon.

On 'April the first', everything was going to be disbanded. We didn't know if we would ever see this money. And on 'April the sixth', we got a brown envelope with a piece of lined paper wrapped around it that said: 'Send to the Tricycle', and all it said on the envelope was 'Tricycle, London'. That's all it said. And had that cheque not arrived, there was no one to rewrite it. Had it not arrived, there was no way of getting that money. And we got another cheque, for the photocopy machine, which also turned up, which just said, 'Send to the Tricycle'. It said 'Tricycle, Kilburn' on that envelope too, so at least they knew roughly where we were. Thank God the post office delivered both these cheques. Neither had a stamp on it.

During the first few years of Kent and Lauder's tenure, the Tricycle presented Irish and black plays. There was also a docudrama and the National Theatre of Brent's *The Greatest Story Ever Told* (cast: Patrick Barlow and Jim Broadbent). And the Tricycle had a notable success with the Carib Theatre production of James Baldwin's *The Amen Corner*.

Mary Lauder: We had achieved so much, particularly in terms of getting the audience mix right. One was always able to say that the mix of plays that we had on in that period seemed to just be perfect for getting in everybody, and it wasn't all about a black audience for a black show or an Irish audience for an Irish show. It just felt like everything was buzzing.

The fire

On 21 May 1987, coinciding with a production at the Tricycle titled *Burning Point,* a fire broke out in the timber yard next door to the theatre. Lauder was called at five in the morning by the alarm company, informing her that the Tricycle's alarm had gone off. That used to happen a lot, she says. The Tricycle was 'always being burgled and horrible things'. This alarm, the company representative said, might have something to do with the fire in the timber yard. So Lauder made her way to Kilburn thinking she was just going to turn the alarm off. When she got off the train, she couldn't understand why it seemed foggy there, until she realised that it wasn't fog. It was smoke. Nearing the Tricycle, she reached a barrier and asked to be let through.

Mary Lauder: Then I bounced up to this enormous fireman in all the yellow fluorescent stuff, helmet and all that, said, 'I'm the keyholder for the Tricycle Theatre. Would you like me to let you in?' And he said, 'Come with me, love'. He put his arm around me and guided me up to the shutter at the end of the corridor, and said, 'Actually, we don't need your keys'. They had belted their way in already, which they had to because the fire by that time had gone into the roof space. And they were training the hoses on the fire in the roof space, and the water was just gushing down that long corridor. Gushing, gushing, gushing. I stood there in amazement. In the foyer, everything looked just the same. It didn't look different apart from the fact that there was obviously something happening beyond the auditorium doors and there was water coming down.

I rang [Nick] just after seven and said, 'You need to come in. There's been a fire.' And he was very calm. I was very calm. He said, 'How bad is it?' I said, 'Well, the theatre roof's gone'. So he came in, and we started phoning people, and by noon, we had a representative from each of the funding bodies plus the architect, Tim Foster. We all just stood in the yard, looking at the mess, and everybody just assumed that it was going to be rebuilt really quickly, and whilst we were being rebuilt (which at the time foolishly we imagined would take six months), that we would continue the work either in the remaining part of the building, because all the front of house was still fine (the bar and gallery were fine), or we would take shows elsewhere to other theatres. And there was never any question, really.

There was an immediate outpouring of support, Kent wrote, numerous phone calls and messages. Many people 'came in to offer help' and 'commiserate': from the Arts Council's secretary-general Luke Rittner to playwrights Shane Connaughton and Mustapha Matura to representatives from Brent.[12] Pamela Howard, then director of theatre design at the Central Saint Martins College of Art and Design, says that after Kent called her, she and her students went to the Tricycle with buckets and mops.

Pamela Howard: We were only in Holborn, and it wasn't far away, and we helped with the cleanup. We put on our rubber boots and aprons and came down. We borrowed buckets and stuff from the cleaners at the school. I remember saying to the students, 'Everything stop. Get your cleaning things. We're going down to clean up.'

Kent recalls remarking to Lauder a couple of months before the fire: 'For the first time ever, we can see the way ahead. We have some funding for the next year, and I know what we're going to do.' After the building 'disintegrated in the fire', Kent says, 'I thought, Well, you can either leave it or you can fight and try and get it back again'.

Nicolas Kent: We'd opened *The Amen Corner* [in January 1987], which the Minister of the Arts [Richard Luce] had come to see, and he was almost the first to ring up on the day we burnt down. He was a Tory Minister of the Arts, and he rang the box office, the only number he could get through to, and said he wanted to talk to me. He said he would do anything in his power to help us rebuild. We were known as a left-wing theatre, and it was an extraordinary, generous, warm gesture from a man who was part of Margaret Thatcher's government. And he was as good as his word.

Both Foster and Theatre Projects' Iain Mackintosh had turned up the morning of the fire, and Kent told them he wanted the theatre back as it was.

Tim Foster: Now I take that as a compliment. Because I can think of very few theatre directors who having lost their whole theatre would want it back the same as it was before. Most of them would wish to develop something new or different. That was a great tribute, really.

The new theatre after the fire is . . . mostly the original scaffolding, which was simply sent away to be repainted. We made some minor improvements, which you wouldn't notice. The original theatre had some columns at the side of the stage, which were a nuisance, and we got some more seats in, put an extra row at the back of the balcony and an extra row on stage right of the side galleries and also put air conditioning in. To actually put air conditioning into a fringe theatre in 1987 was unheard of.

Nicolas Kent: We raised the roof a bit. And we made a proper control box. We made various small adjustments to it. But the footprint remained the same in that obviously though it had burnt down, we still only had that amount of space available, so we could either start from scratch and come up with something different within the confines of that space, which would have been about the same size whatever you do, and my attitude was, if it ain't broke, don't fix it.

I always think theatres work better in converted spaces. It takes time to understand how to build a theatre. And they had sort of found how to build this, through the good offices of Iain Mackintosh and Tim Foster. And there was something rather makeshift about it that worked. The bench seating has problems, but at least 12 people met their wife in this building. Or the wives met their husbands. Mike Attenborough, who runs the Almeida, met his wife in this building on one of those benches. I just thought this is a theatre that really works.

The rebuilding included the addition of a workshop for props and electrical equipment on the ground floor and a community room on the floor above (the James Baldwin Studio); improvements to the backstage area; and, in the front of house, a remodelled bar and gallery.

The Tricycle kept on with its programmes for quite a while during the construction.

Mary Lauder: There was still loads of work going on because we did the children's shows at Hampstead, and we did a show at Lyric Hammersmith; we did another one at the Donmar. The bar was open. There was lots of music and improv and stuff like that happening in the gallery. It took two years rather than the six months, and certainly towards the end of that two years, we made a conscious decision that we wouldn't be trying to do other stuff as well because it was taking all our energy.

The reopening

The Tricycle had been restored and improved, with a price tag in the range of £1.4 million to £1.5 million, according to press reports. (The original conversion was estimated at £130,000.)[13] The theatre was finally scheduled to reopen in autumn 1989. Then a harrowing backstage drama threatened the opening production, Caryl Phillips's *All or Nothing at All*, a new play about Billie Holiday. Early in rehearsals, Phillips sought to have Kent replaced as director of the play. When that failed, he took legal action against the show to bring it to a halt. The court ruled in the Tricycle's favour, and *All or Nothing at All* premiered that September, with Pauline Black starring as the singer. The theatre was back in business.

The cinema

Thanks to Arts Council Lottery funding for capital projects, by 1998, the Tricycle was able to add a building extension that housed a 300-seat cinema, designed by Tim Foster. I asked the architect about the concept behind creating a modern space to join up with the 1920s building.

Tim Foster: We were building a fairly major new building, which, although it's an extension, is as big as the original building. One of the important things about the site was that it gave the theatre a street presence for the first time ever, although it's on the side street [Buckley Road], not on the main high street. And I believe that you don't do fake buildings. You don't do reproduction buildings. We wanted to do a good modern building.

Brent gave its permission for the modern building provided it didn't overwhelm the Victorian houses on the street, says Foster, which is one of the factors that went into putting the cinema itself below ground. The new building also has a rehearsal room (named for patron Cameron Mackintosh). Plus it has an office space and an art studio.

Administrative manager Trish McElhill, who started working at the Tricycle in 1989, remembers when Kent announced the project.

Trish McElhill: 'I'm going to make the undertaker's next door a cinema' (and that's laughing), and he actually achieved it. That became very special. We were on the other side of that wall [where the old and new buildings connect] in the theatre's bar on a Friday evening, and the cinema was opening on Sunday. We were leaning up against the wall having a drink, smoking, which we were allowed to do at that point. Then Sunday lunchtime we came in and saw this whole layout of the cinema – we hadn't seen it – and it just looked like a theatre set. And it took weeks to actually get used to the idea that it didn't move, that it was a permanent thing.

The education programme

According to the Tricycle's 2011 annual report, there were '50,000+ attendances in 2010/11' in its education and social-inclusion pro-grammes.[14] The education department runs creative workshops for children, starting at age 18 months. That's in addition to the mati-nees for school groups and Saturday entertainment for children. For the older kids, there is the youth theatre as well as workshops that generate productions like *Cricklewood Broadway*, a multicul-tural musical exploration of the community. A Jewish and Muslim youth-theatre group, which is now an independent charity (MUJU Crew), was started at the Tricycle in 2004.

Gillian Christie, then education director, talked with me in 2006 about the special nights sponsored by Bloomberg, when students in the area come to the theatre to see the main show and have supper for £1.50.

Gillian Christie: I'm always pleased, especially if there's a show . . . where you know they're going to absolutely love it, they're going to come out buzzing, they're going to be talking about it. They come out, there's this whole buffet laid on, with food and fruit and biscuits and chocolate, and then in ten minutes the actors are coming out and sitting down and eating, and they can go up and talk to them and ask them questions. I've never had a bad Bloomberg night.

To supplement the theatre's subsidies and a very respectable self-generated income, the Tricycle's development director (from 1996 to 2008, that was Caroline Keely) raises money from membership schemes, trusts, foundations, and, supported by a board committee, puts together fund-raising events, much of that connected to the education department.

Mary Lauder: Where we're at is that we never call it an arts centre. We call it a theatre, a cinema, and a gallery, with an education programme running through the whole thing. The Tricycle train that keeps the three art forms moving is the education programme. But in our heart, the theatre is absolutely at the forefront of what we're doing.

The South Africa connection and the Nelson Mandela clause

Typically the Tricycle has presented about 10 to 12 productions each year: homegrown plays, coproductions and visiting companies, most from Britain and Ireland, and over the years, imports from South Africa.

Mary Lauder: We used to get a bit of flak for bringing work from South Africa [during apartheid], people standing on the pavement handing out leaflets to the audience as they came in. But we were doing work from the Market Theatre in Johannesburg, an integrated company. We believed it was right to bring those performers over.

A Market Theatre production that played at the Tricycle in the 1980s had a profound effect on actress Jenny Jules, who was in the Tricycle's youth-theatre group then. Jules attributes her political education to the Trike.

Jenny Jules: As part of that group of teenagers, I had the best upbringing I could ever have. I was politicised at the Tricycle as well. Because when I decided to be an actor, I was going to go to RADA and I was going to be a star. Then I saw plays at the Tricycle that just blew my mind. I saw a play called *Black Dog – Inj'Emnyama* [1984], and that was by the Market Theatre, Johannesburg. And that changed my life, literally. I learned about apartheid and what that meant, what that did to people's lives. And it made me become much more focused on injustice in the world.

The Tricycle maintained a very special feeling for Nelson Mandela. 'This theatre will only close the day Nelson Mandela dies', actor David Ganly recalls Kent saying to him. It was 7 July 2005, the day terrorists attacked the London transportation system. Ganly was in the cast of Robin Soans's *The Arab-Israeli Cookbook* playing at the Tricycle. (In fact, they did later decide to cancel the performance that night.) Kent's statement had referred to a longtime clause in the Tricycle's contract, which Mary Lauder had explained when I interviewed her in 2006.

Mary Lauder: In the visiting companies' contracts, if I'm ever dealing with a new company, it is guaranteed that the moment they've read through the standard contract, they will ring me up and say, 'What is this clause about when Nelson Mandela dies we're going to cancel the performance?' It's a standard Tricycle clause. It's been in there for a very long time. It has been amended slightly. Originally, it was: we cancel the performance that night as a tribute. But when I negotiated the contract with Talawa Theatre Company, who brought us *Blues for Mr. Charlie* [2004], Kate, who is my equivalent, did the usual, 'What is this? What is this all about, Mary, for goodness' sake?' Then [director] Paulette Randall rings me up and says, 'Look, I'm black. I couldn't be a more ardent supporter of Nelson Mandela, but I am not having you cancel the show. Can we not say that we will nominate a subsequent performance as a tribute to him?' I said, 'That's fine'.[15]

Late breaking news: Kent steps down, and a new artistic director is appointed

In July 2011, in response to yet another budget crunch, with cuts coming from a number of directions, Kent sent this e-mail announcing his resignation:

> **Nicolas Kent:** I am writing to let you know that I am stepping down as Director of the Tricycle in March next year. [He stayed till May 2012.] The cuts in Government funding mean that the Tricycle will receive £348,000 less funding from statutory bodies in the next financial year than it did in 2009/10, and our Arts Council support will be on a par with that received 6 years ago – without even thinking about inflation. This has made maintaining the level and quality of work for which we have become known a hugely difficult challenge, and one perhaps more suited to new hands.[16]

Some months after Kent's departure, I heard from Mary Lauder that she too was leaving the theatre, in October. This was truly the end of an era at the Tricycle, but the theatre was secure with its new leader in place.

Indhu Rubasingham had been appointed as the Tricycle's next artistic director in November 2011. Rubasingham's association with the Tricycle went back to 1998 when Kent asked her to direct at the theatre. In the almost 15 years that followed, while also working in theatres like the Royal Court and the Young Vic, Rubasingham was involved in major projects at the Tricycle in black theatre and political theatre – and by the winter before she assumed the leadership, she had directed an Irish play at the Tricycle.

2

Black theatre at the Tricycle

In creating theatre for a borough – and a city – of diverse cultures, the Tricycle staged comedies, dramas, and musicals about black Britons, Afro-Caribbeans, African Americans and South Africans. It commissioned plays from black dramatists and hosted black theatre companies. As director Paulette Randall says, the Tricycle 'put black work on the theatrical map in a major way'.

The repertoire of plays by writers like August Wilson and Kwame Kwei-Armah provided meaty roles for black artists. Actor Joseph Marcell remarked that the work he gets to do at the Tricycle 'is off the beaten track, and it's wonderfully challenging, and it stretches me as an actor and also as a human being'. Marcell was a member of the company Kent put together for a season of African American plays in 2005–6. Three years later, Kent engaged a company for a season of black British plays.

Marcell is one among many prominent black actors who have performed at the Tricycle. Norman Beaton and Thomas Baptiste, for example, graced the Tricycle's stage in its very first production.

Samba by Michael Abbensetts (1980)

For the Tricycle's grand opening in 1980, Ken Chubb and Shirley Barrie looked close to home. They commissioned a play from the London-based, Guyana-born playwright Michael Abbensetts. Chubb says they 'were quite determined to open with a theatre piece with music', something with a big-band feel.

Ken Chubb: We also wanted to say right from the beginning that the theatre was going to be presenting work reflecting the varied ethnic communities that made up a big part of Brent. We'd known Michael Abbensetts for some time and he lived right around the corner from the theatre, so it seemed a good pairing.

Samba, directed by Chubb, starred Norman Beaton in the role of Alfredo Lamas (formerly Alfred Lewis). As a West Indian in England, Lewis had changed his name and transformed himself into the Latin American Samba King, a successful bandleader of the Gauchos – that is, until rock 'n' roll put him out of business. Now, 20 years later, Alfredo is the owner of the not-so-successful Samba Mini-Cabs in London, dispatching cars alongside his old friend and fellow musician, Selwyn Hall (Thomas Baptiste). In flashbacks, we see and hear the Gauchos in their glory days and learn about some of the low points, including a tour to apartheid South Africa. The play ends happily with a comeback in the offing, but there's also a suggestion that Alfredo needs a political awakening. As he gathers his band together and slips into his Argentinian identity, his daughter (Angela Bruce) takes him to task, saying that times have changed and that he no longer has to pretend – he can be proud of being West Indian.

It was clearly ambitious to open a theatre as well as stage a brand new play. Abbensetts says it was very hectic because they were still building the theatre. He was concerned that his play wasn't getting enough attention. 'There was just too much happening.' But, he says, 'I was more amazed and pleased at what they managed to pull together. And I don't think anyone but Norman could have done it. I'm not saying there aren't actors now, but certainly back then. Norman really was quite an exceptional person.'

Ken Chubb: That cast of Norman and Tom Baptiste, these were senior actors in the community who came and who acted and sang and really gave the place the first sense of what it could be and the aura of what it could be.

Reviewers were enthusiastic about the colourful and comfortable new theatre. Some critics, like Benedict Nightingale, thought the play might have been more hard hitting in dealing with such issues as 'racial identity', but the production was found to be 'good humoured'.[1]

Love in Vain by Bob Mason (1982)

Chubb directed another commissioned theatre piece with music in 1982, but this time the music was the blues. Bob Mason's *Love in Vain* imagines the life and career of the American musician Robert Johnson from 1927 to his violent death in 1938 at age 27. Johnson (dubbed the 'King of the Delta Blues Singers') has folkloric stature, and although he made only two recordings, his songs have been widely performed. Mason wrote that he had been entranced by the myth of Johnson. He used what he learned from Johnson's body of work and 'mixed that with the few facts' known about the singer/guitarist to 'bring him back to life'.[2]

In a cast of seven playing twice as many roles, Julian Littman portrayed Robert Johnson and Pauline Black, the lead singer of Selecter, made her Tricycle debut as his girlfriend Betty Mae. Black was rehearsing for her first acting job when she heard about auditions for *Love in Vain*. She didn't know 'the protocol', so she rang the theatre up, went down to the Tricycle, and auditioned for Chubb and Mason: 'They looked so much like a couple of really lovely uncles, and you just performed your socks off to them.' She got the part of the 'feisty little character', who, she says, 'fitted me like a glove at that particular time'.

Pauline Black: The audiences as I recall were just fantastic . . . I'm sure there were nights when it wasn't particularly full. But I do remember there being quite a sizeable contingent of black people who would come on Monday nights. I think they ran a policy of having it cheaper on one night to attract audiences from some of the ethnic communities who wouldn't normally go to the theatre.[3] And of course because of my background in the music, people knew me from that. They also knew Paul Barber [who played Leroy, the rival for Betty Mae's affections] from various things he had done on the TV. He's a Liverpudlian actor, and he's very full of character. You just had to look at him, and he was funny. Everybody who came to it just entered into the spirit of it. And also it's a fabulous story.

In the Tricycle's early days, 'the work had to be simply done', says Andrée Molyneux. 'There was no money for big sets or anything like that. And yet there were some very interesting things done, in which amazing results were achieved.' *Love in Vain* was an example of that achievement.

Andrée Molyneux: Considering they were doing it in England, in a fringe theatre – I hope it isn't quite a 'fringe' theatre now; because of its reputation it's much more in the mainstream than it was then – it was amazing how well they managed to do it.[4] And to get somebody who could play and sing, and to get one or two American actors who were around [Guy Gregory and Billy J. Mitchell] into this very small cast. Most things had to be done with very small casts, again because of money.

Playboy of the West Indies by Mustapha Matura (1984)

Kent's 1984 production of *Playboy of the West Indies* (Oxford Playhouse Company) had brought him to the Tricycle, and he restaged the play as a kind of anniversary celebration in 1993–4 and again in 2004–5. Kent says this adaptation of Synge's *The Playboy of the Western World* was ideal for the Tricycle. It appealed to the Afro-Caribbeans and the Irish in the area, both groups from a storytelling culture.

Matura's *Playboy* is a lusty version of the story about the young man who believes he has killed his father and on the telling of that deed becomes a local celebrity. It's 1950, and the locale is the Trinidadian fishing village of Mayaro. Ken, the supposed father slayer, finds his way to a rum shop where he seeks refuge. The ladies quickly fall for the stranger. There's Peggy, who runs her father's rum shop, an Obeah woman named Mama Benin, and two impressionable village girls. It's not long before Ken's father appears, very much alive. The two of them fight, and it seems as though this time Ken really has killed the old man. Faced with an actual murder, the locals – including Peggy, his love interest – turn on Ken, going so far as to tie him up. Of course the father revives, and Ken departs, emboldened by his adventures in Mayaro. Poor Peggy is left to lament the loss of the playboy.

In the eighties, Ken was portrayed by Jim Findley, Peggy by Joan-Ann Maynard, and Mama Benin by Mona Hammond; in the nineties, those parts were played by Cyril Nri, Cecilia Noble and Pat Bowie; in 2004–5 by Kobna Holdbrook-Smith, Sharon Duncan-Brewster, and Joy Richardson.

A decade before she acted in the play herself, Cecilia Noble saw the Tricycle's 1984 production.

Cecilia Noble: My relationship with [the Tricycle] goes right back to when I was studying for my A levels . . . We were doing *Playboy* *of the Western World,* so we came to see Mustapha Matura's *Playboy of the West Indies* in 1984. I came here as a student to see it, and little did I know years later I would be playing the same part that I saw. I remember watching them, thinking, I want to be onstage . . . I went to a girls' school, so we didn't go out a lot to trips, and we were all really excited, and I was particularly excited because I was harbouring this ambition to be an actress. It was something I'll never forget, watching it. I sat in the balcony and just watched, and I took it in from an actress's point of view. And ten years later I was in it.

When the play had first been produced in Oxford, Kent told TheatreVOICE in a 2004 interview, people had difficulty under-standing the patois: 'We could have been doing the play in French.' By the nineties, in London, he said, there was 'hardly a problem at all'.[5] But even in the 2000s in the multicultural capital, critics were struggling a bit with the dialect. Alastair Macaulay wrote in his 2004 review for the *Financial Times* that 'there are minutes on end when it is virtually impossible for your average white Londoner to make sense of what these characters are saying'. Yet the *Spectator*'s Lloyd Evans enjoyed the music of the language, saying the dialect was a 'treat to listen to, although it takes a few minutes to attune the ear to its bristling harmonies'.[6]

A glossary was provided to help the audience with some of the local terms like 'bazodee' (meaning crazy) and 'put goat mouth on him' (to wish someone bad luck).[7] Then there was the Trinidadian accent, which Duncan-Brewster knows well because her parents are from Trinidad and Tobago.

Sharon Duncan-Brewster: They were looking for somebody who had a real good Trinidadian accent. When I walked in [to the audition], I don't think Mustapha Matura was sure about me. But when I opened my mouth and started speaking in Peggy's character, his physicality changed. . .

We had some cheeky, cheeky guys on that, real lovable actors, Shango Baku, Malcolm Frederick, Larrington Walker [see Figure 2.1]. It was like having 6 million daddies onstage at the same time. So many jokes. Then alongside Nick in rehearsals. Nick knows West Indian culture. I don't know how, but he knows it. It's in his belly. So he knows about the whole swagger, the pace. In rehearsal, around the table, we couldn't wait to get up. It was flowing. It was such a vibrant play, and physically, we just wanted to get on with it.

Joy Richardson had been one of the village girls (a very giggly one, she admits) in the original production. By 2004, she got the part that she had hoped to play someday: Mama Benin. Richardson says to create the character, she looked to people she knew from Guyana (where she was born) and from Africa for the qualities that the Obeah

FIGURE 2.1 *(From left) Sharon Duncan-Brewster, Malcolm Frederick, Ben Bennett, Shango Baku and Larrington Walker in Mustapha Matura's* Playboy of the West Indies, *2004–5.*

Source: Photograph by Graham Brandon © Victoria and Albert Museum, London.

woman had: 'earthy, playful, witty, sexy, daring, knowledgeable' (see Figure 2.2). However her costume and her makeup sent out a different message. Benedict Nightingale described her as a 'commanding old bat in beads, bangles and an orange dress that looks as if it's been worn for two centuries'.[8] During the tech rehearsal, Richardson says, Kent had asked for her to look dirtier, as if she smelled, as if she dealt in all kinds of dead things.

Sharon Duncan-Brewster: She used to make me laugh onstage. She had this blacked-out tooth going on, and she would come onstage and I'd be laughing inside. She would corpse me; the eyes would be going and the teeth rolling. And Joy is such a very calm, spiritual, artistic lady. She's so soft-spoken. And this thing comes onstage, bounding onstage, this energy like a fireball almost.

FIGURE 2.2 *(From left) Remi Wilson as Alice, Kobna Holdbrook-Smith as Ken, and Joy Richardson as Mama Benin in Mustapha Matura's* Playboy of the West Indies, *2004–5.*

Source: Photograph by Graham Brandon © Victoria and Albert Museum, London.

Apparently the audiences were equally spirited. Andrée Molyneux remembers a matinee, when the audience were 'shouting out and joining in'. Duncan-Brewster says the audiences were generally very vocal: 'Sometimes as audiences go, Monday night is cheap night, so they're a bit rowdy. But it would be every night.' Kent related an anecdote he enjoys telling about the 1984 production of *Playboy*.

Nicolas Kent: That play was brought here from Oxford, when I was running the Oxford Playhouse Company. It was very popular, and we did a short season here. Then we brought it back because it sold out. It was the first black play to sell out here. It really hit a nerve. And I remember standing by the box office, and there was a rather large West Indian, Jamaican lady who was getting very irate with the box office and said, 'What do you mean you don't have a ticket?' And they said, 'We're sold out'. And she said, 'What do you mean sold out? You weren't sold out last night; you weren't sold out the night before; you weren't sold out the night before that. I got a ticket on all those nights.' And I said, 'How many times have you seen this play?' And she said, 'I've seen it five times. And they always say the same lines every night, you know.' Which I thought was terrific. And I said, 'Have you seen any other plays?' She said, 'No, I've never seen another play'. We got to an audience who'd never ever seen other plays.

Lonely Cowboy by Alfred Fagon (1985)

As part of the black theatre season in 1985, Kent directed the premiere of *Lonely Cowboy (A Brixton Café Western)* by Alfred Fagon. All the characters in this contemporary play are English second-generation blacks.[9]

As the play opens, so too does a café in Brixton called the Lonely Cowboy (see Figure 2.3). For owner Flight (*Playboy*'s Jim Findley)

FIGURE 2.3 *Jim Findley as Flight and Beverley Michaels as Thelma being directed by Nicolas Kent in* Lonely Cowboy *by Alfred Fagon, 1985.*

Source: Photograph by Joy Richardson, courtesy of Joy Richardson.

and his partner Gina (Angela Wynter), both in their twenties, the café is meant to be what Flight calls their base. Throughout the play, the front line (Brixton's area 'with high police activity, drug dealing') is a palpable presence.[10] Outside the café, police sirens are heard with regularity. The couple and their patrons all know one another from the neighborhood. And they know the policeman on their beat (Calvin Simpson), whose joining the force is seen as a betrayal of his fellow blacks. The food is hardly abundant, however there is root drink. And there's the occasional poem from one of the regulars. But trouble soon walks into the café when a well-heeled stranger arrives with a box of ganja (marijuana), which leads to a theft and a battle of wills. Then little more than a fortnight after its opening, the café is the scene of a violent, deadly showdown.

Joy Richardson, who played a young woman in love with the wannabe poet, says Fagon's writing about second-generation blacks was 'very fresh'.

Joy Richardson: He was really leading the way. And the whole thing of having the black policeman as well. I remember in Hackney seeing a black policeman for the first time, and thinking, my gosh. And then when I saw it represented onstage, I thought, I hadn't seen this before. Of course, the play deals with how the black policeman is treated by the community. He's part of the community, but at the same time, whose side is he on?

Tragically, Fagon died the following year at age 49. The writer had been jogging and collapsed near his home. His agent Harriet Cruickshank described the sad circumstances surrounding the writer's death in a 1998 programme essay about the Alfred Fagon New Play Award. The police had 'failed to inform any of his family, friends or associates of this death' – and because no one came to claim the body, the authorities had him 'cremated in a pauper's ceremony'.[11]

Shane Connaughton reminisced about the monthly dinners for writers that Kent had hosted. Alfred Fagon ('a wonderful man') was one of the group.

Shane Connaughton: *Lonely Cowboy* . . . was a wonderful play . . . I loved his characters, and I loved his writing. His death was a blow. He had a real talent and a real punch. He was an ex-boxer, ex-soldier. He had such a wonderful insight into characters and into his own society. I thought he could have been a London West Indian version of Sean O'Casey.

The Great White Hope by Howard Sackler (1985)

Toward the end of 1985, Kent staged Howard Sackler's 1960s Pulitzer Prize–winning drama *The Great White Hope*, which demanded a large-scale production, and, as Kent said, was a strategy to deal with the abolition of the GLC and the threat of a funding crisis. Hugh Quarshie starred in the play based on the life of Jack Johnson.

Episodic in structure, it follows the hounding of the boxer, renamed
Jack Jefferson, after his win in the early 1900s as the first black world
heavyweight champion in a match against the racist establishment's
White Hope. It dramatises his arrest on trumped-up charges of 'tran-
sporting' his white lover, Ellie, 'across a state line for immoral pur-
poses'[12]; his skipping out on bail, wandering throughout Europe; and
his relocating to Mexico at the time of World War I (see Figure 2.4).

FIGURE 2.4 *Nicolas Kent directing Hugh Quarshie as Jack Jefferson and
Jenny Quayle as Ellie in Howard Sackler's* The Great White Hope, *1985.*

Source: Photograph by Douglas H. Jeffery © Victoria and Albert Museum,
London.

After Ellie (Jenny Quayle) commits suicide, he agrees to a match and finally loses the gold belt to a white boxer. There were 18 scenes with almost as many locales, more than 55 characters portrayed by a cast of 27 – and Jenny Jules was a supernumerary. A band of eight actor/musicians was led by Terry Mortimer.

The feat of staging a play of that breadth with such a large cast in the small theatre drew critical attention. Michael Coveney noted in the *Financial Times* that the production was 'the sort of large-scale affair the fringe has studiously backed away from for years', adding that it compared more than favourably with a National Theatre boxing 'extravaganza'.[13]

On one occasion, the show received unsolicited endorsements.

Nicolas Kent: Jane Birkin came to see *Great White Hope* and absolutely loved it. And I drove her home afterwards – met her for the first time. And she said, 'Watch the television tomorrow; listen to *Breakfast Time* news because I'm on'. So I watched it, it came up at 7.45, and they interviewed her about her film. It was Frank Bough, and he was in a sweater, and he was interviewing her, and she said, 'No, I don't want to talk about the film. I want to talk about this fantastic play I saw at the Tricycle Theatre, *Great White Hope*.' And she went on and on about it, and Frank Bough said, 'We have to talk about your film', and she went on, and he said, 'Listen, we're running out of time. We have to talk about it.' And she said, 'No, I want people to go and see this play because it's so fantastic, and I had such a good time'. And he said, 'Listen, Jane, we've now overrun, so I'm going to do something I never do. I'm going to ask you – the programme goes on after the news – so at 8.05 this morning, could you come back on, and we'll talk about your film? But you have to make a promise that you won't talk about *Great White Hope*.' And she said, 'No, no, that's fine, I'll do that'. And he said, 'And now, over to John Kettley who will give you the weather'. And John Kettley said, 'Before I talk about the weather, I just want to say I saw *Great White Hope* at the Tricycle

Theatre too, and you all have to go and see it'. And I was in fits of laughter. It was like a conspiracy to give us a plug.

While the fire-damaged theatre was out of commission, Kent directed a Royal Shakespeare Company production of the play at the Mermaid (1987), again starring Hugh Quarshie, but with cast changes that included past and future actors at the Tricycle: Mona Hammond, Joseph Marcell, Patrick Robinson and Tony Armatrading. Terry Mortimer reprised his gig as musical director.

Terry Mortimer: What was so great about the Tricycle was . . . the big fight scene, which you learnt about through each of the characters describing what was happening, and they were all facing out front, they were climbed up the scaffolding, the theatre was bursting at the seams, really fantastic kind of energy was exploding from that central stage right out. The same scene didn't work in a much bigger theatre. You didn't get that sense that you've got this auditorium full of people and the whole thing was bursting at the seams; the planks and the scaffolding were almost tumbling down. You didn't get that sense, and we lost a bit of focus when it did transfer.

There's another story connected with *The Great White Hope* at the Tricycle that both Kent and Mortimer told me about: Colin Salmon busking outside the theatre. (He soon became the Tricycle's official 'busker-in-residence'. And, obviously, Salmon is better known now for his TV and film roles.)

Nicolas Kent: Colin was playing the trumpet outside because Miles Davis wrote an homage to Jack Johnson, the boxer, and when Colin saw the play was being done, he thought he'd come and busk outside as an homage to Jack Johnson too. The musical director and other people thought he was wonderful. One day they insisted he come and talk to me, and we got to know each other.

The Amen Corner by James Baldwin (1987)

Just months before the May 1987 fire, Carib Theatre presented *The Amen Corner* by James Baldwin at the Tricycle, directed by Carib's Anton Phillips.

Anton Phillips: It was a play which I had for years and wanted to do, but it's such a big cast [12 roles along with congregation members/singers], how do you afford to do it? Finally, I managed to get hold of the money from the London Arts Board . . . And then I went to Nick and gave it to him, and he said, We'd love to do it. Do you have the rights? Which was my one big problem. I didn't have the rights.

Phillips tried to track down the rights holder. He finally got Baldwin's number and called him at his home in the south of France to get that information. Baldwin told him, 'I own the rights, baby'. Shortly after Phillips visited the writer, Baldwin gave his permission for the production and said he was available to come to London for the show. 'Sure enough', says Phillips, 'about a week before we opened, he came, looked in at rehearsals, met the cast and was very pleased. And I subsequently heard that he could be a really difficult guy.'

The Amen Corner takes place in a 1950s Harlem 'storefront' church and the downstairs apartment of the pastor, Sister Margaret Alexander. She lives there with her 18-year-old son and her sister Odessa. Margaret has been pastor for ten years, but the elders are growing restive, and a crisis erupts when her jazz musician husband, Luke, whom she left years before, reappears (see Figure 2.5). She had abandoned him after the stillbirth of their daughter, seeking refuge in religion and righteousness. Luke is now deathly ill, and her belief system is being sorely tested. Her musician son rejects the religious path and goes off to follow his own dreams. Right before Luke dies, she realises the love she had for her husband was precious. A shaken

FIGURE 2.5 *(From left) Stacey Zuckerman (seated), Carmen Munroe, Sylvester Williams, Al Matthews (seated), Clarke Peters, Claudette Williams and Alibe Parsons (seated) in James Baldwin's* The Amen Corner, *1987.*

Source: Photograph by Douglas H. Jeffery © Victoria and Albert Museum, London.

Margaret cedes the church to the elders who have been plotting against her.

But that's just the story of *The Amen Corner.* Baldwin's play calls for gospel singing and impassioned preaching. Alex Renton in the *Independent* recapped the 'first twenty minutes' of the production: 'Three gospel anthems sung at full whack and a virtuoso jive sermon on Isaiah in the wilderness. This Force Ten opening tells us that we are in for an experience on the grand scale.'[14]

Carmen Munroe starred as Margaret, and Claudette Williams, a young actress at the time, got the role of her older sister, Odessa. Although Williams was called in for a younger part, she went after this one, she says, because she wanted to understand those black women 'who are so supportive and are the pillar of society'.

Claudette Williams: It was an illustrious cast. It was Caribbean and African-American actors, so it was quite a big mixture – and also established actors and young actors. It was the first time I met Carmen Munroe and Clarke Peters and Al Matthews, who played the father. It was a great structure to play that afforded you a journey and a character. You weren't playing an attitude or political stance. You were trying to uncover the humanity of the character, and I enjoyed that challenge.

The Tricycle has always been the home of black theatre, or giving black actors a voice, and so you felt passionately about the theatre and the fact that it allowed Anton to direct. It was very amazing on the part of Nick Kent, that he was promoting black art in this way. We were allowed space, and everyone was supportive, and it was an amazing atmosphere to work in. And we were privileged to have London Community Gospel Choir and Bazil Meade coming in and working with us.

And Anton as a director was very shrewd in allowing you as the performer space to be creative. I think that's why it worked, because of his nature. You felt we were all called to be together and terribly protected in the fact that we all got on, and our main focus was on the work, because it is quite a large cast of people.

Opening-night stories included one about the part that the audience had played.

Claudette Williams: I remember on the opening night, Carmen Munroe got up to preach that wonderful opening in which she says, 'Let the church say amen!' And as she got up to speak and she said the line, somebody from the audience said, 'Take your time, sister'. And she started it again. Just that statement, really, solidified us and the audience. And she took her time to preach it. It's that responsiveness of a black audience – they were totally within the story. People wanted to talk about the production. People spoke during the production. I remember I have a fight with Sister Moore, and people were voicing their opinions. And every time Sister Moore came out, she was the evil woman. It was responsive. It was alive. It was always packed. And we were just having fun in telling this story.

In March, *The Amen Corner* began a run in the West End, said to be a first for a British-based black company in a straight play.[15] Clare Fox, a Tricycle board member from the early 1980s through 2004, was a coproducer for the transfer to the Lyric Theatre on Shaftesbury Avenue. She tells a story about James Baldwin at opening night in the West End.

Clare Fox: He was in a box to see the opening night, and I said to Carmen Munroe, 'Look, if the audience is clapping loudly, give him a call'. And she did, and the whole audience stood up. That was great. We went to a restaurant that evening, and the whole restaurant stood up.

Phillips says the 'set fit exactly' in the Lyric, and the play worked well even in the bigger space. However, it ran for only a few months because it didn't do well enough, he says: 'And the feeling is that the timing was bad. It was in between the end of winter and the start of summer. The tourists really hadn't kicked in.' Still Fox maintains she was thrilled to have been part of it: 'The reviews were fabulous, and it was good work. And that's all that matters. We didn't make our fortunes, but we were very proud to have done it.'

All or Nothing at All (1989)

One of the plays Kent directed off-site while also overseeing the restoration of his theatre was *Trinidad Sisters* (1988) by Mustapha Matura, based on Chekhov's *The Three Sisters*, and featuring Pauline Black. Right before the fire, Black had been cast as the lead in the Tricycle's production of the play about Billie Holiday. (It was postponed when the theatre was destroyed.) She had heard about the auditions for the Billie Holiday play, rang the theatre, and was told to come down to rehearsal.

Pauline Black: And these were very much open rehearsals, and I remember just wandering onto the stage and singing a cappella, I can't remember what now, to Terry Mortimer, who was the musical director on *All or Nothing at All*, and being told that they were doing this play, would I like to read, and I read. These auditions went on for a while. I got a recall, then I got another recall, and I think it was down to me and somebody else, and it was all getting a little bit fraught by that time. But in the end, I got the play. So I was absolutely over the moon. I can remember Nick Kent ringing me up and saying we'd like to offer you the part. The next day the theatre burnt down.

Black was involved with the preproduction for the play. She says she 'saw various stages of the script. I can't remember how many now, something like four or five drafts. I had various meetings with Nick Kent, and obviously my relationship with Nick Kent was built during that time. But also with Caryl Phillips, who wrote it. And we would either meet at the Tricycle or at Nick Kent's apartment.' In spring 1989, she got the call that the Tricycle was set to reopen and rehearsals would begin in the summer. But then as rehearsals began, Phillips filed the unsuccessful injunction to stop the production.

Nicolas Kent: I'd been working with Caz for three years on this project. It was my idea to do it. Caz was the writer. We met on various occasions. He had approval of the set, and I had problems getting the set designed because the designer took forever. But eventually the set was designed and finished, and he came to the first rehearsal. I think he thought I was not well enough researched about Billie Holiday, but I was, and I was working organically, rather slowly. After the first rehearsal, which was the read-through and I talked a bit, he told his agent he wanted me removed from the show. I was trying to get the building open at the time, after the fire, and there were all sorts of stresses. I thought, 'I don't really need this. I'll walk away, and let them get another director.' My board were outraged and said no, including Mustapha Matura, who was on the board. There were a number of writers on the board. They said, 'This cannot be allowed to happen. You have to direct it. He's got no right to do this.' Meanwhile [he and his agent] were looking for another director, and I had to continue rehearsing because it was evident that we had to go on because there was only a limited rehearsal time. I had a very good cast. Eventually, he came up with a director who was completely unacceptable to all of us. Various directors who had been offered it all turned it down, knowing what had happened.

He then put an injunction on the production, and the cast all signed an affidavit saying they wanted to work with me and they couldn't see the problem – which they did independently of me. They had a meeting and decided to sign an affidavit saying that, and they put it into court. When the case was heard, the judge threw out his complaint. There was a settlement that as the author couldn't be present in the rehearsal room, the play could not be changed. Not a word of the play could be changed, which was rather inhibiting because obviously during rehearsals, plays get changed with the consent of the author.

Pauline Black: I knew Caryl Phillips from before this play. We had mutual friends. I knew he was a relatively temperamental person, in the best sense of the word, in an artistic sense. And I fully respected him. When this bombshell hit that suddenly he wanted to take his name off the credits and we couldn't change any of the words within the script, I actually went round to his house . . . He wasn't in. And I sat on his doorstep for a long time just crying. And eventually he came back. And we sat, and I said to him, 'Why are you doing this?' And he turned round and said, Look, it's nothing personal, blah, blah, blah. It's just that we've had a difference of opinion (I think that's between himself and Nick), and he didn't want his name on it anymore. There was no persuading him.

To a certain extent, it crushed us during that period. But out of that I felt the whole of the cast really pulled together, particularly Henry Goodman, who played the manager of Billie Holiday. He was absolutely fantastic. And I'm sure that none of us, to be perfectly honest, would have got through it quite so well. It was just his energy, the energy that he put into the production. Everybody's energy that they put into the production was great, but I really felt his energy much more, I think, than anyone else's within the cast. Nick Kent was absolutely there and right on it. It was a real learning curve for me, and I learned an enormous amount both from Nick Kent and from Henry Goodman.

Black says she sang more than a dozen songs and was rarely offstage (see Figure 2.6). The play follows Holiday's rise and fall, her story illuminated in songs like 'Strange Fruit' and 'Lady Sings the Blues'. Colin Salmon, formerly busker-in-residence, was in Holiday's band, playing the trumpet and making his acting debut in London. The song 'Sophisticated Lady', which opened the show, had a very high note, says Terry Mortimer. Colin 'came in on B flat, and wow, he could do it. Colin could do it. He did it each time.'

The reviews referenced the public controversy and bemoaned the problems of the untouchable script.

Pauline Black: Reviews are reviews. One tries not to get affected by them. Obviously one does. It was unfortunate, but it was obvious that reviews were going to be fairly unkind in that respect about the length of the play and things like this because they knew we couldn't do anything about them . . . I always remember Joan Bakewell was really wonderful about it, and I thought, well, if she likes it, that's great . . . She's a broadcaster here, and she was in one night, and I thought, That'll do for me.

FIGURE 2.6 *Pauline Black as Billie Holiday and Alan Cooke as Lester Young in* All or Nothing at All, *1989.*

Source: Photograph by Douglas H. Jeffery © Victoria and Albert Museum, London.

Kent says the show played to good houses, and 'we weathered the storm'.

> **Pauline Black:** Once we'd opened and got over the trauma of all that, it was like a real party atmosphere. There were 17 people in the cast and live music onstage, and we really did have a ball. It all flashed by so quickly, and I was very happy doing it because Billie Holiday had been a hero of mine for a long, long time, before it became trendy to be into Billie Holiday. And even though the script was not great in terms of what we could do to it or change, I felt it was an awful lot better than the *Lady Sings the Blues* movie in trying to portray what Billie Holiday was about.

Despite the fact that they couldn't touch a thing, Mortimer says one afternoon they did make a slight change – in the background music.

Terry Mortimer: Adelaide Hall was in the audience. She was the singer originally, I believe, when Duke Ellington recorded 'Creole Love Call', back in 1927. The thing that goes: [Mortimer sings] *doo dah, doo dah, doo dah, doo daaaah*; then you hear this voice going, *waa, waa, waa, waa*. That was the voice of Adelaide Hall. When Duke Ellington first recorded it, he didn't write that in. She improvised it, and it stuck. And it's one of the most memorable elements of that particular song. It's such an important ingredient, everyone can remember it. I think Mary came around to us just before we went up: 'Adelaide Hall's in.' I thought, How wonderful. And you could see her sitting down one of the side aisles quite close to the band.

Usually what we did to start the second half was a fairly laid-back club scene where the band played very quietly in the background, 'Body & Soul', a song that Billie Holiday sang. And at the interval, I said to the guys, 'How about this? Instead of playing "Body & Soul", why don't we do "Creole Love Call"? Adelaide Hall's there.' They said, 'Do we know it?' And I said, 'I'll sing it'. 'Oh, yeah, we know it.' 'Let's rehearse it.' And I said, 'Colin, you do *waa, waa, waa, waa* on the trumpet'. We rehearsed it and got it up, and the lights went up on the second act, and the club scene's there, and I was sitting there as one of the club members reading a newspaper, and they launched into this very gently, and I heard this voice from the audience saying, 'Hey, they're playing my song'.

Joe Turner's Come and Gone by August Wilson (1990)

This was the Tricycle's first August Wilson play; by the end of 2008, the theatre had produced six British premieres of Wilson's ten-play cycle about the African American experience in the twentieth century. Early on in *Joe Turner*, set in 1911, Herald Loomis and his young daughter make their way to a boarding house in Pittsburgh. Loomis (Tony Armatrading) is looking for his wife. He rents a room at the house, where he finds out that a pedlar who does business there once a week is known to be a people finder. The backstory is that Loomis was a deacon and a sharecropper down south, but he was picked up and forced to serve for seven years on Joe Turner's chain gang. Upon his release, he sought out his wife and found only his daughter, who was staying with her grandmother. Loomis has been on the road since then. He believes he must see his wife so that he can start again. When she finally appears at the boarding house, he hands their daughter over to her, and the broken man begins to reclaim himself.

Joseph Marcell portrayed Bynum Walker, an otherworldly character who lives at the boarding house. Known for his ability to bind people, Bynum uses the power of his Binding Song and works spells with his roots and powders. But he also has an understanding of other people's pain. It's Bynum who brings Herald Loomis out of a sudden fit, talking the man through his terrifying vision of bones walking on the water and black men washed up on the shore. Michael Billington wrote in the *Guardian* that Marcell 'as Bynum exudes a grizzled wisdom and mature serenity that never makes you doubt for a second this conjure-man's healing properties'.[16]

The play was directed by Claude Purdy, who had been a longtime friend and associate of Wilson's. I asked Marcell what it was like to work with an American director.

Joseph Marcell: It was less intense in the sense that we were expected to know a little more about the subject that we were dealing with. Whereas with a British director, with British plays, although a lot is understood, there's more of a give and take between the actor and the director. I found with the American director, a lot of things had to be accepted as given. It was a different experience, but interesting as well and very challenging and wonderfully stimulating.

Claudette Williams played Loomis's wife Martha Pentecost. That was the beginning of her love for August Wilson, Williams said in her 2006 interview, 'and the journey that he's taken African American theatre through in the telling of our stories. They're important plays to do over here, as we are in the process of defining the theatre that we want to create.'

Pecong by Steve Carter (1991)

Calypso and carnival came to the Tricycle in autumn 1991 with Steve Carter's *Pecong*. It is a variation of the myth of Medea (renamed Mediyah); the locale is an imaginary Caribbean island. This tale of love, betrayal, and murderous revenge introduces Mediyah before she meets Jason. When the play opens, Mediyah's Granny Root is about to die and pass along her powers as Obeah Queen to her granddaughter. But death doesn't take Granny out of the action. Jenny Jules, who played Mediyah, explains.

> **Jenny Jules:** Her grandmother has physical magic, and she says, 'Don't worry, I'll never leave you'. And then you see grandmother sitting at the top of this ladder for most of the play. She's like the puppet master. And we're all telling the stories she wants us to be telling. She then gives me all of her magic power, and I become this witch, this magic woman.

The stories are fuelled by Granny's desire for revenge on the man who broke her daughter's heart, although she leaves room for some fun too. Mediyah meets and falls for Jason (his not-so-subtle surname: Allcock). She uses her considerable magic to help him when he shows up wounded, and she does the unthinkable: she falls in love with him, losing her powers and her hold over her man even though she is pregnant with his twin sons. Jason and Cedric, Mediyah's brother, face off against each other in the carnival's pecong, a down-and-dirty calypso contest of rhyming insults. Jason not only wins the pecong, but he also captures the heart of the magistrate's daughter. Although the play ends with Mediyah's vengeance and a pileup of corpses, by most accounts the show was 'exuberant'.[17]

Pecong was director Paulette Randall's first production for the Tricycle. Randall says she was hesitant about taking on the assignment.

> **Paulette Randall:** Nick sent me the script and said, 'Read it and tell me what you think'. I nearly lost out on doing it because when I read it, I loved it, but I was really afraid of it. You know what it's like with life. I'd been through a bit of a time, and I hadn't done any theatre for a little while. The last show I'd done was *Five Guys Named Moe,* and I left [that]. So this was my first time going back into theatre. I read the play, thought it was wonderful, and felt, 'I can't. It scares me. I can't do this.' So I *um de ummed de ummed.* Nick rang me back and said, 'If you don't give me an answer, I'm going to give it to someone else'. So I said, 'Yes, I want to do it'.

Her concerns about taking the job proved to be unfounded. 'The achievement of Paulette Randall's production is to accommodate magic, broad fun, and tragic horror on the same dramatic canvas', wrote Irving Wardle in the *Independent on Sunday.*[18] The critical acclaim was extended to her designer Kendra Ullyart, and her cast: Jenny Jules, Pat Bowie (Granny Root), Cecilia Noble (Persis), Victor Romero Evans (Jason Allcock) and Eamonn Walker (Cedric/ Damballah).

> **Jenny Jules:** How we did it was, we started by saying this was a carnival, and out of this carnival troupe of people, we were going to tell this story of Mediyah. That's why it was so vibrant and magic and colourful, and everyone was dressed in colours.

There was so much music in the play (composed by Felix Cross), Jules says, that it was close to being a musical.

Paulette Randall: Every Caribbean island I know of is very musical. So I couldn't imagine doing a play that's set even in a mythical Caribbean island without music. The fact that it's called *Pecong*, and pecong is about rhyme and using words, like song in a way, like a very early rap, I thought this cries out for music.

The audience response was 'massive', Jules told me. 'People absolutely loved it. People would cheer, give us standing ovations. People would shout, they'd interject, people would be angry.' The *Evening Standard*'s reviewer reported that Jules's avowals of vengeance 'gained vocal endorsement from several women' seated in his row.[19] Jules says, 'People still stop me in the street and say, "Were you in *Pecong*? Did you do Mediyah?" It's an incredible play.'

Pinchy Kobi and the Seven Duppies, devised by the Posse (1992–3)

Paulette Randall was back in 1992 directing a rollicking holiday-season show, a kind of Afro-Caribbean *Christmas Carol* titled *Pinchy Kobi and the Seven Duppies*, performed by the Posse: Brian Bovell, Michael Buffong, Robbie Gee, Roger Griffiths, Gary McDonald, Eddie Nestor, Victor Romero Evans, and Sylvester Williams. The company, Randall says, 'came out of a benefit that was done at the Theatre Royal Stratford East'.

Paulette Randall: There was an actor called Calvin Simpson, who sadly died. [Simpson was the policeman in *Lonely Cowboy* at the Tricycle in 1985.] He got hit off his push bike. In between jobs. He had a family – a wife and two kids – and no insurance or anything like that, nothing. Anyway, he got killed, so we, the community, did a benefit to raise money for him. There were different groups of people who got together to do things. These guys got together to do a sketch. Then after that, they formed the company, the Posse.

Randall was brought in about ten days before the opening to help the company finish constructing the full-length entertainment (music by Felix Cross) for the Tricycle. In the play advertised as 'a seasonal tale with lots of spice', landlord Pinchy Kobi is haunted by the seven duppies, 'souls trapped in limbo' – or 'semi-delinquent spirits', as *Time Out* described them – who set out to reform the hard-hearted miser.[20] Randall says the long rehearsals and the pressure of getting the show together in less than two weeks was 'insane, but very funny. One of the best experiences I've ever had in my life.'

The Piano Lesson by August Wilson (1993)

The second August Wilson play for the Tricycle, *The Piano Lesson*, was Paulette Randall's first time directing the playwright's work. She travelled to America to meet him.

Paulette Randall: I was offered it, and I read it, and I said, 'God, I would love to do this'. I hadn't seen *Joe Turner*. I didn't see *Fences*, either. In fact, I hadn't seen any of his work. Somehow I'd managed to not see any of this man's extraordinary work. So of course, Nick said, 'Well, you must read'. I've never been good at cramming for exams. I thought, I could read these plays and then go and bullshit or try to, but there's no point. I'm going to go and be honest . . .

When we met, he was at the Eugene O'Neill Theater Center in Connecticut . . . I was very nervous, not so much about talking about everything else. I knew I needed to get the thing out, at the very beginning, that I hadn't seen any of his work. Because I couldn't have a conversation with him with that in my head . . . We sat down, and I said, 'The first thing I want to say is I loved *The Piano Lesson*, and I'm thrilled that I'm going to be doing it. And the second thing I have to say is, I've never seen any of your work. I needed to get that out of the way. It's not been deliberate, you understand. It's just one of those things. I'm really sorry.' He looked at me and said, 'I wouldn't worry. I don't go to the theatre much myself.' And I fell in love with him instantly . . . For the next three, four, five hours, we sat, chatted, laughed, and got to know each other. Didn't talk about the play once.

August Wilson came to see her production of *The Piano Lesson* after it opened.

Paulette Randall: It was a great cast. In the lead [Boy Willie], we had Lennie James, who was astonishing, amazing to see that man. It's a wonderful part, and he put it to bed. He did it with such clarity and speed and love and joy and passion that you understood every breath that he didn't take and all the rest that he did . . .

[Wilson] gave me two notes. One I can't remember. It was very simple. It was one of those ones that you go, Oh, god, of course. And the second one, there's a character, Wining Boy, and at the end of the play, he was still there, left in the house. So August said, 'He shouldn't be there. Why is he still there?' I said, 'Let me get the script'. I went, 'He's still there because it doesn't say that he leaves'. He just laughed.

The Piano Lesson is Wilson's 1930s play, set in the Pittsburgh home of Doaker Charles, a railroad cook; his widowed niece Berniece; and her 11-year-old daughter. African American history is embodied in the Charles family's upright piano bearing carvings on its legs and now standing in the parlour. That piano is at the heart of the conflict between Berniece and her brother Boy Willie who arrives from the south wanting to sell their inheritance. He needs the money to buy land from the family that once owned his ancestors as slaves so that he can have land of his own. But Berniece insists on keeping the piano, which was polished with her mother's tears, she says. Their great grandfather, the slave of Robert Sutter, had carved the family's stories on the piano after his wife and son were traded for the instrument. Berniece and Boy Willie's father was burned to death in 1911 when he and his brothers took the piano from the Sutter home. The Charleses and the Sutters are still so bound by the piano that the ghost of a recently deceased Sutter (slave-owner Robert's grandson) also arrives up north at the Pittsburgh home and becomes a key player in resolving the clash between brother and sister.

Cecilia Noble played Berniece. Her character blames Boy Willie for the death of her husband in an incident over stolen wood, and she is stern and all bottled up. Michael Billington wrote that Noble 'movingly suggests that Berniece, in preserving her family's heritage, also hoards her own womanliness'.[21] Noble says she was very happy to play that role, a great part in a great play. However, there was some language in the play that bothered her.

Cecilia Noble: I do remember a debate at the time because there were a lot of references to African Americans calling each other 'niggers' in the play. And I found that very uncomfortable because we just don't do that here. It's an offensive word. It's not something that you really at that time called each other. Maybe it's changed for the youngsters now. I researched the history of that and of claiming that word back and why black men would call each other that. That was one particular challenge, apart from obviously the accent and getting into the rhythm (Americans have a different rhythm), and all the other acting things.

At the end of the play, the family tries to rid their home of Sutter's ghost. Berniece's preacher friend performs a ceremony, reading from the Bible, and Boy Willie literally wrestles with the ghost. But the ghost is vanquished only when Berniece – who had stopped playing the instrument years before – plays the piano, calling on her ancestors for help with her song. That meant Noble had to learn to play some chords on the piano, she says. 'I remember practising an awful lot (I can still remember the song) with Felix Cross. It was a first for me. It's great, those parts when you get to exorcise your demons.'

Since staging *The Piano Lesson*, Paulette Randall has directed all the Wilson plays at the Tricycle. Joseph Marcell offered a reason for Wilson's wanting Randall to direct his plays.

Joseph Marcell: He thought she was the woman who understood what he was trying to put over, who went beyond the superficial history of the African-American experience, but more the struggle of the artist, the struggle of the worker, and mostly the poetic import of his work.

Ain't Misbehavin': *The Fats Waller Musical Show,* based on an idea by Murray Horwitz and Richard Maltby Jr (1994–5)

The Tony Award–winning musical *Ain't Misbehavin'* also scored a hit at the Tricycle. After previewing in December, it welcomed in the new year with a 9 January opening. The 'joyous' production earned plaudits for its energy and its evocation of 1920s and 1930s Harlem and for the glorious songs: 'The Joint Is Jumpin'', 'Honeysuckle Rose', ''T Ain't Nobody's Biz-ness If I Do'.[22] After a two-month-plus run, the show transferred to the Lyric Theatre in the West End (where *The Amen Corner* had played eight years earlier). Directed by choreographer Gillian Gregory and Nicolas Kent, *Ain't Misbehavin'* featured Ray Shell, Debby Bishop, Dawn Hope, Melanie E. Marshall, Sean Palmer and musical director Clement Ishmael at the piano.

Shell says that from the beginning, 'people just seemed to like it', and it was clear that this was a winner.

Ray Shell: I think it was the first preview of *Ain't Misbehavin'* . . . and people were literally hanging off the rafters. After the first act, before Nick had even told me, Debbie, Dawn, we knew we were going to transfer. When a show transfers to the West End, it's a very special kind of thing. You can actually feel it happening, and it did happen.

The play was noteworthy for another cast member: Roy Williams as stage manager/police officer. Mary Lauder recalls that 'the first time we knew Roy, he was an extra in *Ain't Misbehavin*'. The very end of act 1, he came on dressed as a New York policeman and waved a gun about'. Williams would return to the Tricycle in 1998, this time as the playwright.

Starstruck by Roy Williams (1998)

It was Indhu Rubasingham who suggested Roy Williams's play to Kent after he invited her to direct at the theatre.

Indhu Rubasingham: Nick had seen one of my early productions of Roy's play *No Boys Cricket Club* at Theatre Royal Stratford East [1996]. He'd introduced himself to me then [and said] how much he enjoyed the production, and jokingly said, 'If you've got any Asian plays, you must bring them'. And I thought, 'No, I'm not going to bring him any Asian plays. I'm not going to talk to him now.' I was a bit piqued at that comment because [of] the assumption. He'd just seen this play which he said was well directed, and it was nothing to do with being Asian. But we had a joking relationship because of that. Then again we met, and he said, 'Please tell me if there's anything you'd like to do'. And I said, 'Well, I won't bring an Asian play, but I do know there's this play, Roy's second play'. And he was very interested in reading it. What's great about Nick is that once he responds to something, he'll make it happen really fast. He decided very quickly once he'd read it.

In the family drama set in Kingston Town, Jamaica, in the 1970s, Eddie Nestor played Gravel, the head of the household, a man who is an object of derision in the town. He's bought a beat-up car that he intends to repair to start his own cab company, a plan he doesn't live to fulfill. That car, sitting in his backyard, becomes a perch from which the starstruck others (including Gravel's unfaithful wife Hope played by Adjoa Andoh) try to view actor Stewart Granger and company on the set of a film being shot nearby. The son Dennis (Martin Cole) envisions becoming a star himself and manages to get a closer look when he nabs some work in the movie.

The car got publicity of its own in the local press because of the effort to get it into the theatre. It was 'a very specific model of car that you would have found in Jamaica' in that period, says Rubasingham. 'They had to crane it in because of the building works. It was this incredible feat.' The set, she says, designed by Rosa Maggiora, was 'transportive, but real. It was a real car rather than a made-up car.' The *Observer*'s Susannah Clapp found the design 'evocative', with its 'corrugated iron, a splash of red flowers, a pile of crates and a tacked-together chicken coop'.[23]

Rubasingham went on to collaborate with Kent on a number of the Tricycle's innovative projects and, in 2011, of course, was appointed artistic director after Kent resigned. But back in 1998, she was finding her way there.

Indhu Rubasingham: Nick is an amazing character, but he can be an incredibly controlling character. So for my first job in that theatre we got on really well, but my god he wants to have his finger in every pie. And I was a young buck kind of director trying to do my own thing. It was absolutely fine, but we did have our clashes . . . I didn't appreciate it then, but what I really appreciate about Nick is that you can have a confrontation with him, you can have an absolutely big argument, but it's then forgotten. It's not held against you.

One disagreement had to do with the marketing of the play as a comedy, which she and the writer felt was inappropriate for the piece. 'It was a very funny play', Rubasingham says, 'but the main character dies at the end . . . In the print image, there was a very buxom young character that doesn't feature in the play at all . . . But it was Nick's way of trying to make it tantalising, exciting to an audience.'

While sex offers forbidden pleasures in *Starstruck* – Hope with her nephew, Dennis with his girlfriend – an unplanned pregnancy causes Dennis to give up his dream of leaving Kingston to pursue an acting career. Before he makes that decision and before Gravel dies, family infidelities come to light. Dennis learns that Gravel, the man he thought was his father and with whom he has had an uneasy relationship, is really his uncle. His actual father had abandoned the pregnant Hope. In a programme interview, playwright Williams said that for him 'the characters are the key: they come first and . . . I go along with them'.[24] Those characters, wrote the *Guardian*'s Lyn Gardner, 'burst with life, emotion and contradiction'.[25]

Water by Winsome Pinnock and *Wine in the Wilderness* by Alice Childress (2000, 2001)

A double bill in autumn 2000 by women writers, the late American playwright Alice Childress and Britain's Winsome Pinnock, addressed art, identity, and authenticity – *Wine in the Wilderness* taking place in 1960s Harlem, and *Water* in present-day London.

Pinnock was commissioned a couple of months before the start of rehearsals to write a curtain-raiser for the 80-minute Childress play. The 'spontaneous project', she says, was to come up with a contemporary piece that contained a debate of the issues in *Wine in the Wilderness*. The subject of identity has a strong appeal for Pinnock.

Winsome Pinnock: It is something that fascinates me as a black woman, a black person who grew up in London and the way in which an identity was imposed on me . . . That's a theme that I write about, and in *Water*, it's more obviously what I'm looking at.

I remember years ago an actor saying that he became black when he became an actor. That always interested me. When actors were playing Jamaicans, rather than Londoners or black British, they were playing black, and there were certain prescribed notions of what that meant. Often when you were working with black actors, that would be a topic of conversation, about stereotyping [the] black community in its representation onstage. That fascinates me. And that's why *Water* does deal very obviously with that whole idea of the commodification of race and the sexiness of certain kinds of representations of black identity.

In *Water*, a journalist (Gary McDonald) is on assignment to interview the black artist SJ (Cecilia Noble) whose work depicts drug use and prostitution and also her mother's suicide, and whose subject matter is said to come from her own life. She eventually admits that she co-opted the experiences of a girl from her school for the paintings. SJ is saying, the playwright told me, that 'what I really am isn't interesting enough or sexy enough to be of commercial value because I'm supposed to represent the darker side of things, literally'.

I asked Pinnock whether it was significant that she changed the artist's gender. (In *Wine in the Wilderness,* the artist is male.) She says the choice might not have been conscious, but she 'was interested in the work of people like Tracey Emin at the time . . . A lot of her work is seemingly about her, her own identity, herself as artist, the woman who holds the paintbrush. All of that fascinates me.'

Wine in the Wilderness, directed by Kent, starred Jenny Jules as Tomorrow Marie (Tommy), the woman who is brought to an artist's Harlem apartment to pose for his latest project. The artist, Bill (Ricco Ross), is working on a triptych, *Wine in the Wilderness*, two-thirds of which he has completed. One painting is an image of a little girl in her Sunday best. The central painting is a noble woman, a kind of African queen. For the third canvas of his study of black womanhood, he wants to represent someone at the bottom of the heap. On the night of a riot in Harlem, the artist's friends, a middle-class black couple (Cecilia Noble and Gary McDonald), meet the factory worker Tommy. She has just lost most of her belongings in a fire started by the rioters. Judging by her manner and the way she is dressed, the couple think they've found the model their friend is looking for, so they bring her up to meet him. Although Bill and his friends profess to believe in black solidarity, they treat Tommy as a visitor from another class in need of education, correcting her when she uses a pejorative term for blacks while she's describing the trauma of the riot. (They've also befriended a neighborhood geezer, Old Timer, played by Ray Shell.) As the night wears on into the next morning, Bill begins to recognise Tommy's innate intelligence and her beauty as a black woman (see Figure 2.7). At the play's end, the triptych is about to be reconfigured, with Tommy taking her rightful place as the genuine Wine in the Wilderness.

Jules says Kent sent her the script during a low point in her career.

> **Jenny Jules:** I read it, and I cried. Because that's exactly how I was feeling at that time. I just felt like I was on my own, isolated, wanting to say things but not being able to have a voice, not being listened to and not feeling that my experience was valid. And I gave my heart to Tommy. When I think about it, I want to cry sometimes. It was such a beautiful play.

Critics and audiences were taken with Jules's portrayal ('a stunning central performance . . . she combines an attenuated frame with a spirit as big as Grand Central Station', from Michael Billington). The *New Statesman* reviewer of the remount reported that several audience members shouted out to Jules's character: 'Don't listen to them!'[26]

> **Jenny Jules:** They would call out to try and protect my character, Tommy, 'cause she was simplicity in itself. Some of the women would just get so angry that she was being exploited.

FIGURE 2.7 *Jenny Jules as Tommy and Ricco Ross as Bill in Alice Childress's* Wine in the Wilderness, *2000.*

Source: Photograph by Douglas H. Jeffery © Victoria and Albert Museum, London.

Actress Joy Richardson is also a visual artist, and her work has been exhibited in the Tricycle gallery. She was commissioned to do the artist's paintings for the production, and that included the triptych. Richardson told me that she found the face for the idealised woman in Clissold Park, Stoke Newington: the mother of a 4-year-old who agreed to be photographed for the portrait. To avoid a photographic quality in the painting, Richardson says, she sat in front of a mirror, dressed in ethnic fabrics, and the painting became an amalgam of the two women. The final portrait represented Bill's fantasy vision of perfection: a regal beauty adorned with jewels and a headdress.

One Under by Winsome Pinnock (2005)

Winsome Pinnock's next production at the Tricycle was a full-length play, *One Under*. She had sent a working version to Kent's literary agent to get some feedback; the agent forwarded it to Kent, who called Pinnock saying he had a slot and wanted to put it on. Pinnock says, 'It was very quick. He was speaking to me in November, it was going to go on in January, and I didn't feel I'd finished with it because I'd sent it to this woman to have a look at.[27] But it was exciting because I hadn't expected that.'

Scene 1 finds Tube train driver Cyrus shaken after his first 'one under': a young man waving at the driver had deliberately fallen off the platform into the path of his train. The incident throws Cyrus (Brian Bovell) off-balance. He begins to look for clues as to why that young man called Sonny did it, convincing himself along the way that Sonny was the son Cyrus had to give up for adoption 30 years before. The scenes of Cyrus's searching for answers alternate with flashback scenes of Sonny's last hours on earth. The younger man is guilt ridden because he believes he's responsible for a hit-and-run accident and is trying to make amends to those he hurt. Motivations and connections eventually become clear.

The playwright says the structure of the piece evolved, developing itself.

Winsome Pinnock: As you start thinking about these things and asking questions about the characters, a structure kind of imposes itself on the piece, or you find it. And half the work is finding that. It was really interesting to try and think it through. Because if you're telling two stories [with] the usual structural demands of a play, you're obeying all those principles of the climax in each scene and the overall structure, but you're doing it twice. So then you run the risk of it lacking energy because you have a climax in a story, then go to another story and have another climax. You actually need one climax throughout the whole play, so the two have to fit together as one whole play and not be two completely separate stories.

The *Daily Telegraph*'s Charles Spencer called *One Under* 'a fine new play, at once a gripping urban thriller and a moving examination of the power the dead can exert over the living'. Spencer wrote that Kent alerted him to 'another remarkable feature' of the play: although the writer is black and a number of the characters are black, 'this is a drama that never mentions race issues once'.[28]

Winsome Pinnock: That play on my part was a reaction against something. It's a continuation of having an identity forced upon one. It was a reaction against that that you don't mention it and write about these characters who have interesting relationships with each other, all of whom are different races. I didn't [write the race of the characters] in the character list, and I should have done. It actually is important, because the main female has a mixed-race child . . . I was experimenting with doing that because you very rarely see plays with black characters where race isn't the main theme, and race in a particular kind of way isn't the main theme, race as some sort of problem or the cause of the ensuing drama. I was just playing around, for myself, with getting away from that for one play at least.

The African American season: *Walk Hard – Talk Loud* by Abram Hill; *Gem of the Ocean* by August Wilson; *Fabulation* by Lynn Nottage (2005–6)

In the 2000s, the Tricycle continued to present African American work: August Wilson's *King Hedley II* (2002–3), a coproduction with the Birmingham Repertory Theatre, and James Baldwin's *Blues for Mr. Charlie* (2004), in partnership with Talawa and the New Wolsey. Then in 2005, Kent produced an African American season, running from late November to mid-March 2006. The plays spanned some 100 years. Kent gave his reasons for delving into the African American canon in our 2008 conversation.

Nicolas Kent: Basically we don't have a large African-Caribbean history in this country which can be mined to produce work. Nor did the States have such a history before slavery. We didn't have much of a history before 1950 or so when this large influx came in from the Caribbean, and has continued to come in since then. So to find playwrights who told about the racist story – good storytelling, mature playwrights – in a society that had begun to assimilate its black members was quite difficult. Yet if you look in the twenties, thirties, forties, and fifties in the States, there was already that body of work, be it Alice Childress, James Baldwin, Lorraine Hansberry. There were writers who were dealing with that. And then later August Wilson, who did a whole summation of the twentieth century in those ten plays.

That story wasn't being told so that people could put their lives in a perspective in a parallel way to what was happening in the States when people were trying to get civil rights – and pre-civil rights. People arriving in this country from the Caribbean were walking in and going to see landlords and were suffering very similar racism to what was happening in the southern states in

America in the late forties, and a similar period to some extent . . . Those stories coming out of the States that had that background had resonances with people, so I felt they were useful stories to tell, and they certainly drew an audience.

Kent engaged a company of actors for the 2005–6 season. One reason, he told the *Evening Standard*, was financial: The Tricycle 'didn't have enough money' to do the three British premieres together, but 'I realised that if we held a company together over the three plays, we could cut down considerably on expenses . . . And the cast we have got are the crème de la crème.'[29] That core group of actors included Kobna Holdbrook-Smith, Jenny Jules, Joseph Marcell, Lucian Msamati and Carmen Munroe under the direction of Kent, Paulette Randall and Indhu Rubasingham.

Joseph Marcell had been a member of the Royal Shakespeare Company. I asked him how the Tricycle's rep season was different.

Joseph Marcell: It was different because it was an African-American season. It was a season of plays by black playwrights. There were black and white directors. There were black and white actors. But the actual plays were written by blacks . . . that was what was important.

When asked about the Tricycle's idea of engaging an ensemble for the three plays, Marcell called it 'marvellous'.

Joseph Marcell: For us, the actors, [the company] was the most wonderful thing 'cause you were able to move on after the first play. Like all rehearsals and performances, it starts off as an endless audition. So by the time you'd started the second play, everybody was relaxed. Everybody knew what the other person's capabilities were, and it was wonderful fun. Learning became much easier because you were playing and learning at the same time. I think for the black actors of London, it was the first time in modern times that had been done. It was priceless.[30]

Kent directed a cast of 16 in the opening play of the season, *Walk Hard – Talk Loud* by Abram Hill. The playwright was a cofounder in 1940 of the American Negro Theatre, a company with a special interest in developing plays of protest and social significance.[31] *Walk Hard*, first produced in 1944, takes place in New York City in 1939, near the end of the Depression. It's the story of Andy Whitman (Kobna Holdbrook-Smith), who is 19 years old and shining shoes. He becomes a professional boxer after he is spotted in a street fight by a boxing manager. Andy is a powerful fighter and achieves success, but he comes up against racism within and outside of the profession, from boxing honcho to hotel management. His new career seems to be finished after he has a violent clash with the racist headman who had been demeaning him from day one. Yet when Andy is offered a second chance by another organisation, he turns his back on the boxing world. And with the coaxing of his idealistic girlfriend (Ony Uhiara), Andy decides to commit himself to the people's struggle.[32]

Kent 'approached it as a history play, which made it work', says Marcell, who played Andy's father. He 'put it in context and in time, and so you could see it for what it is, a play of another time'. Although there were comments about the play's not being a 'master-piece', reviewers noted *Walk Hard*'s 'theatrical verve', its lively use of language, and the considerable talents of the company.[33]

The second play went back in time to 1904, for the first decade of August Wilson's chronicle of black Americans in the twentieth century. Sadly, Wilson had died in October 2005, shortly before the Tricycle's production of *Gem of the Ocean*, directed by Paulette Randall. (The play had opened on Broadway in 2004.)

Gem is set in the Pittsburgh home of Aunt Ester (Carmen Munroe), the 285-year-old spiritual adviser. Citizen Barlow (Holdbrook-Smith) seeks out this woman who is known as a powerful healer. He is distressed because another man took the blame for a theft Barlow committed (a bucket of nails from the tin mill). The man had jumped in the river and drowned when the black constable Caesar Wilks

(Patrick Robinson) went after him. To help lift Barlow's burden of guilt, Aunt Ester and her companions take him on a symbolic slave-ship voyage to the City of Bones, the resting place for slaves who didn't survive the passage.

Holdbrook-Smith says that ritualistic scene was the most challenging thing he'd ever done as an actor.

> **Kobna Holdbrook-Smith:** I'd get nervous because I knew every night I had to take myself to a certain place. It's exciting, but it's –. Every performance you get the feel of the shift, this colossal, tectonic sliding from one human being and evolving into another. What I didn't do – I couldn't quite take myself to a place where I completely lost it, because I was always aware that I had to be able to play the next X amount of scenes. It would be different if that were the end of the play, and I'd just go home. I didn't really cry tears onstage. I wish I could have, but I knew that scene happens, then Caesar comes in, chases so-and-so out, and then seconds later we're [Holdbrook-Smith and Jenny Jules as Black Mary, Ester's housekeeper and protégé] sitting having the conversation about the girl in the blue dress. And it was one of those choices, those acting choices, where you have to kind of balance going from the outside in and the inside out, 'cause you can do either.

There is a particularly rich character in *Gem*: Solly Two Kings, a friend to Ester's household and a participant in the ritual (see Figure 2.8). Solly had been a slave who escaped and led others to freedom on the Underground Railroad; he is now in Pittsburgh selling dog manure. When the mill incident leads to riots and jailings, Solly burns the mill down. He almost eludes constable Caesar by heading south, but he is drawn back to free the people imprisoned during the riot. Caesar shoots him en route, and in the final scene, Solly (Joseph Marcell) is brought to Aunt Ester's house, fatally wounded. Sharon Duncan-Brewster, who performed in the third play of the season, said she heard a story about an audience member's response to the scene in which Marcell's character dies on the kitchen table.

FIGURE 2.8 *(From left) Joseph Marcell as Solly Two Kings, Kobna Holdbrook-Smith as Citizen Barlow, and Lucian Msamati as Eli in August Wilson's* Gem of the Ocean, *2006.*

Source: Photograph by Graham Brandon © Victoria and Albert Museum, London.

Sharon Duncan-Brewster: I think it was a matinee – I wasn't there, but I was told this story – and a woman shouts in the back, 'Oh, God, Solly dead! Solly dead!' Everyone starts laughing. It was so emotional. That's what happened. They can't help themselves. And poor Joe is on the table, probably wanting to laugh, but keeping it together.

This was Marcell's third Wilson play at the Tricycle, following his portrayals of Bynum in *Joe Turner's Come and Gone* and Elmore in *King Hedley II*. I asked him whether he felt a kinship for playing African Americans or whether he had to figure out the different culture.

Joseph Marcell: It was an absolutely different culture, but there are affinities between a black British person and a black American person, definitely. We seem to approach the plays as a piece of theatre, rather than a sociological tract or an historical analysis of the suffering of African Americans. Although that is part of it, it's simply beside the point, really. The point is to try to put the characters' and Mr Wilson's intentions as clearly as possible. Obviously it requires re-educating yourself into the history of African Americans and the history of the United States of America. And that, we all have to do whenever we do those plays . . . I try to keep my political opinions out of those things; they're really not germane to the point that we're dealing with, and I found that if I approach those plays with a kind of artistic integrity that everything else falls into place.

In autumn 2008, Marcell appeared in his fourth Wilson play at the Tricycle, *Radio Golf*. In that play, at the end of the twentieth century, an African American is planning to run for mayor of Pittsburgh. There are a number of connections in *Radio Golf* to *Gem of the Ocean*, including a dispute over Aunt Ester's house. The Tricycle's *Radio Golf* programme cover – a *Gem* production photograph in Aunt Ester's kitchen – underscores the connectedness. Marcell's character in *Radio Golf*, Elder Joseph Barlow, turns out to be the son of Black Mary and presumably Citizen Barlow. Having seen the two shows at the Tricycle, I was very moved by the presence of Marcell, representing the relationship of those characters as Wilson's play cycle was brought to a close.

To top off the season, the Tricycle produced Lynn Nottage's *Fabulation or the Re-Education of Undine*, which had premiered in New York City in 2004. *Fabulation* is a contemporary comedy about a black female entrepreneur whose life is suddenly shattered. After her Argentine husband runs off with all her money, the title character loses her business, her possessions, and her so-called friends. Plus she has learned that she's pregnant. Undine narrates the story of her return to her family in the Brooklyn projects and the indignities she suffers as she undergoes her reeducation. The Tricycle's production, directed by Indhu Rubasingham, was fast paced, hilarious and so successful by the end of the run, it was remounted some months later.[34]

Rubasingham says she was worried that the actors would be very tired by the time it came to the third play. But that didn't occur, and 'it felt very exciting'.

Indhu Rubasingham: They were really tight and had been working together, but what it meant was unlike a first day of normal rehearsal where as a director the onus is on you to bring the company together, actually because there was this ensemble that had been working at the Tricycle for two shows, the onus really was on them. It was their responsibility to bring the other, new actors in on the show. So from my point of view, it was great. It was a real relief, and it felt much more [that] we were in this together – we were all on this journey.

While the play's locales are in New York, and the characters are distinctly New York types, Rubasingham says its being 'over there' made the message 'more palatable'.

Indhu Rubasingham: There's also a very human story. I think plays work really well when they're specifically located . . . With *Fabulation*, you're dealing with a woman who has left her roots behind and is embarrassed by her roots and, for her aspirations, denies where she's come from, which is a universal story. Then [she] loses everything and in order to find herself has to go back to her roots.

Back in Brooklyn, Undine soon gets arrested on a street corner when she tries to buy heroin for her grandmother, who needs her next fix. Undine is found guilty and sent to drug counselling despite the fact that she herself doesn't take drugs. When she tries to apply for benefits, she is forcibly removed from a social-services office because she protests the mistreatment by the unhelpful, unfeeling staff. Holdbrook-Smith calls Undine's situation an example of a 'bottom rungness' that black people experience: 'I think, wherever you go in the world, the consensus seems to be that they always put black people on the bottom rung, wherever you are, even in Africa . . . *Fabulation* talked about that and in the richest nation in the world.' But through it all, Undine carries on – with spunk and a sharp tongue. Jenny Jules, who played Undine, says she found her character 'absolutely hysterical. I'd be laughing inside at some of the things I'd have to be saying onstage.' The actress didn't leave the stage for an hour and a half, and the role gave her a chance to show her flexibility – and to do a tango, the scene in which she recounts how she met and fell for her Latin lover husband. In a *Time Out* review of the remount, Rachel Halliburton wrote that the tango scene alone was 'a reason to make the journey Kilburnwards'.[35]

The ensemble played multiple roles as the various colourful characters that Undine encounters on her journey. There was Kobna Holdbrook-Smith's embezzling Argentine husband and his recovering-addict nice guy; Carmen Munroe's druggie grandmother; Lucian Msamati's Yoruba priest; Clare Perkins's and Sharon Duncan-Brewster's tough-talking gals sharing a prison cell.

Sharon Duncan-Brewster: I had a boho wannabe, and then I had somebody who worked for Morgan Stanley, a merchant banker, and then I was a drug addict. My favorite character was the girl in the jail cell who decides she's going to slaughter this imaginary man with her shoe. I loved that scene. Because any pent-up thing that was there just got out.

We talked about developing characters. She was the hardest to find. I don't know why. I wasn't sure that going that far would work. But because of the way the show was played, almost farcical – there was the centre character and then all these crazy people around her – it was beautiful. When the play was up and running and on form, the energy that got me to get to that character was great. I always loved looking at Clare Perkins. She'd be with me. She's another lady that the team spirit is there one hundred per cent.

Jenny Jules and Kobna Holdbrook-Smith, who appeared in all three plays, shared some final reflections on the season.

Jenny Jules: I think I was the best that I will probably ever be onstage during that time. My muscle as an actor was so toned because we were rehearsing in the day and performing at night. And I had to relocate. I had to come and live in London, in Wembley where I'm from and where my family still lives. I was a theatre beast. I lived and breathed it, and it was fantastic. What was so brilliant was playing all the different parts and having those roles in my head as well: Aunt Susie from *Walk Hard* to Black Mary in *Gem of the Ocean* to Undine in *Fabulation*. I would be rehearsing Undine and playing Black Mary at night.

Kobna Holdbrook-Smith: I'm going to sound so trite, because I know what I'm about to say, but it feels a bit like after someone's been in a war and only people who were in the war can talk about it. We worked so closely together, and we worked very hard, because when *Walk Hard* went up, the day after it went up, we began rehearsing *Gem of the Ocean*, and none of these plays – *Fabulation* was a little easier on the soul, in terms of applying oneself, but *Walk Hard* and *Gem* were uphill. Plain and simple, they were difficult because they matter in a different way. So straight away, we were in the thick of it. We would rehearse all day and then perform at night, and then you've got two shows on Wednesday, and two shows on Saturday . . .

It was very valuable indeed in terms of finding a way of working that shakes you as an actor. If you're working on one thing, you can become very singular and point all the things in your life towards the one thing. But if you're working on two things or more, then you can't cheat – you can't rest on external things or on the singularity of something to get you through. You just have to get it all right. And I've thrived on it. I was really tired, but I thought, This is living. I like to be made to feel alive.

Let There Be Love by
Kwame Kwei-Armah (2008)

Let There Be Love, written and directed by Kwame Kwei-Armah, starred Joseph Marcell as a West Indian pensioner at the end of his life in his adopted city of London. Sharon Duncan-Brewster was his younger daughter, and Lydia Leonard, his Polish home aide.

I asked Kwei-Armah about a comment he had made, that in casting the lead role of an elderly man, there was only a small pool of black actors he could choose from.[36] An actor himself, Kwei-Armah answered: Britain has been 'so very unkind to the black acting fraternity . . . If I write a black male character 55 to 65, I have three or four I can call upon because there is nobody else out there who has that level of experience who can fill a National Theatre stage because they've not been given it. [Kwei-Armah's *Elmina's Kitchen*, 2003; *Fix Up*, 2004; and *Statement of Regret*, 2007, all premiered at the NT.] Or the others have just simply dropped out of the game.' Kent told the playwright that he saw Joseph Marcell for the role of the West Indian pensioner, and Kwei-Armah says he did too.

Kwame Kwei-Armah: So I kind of wrote it with Joe in mind, knowing that he was an actor I wanted to work with. And if Joe had said no, the play wouldn't have been scheduled until the summer. [It was first produced in January 2008.] . . . And I have to take this opportunity to say what a wonderful experience it was. He's such a gentleman to work with. An absolute pleasure.

Marcell talked with me about *Let There Be Love*, before the show went into rehearsals.

Joseph Marcell: It's a very important play because it is one of the first plays that deals with the kind of immigrant who has been in Britain for over 50 years and their relationship with their children and also the new immigrants who are the Poles and the Eastern

Europeans. And it is written by a British person about his father or his grandfather . . . that generation. I'm really looking forward to it.

The pensioner, Alfred Morris, is foul-mouthed and short-tempered. He has a fraught relationship with his two daughters whom he raised alone after his wife left him. He's terminally ill, but he withholds that information from his family. He's also in pain and fears it will become unbearable as the illness progresses. When his daughters hire a part-time helper to look after him a few days a week at his home in Willesden Green, the prejudiced older man at first mistrusts the aide Maria, a fairly new immigrant from Poland. But the prejudices fall away as they get to know each other. Alfred offers the young woman shelter when she is beaten by her two-timing boyfriend and gets her started in navigating the British system. She in turn stage-manages a trip back to Grenada where he makes peace with his family. More importantly, she reluctantly agrees to bear witness when he takes his own life, which he does in the final moments of the play.

There is a Polish community in Kilburn and its environs, and Kwei-Armah says he took that into account. 'It was a little bit of my brief to myself, that I thought the subject matter would be apt for Kilburn, for the Tricycle.' So when he began to work on the play and 'started to vibe around', he says, 'I knew there was going to be somebody Polish in it. And that probably triggered Polish, immigration, parents, same stories.' Critics noted that the political playwright had moved into a domestic, more sentimental realm, however the subject matter in this play was meaningful for then Work and Pensions Secretary James Purnell. Asked in an *Independent* Q&A for the last play that he had seen, Purnell replied, '*Let There Be Love* . . . beautifully written and acted, but also dealt with important questions about immigration, life, death, compassion. All that in just over two hours.'[37]

Not Black & White: Category B by Roy Williams; Seize the Day by Kwame Kwei-Armah; Detaining Justice by Bola Agbaje (2009)

The Tricycle again took on an ensemble of actors for a season of theatre, this time commissioning three black British writers for issue-driven plays about British society in the early twenty-first century. The *Not Black & White* season covered prison life in *Category B* by Roy Williams; the candidacy of a black mayor for London in *Seize the Day* by Kwame Kwei-Armah; and the problems of illegal immigrants in *Detaining Justice* by Bola Agbaje. Directed by Paulette Randall (*Category B*), Kwame Kwei-Armah (*Seize the Day*) and Indhu Rubasingham (*Detaining Justice*), the plays ran in rep from October through December. The ensemble featured Aml Ameen, Sharon Duncan-Brewster, Karl Collins, Kobna Holdbrook-Smith and Cecilia Noble.

Category B takes a look at the collusion between inmates and their guards, which is deemed necessary for an efficient operation, and which leads to infractions on both sides of the bars. Holdbrook-Smith portrayed a prison officer who was inclined to play by the rules but also had a 'tendency towards violence', says the actor. When Holdbrook-Smith followed an inmate offstage, he would 'flick his truncheon', signalling that the guard would be less than kind when out of sight.

Kobna Holdbrook-Smith: There was a lot of comment on the fact that the first play was set in a prison, and it was suggested that was a negative place to set a play concerning black people. My take on the world is that when people can look at someone black in a prison or someone black who plays a mugger or a negative character and not think it's a comment on the diaspora, that's when we'll be OK. So I quite like the fact that you can set it in a prison, amongst prisoners who are in the majority black, and it be a facet of our experience. Because as a corner of humanity, it's OK to be as good and as bad as everybody else. That's what the facts are. And then you've got this other play in which you've got a mayoral aspirant, and everybody in there is highly qualified and socialised and intelligent in a way that is very different from the prison, and it's all allowed. As a season, it sort of says, all these things are allowed.

Kwei-Armah's *Seize the Day* enters into the back room of black politics. The play opens with Jeremy Charles (Holdbrook-Smith) filming at a shopping centre. The reality-TV star has become a presenter. Jeremy's profile is raised a notch when he breaks up an attack on a young man and smacks a black teenager, knocking him to the ground. The incident was caught on camera. Disciplining the youngster apparently makes Jeremy an appealing 'crossover' candidate, and he is tapped by black and Asian political players to run for mayor of London in the next election. In a move to court white voters, one of the prospective candidate's handlers rewrites an article Jeremy is about to publish. The result is a piece that takes a harsh view of the children of the black underclass and decries the failure of their parents to look after them. That indictment doesn't go down well with Lavelle (Aml Ameen), the teen from the on-camera incident, whom Jeremy has been mentoring as a condition of the young man's probation.

Soon afterwards, Jeremy's house is burgled. When he shows up at Lavelle's home accusing the boy of the crime, Jeremy is given his comeuppance by Lavelle's mother (Cecilia Noble), a politically hip and extremely expressive woman. Noble says the part was difficult because it was 'very concise', just the one scene. She had to 'come on and go *bam*'. And bam she did, giving Jeremy 'a lecture in class and colour wars . . . articulated with unanswerable conviction by Cecilia Noble', wrote Michael Coveney in the *Independent*.[38]

Holdbrook-Smith says that when they were developing the scene in rehearsal, it got physically intense.

Kobna Holdbrook-Smith: She calls Jeremy a race traitor, and he says, But it's fine for your son to carry a knife in shopping centres – great upbringing that is. And I played it especially sarcastically and gave her a clap and leant into her face. And she as a character just grabbed my throat. Literally she went for me like she was going to choke me, and then Aml Ameen's character had to jump in and pull her off. It didn't stay in. The next week, every time we got to that section, I'd laugh.

Jeremy's run for mayor is over before it actually gets off the ground, aborted when one of his handlers is accused of misdirecting funds and when Jeremy goes off script at a conference on education attended by some two thousand black people. Holdbrook-Smith told me about a change made late in rehearsals for the final (post-conference) section, emphasising the importance of making one's own choices, a change that he feels goes to the core of the play.

Kobna Holdbrook-Smith: In the original version, what happens is, Jeremy talks about standing up in front of the audience and seeing the different paths ahead of him and trying to decide which of the two his mother would want him to go down. And then which of the roads Lavelle and his mother would want Jeremy to go down. In the end he elects not to go down any of them. In the version that we performed, it was less to do with what other people wanted him to do and more to do with him realising that his strength as an individual . . . as a man came from courage in his own convictions and the notion that whoever decides on your behalf belittles you . . .

If you were to dig deep, if in a hundred years' time, people say, What did the playwright really mean?, they might decide the play looked at the false choices that the black diaspora in Britain think they have to make. What they think they have to do to achieve, what they think they have to do to excel, what they think they have to do to assimilate. The choices are false, and there's a useful duality to our existence in being able to do it all. You can sound how you sound and still be a professor or a lawyer. Or you can sound not like everybody else in your sphere and still like traditional things.

Bola Agbaje's immigration play centres on a Zimbabwean asylum seeker named Justice (Aml Ameen) who has been detained for using a fake passport to get into England. A hard-nosed black case worker is determined to send Justice back to where he came from, despite the potential danger for the young man. While Justice languishes in detention, he falls out with his sister Grace (Sharon Duncan-Brewster), who was able to get that asylum in England. He believes she is not doing enough to help him. Yet Grace goes so far as to have sex with an enforcement officer – to no avail, however, and she tells no one about what she did. When Justice's mental health deteriorates, his lawyer (Karl Collins) manages to get him a temporary reprieve.

The young playwright earned critical approval for leavening the serious circumstances with humour, which she did with her group of station cleaners: Jovan (Robert Whitelock), an East European working in Britain under a false identity, and the illegal immigrants, Ghanaian Pra (Kobna Holdbrook-Smith) and Nigerian Abeni (Cecilia Noble). Far from home and separated from family, they work together, take meals together, and pray together. Pra is also a pastor and leads a rousing service, complete with microphone and a huge neon cross in the background. Holdbrook-Smith says that style of preaching was something he knew about. It was director Indhu Rubasingham who came up with the staging of it 'and the idea of having the mike and the extent to which we were able to take it into that world' – a scene infused with the spirit, voices raised in song.

Outside services, Pra and Abeni, the 'splendidly comic double-act' (Charles Spencer, *Daily Telegraph*),[39] argue about almost everything, even about how to make an ethnic rice dish.

Kobna Holdbrook-Smith: I know my way around comedy, but I don't often get to play with comedy onstage. So it was a chance to flex those muscles, too. It was lovely. And that scene where she throws the shoe, that was pure invention on Cecilia's part. We were in rehearsals, and Indhu said, 'Just take it as far as you want, and I'll bring it back'. That was a carte blanche. She's cooking, and I say her food smells, I ruin her food, and we break away from text and start running around the room.

Not Black & White did nicely at the box office, especially Kwei-Armah's *Seize the Day*. The night I went to see it, friends wanted to join me, but it was sold out. The Tricycle's ability to put on a season of black British theatre and attract an audience, many of whom saw all three plays, says Noble, hasn't 'happened overnight'.

Cecilia Noble: The Tricycle has got such a community feel about it, and because they're continually doing interesting plays – it's not like some theatres where they will do a 'black play' unquote, and then expect everyone to go see it once – they've built up over the years a very good audience and a good connection with schools. Their networking is very good. So they can do something like this.

Nicolas Kent: When I first started, there was so little African-Caribbean theatre in London, we were an oasis, and people came to us a lot. Then the volume of work increased throughout London and in the country, but we consistently went on with the work we were doing. We were one of many. Then gradually we've become a beacon of excellence. People realised that some of the best black work happens with us.

. . . and from South Africa

David Kramer and Taliep Petersen's *Kat and the Kings* (1997, 1998, 2003–4)

Kat and the Kings, says Kent, 'was an extraordinary adventure that went completely right'. A highly discerning friend of his who had emigrated to South Africa sent him a fax saying, 'I have just seen the most wonderful thing in the world, *Kat and the Kings,* and you must take this to the Tricycle'.

Nicolas Kent: And had it come from anyone else, I would have taken no notice at all. But because of her record of being so much a perfectionist, I thought I'd better take some notice of this. I rang up Patricia MacNaughton, who was chair of our board, and said, 'Do you know David Kramer?' And she said, 'Yeah, I represent him'. I said, 'Do you know *Kat and the Kings?*' And she said, 'I know something about it'. No one seemed to know much. So I rang [producer] Renaye Kramer and said, 'Look, I'm stuck. I've got a gap for three weeks. Would you like to come to London?' And she said, 'Well, it's a complicated show, but we'd love to come to London'. So we arranged it, and I put them together with [set designer] Saul Radomsky . . .

The music just took off, and people loved it. And it was such a hit, I decided to bring it back [in 1998]. We got it into the West End. And when we transferred, it won the Olivier [1999] for best cast and Best [New] Musical, and went to Broadway, and the rest is history.[40] It was a really fantastic moment for us, and helped us tremendously. Everyone loved the show. And it was a politically important show too.

Just as the opening number announces, *Kat and the Kings* is a memory play. The elder Kat is now shining shoes, but he conjures up his teenage self in the fifties, when Kat Diamond and his friends formed a singing group called the Cavalla Kings (the name is taken from a cigarette brand). Harmonising and singing doo wop, they fashion themselves after American rock 'n' roll groups like the Drifters and the Ink Spots.

The Cavalla Kings are a 'Cape coloured' group from District Six in Cape Town – a place that was different because it was open to all cultures and races. Then in 1966, the apartheid government declared it a whites-only area and levelled it. Kramer wrote that he heard stories about growing up in District Six in the fifties from his collaborator Taliep Petersen and from Salie Daniels, who spent his formative years on the streets of District Six, where he and his friends started their own vocal-harmony group, the Rockets.[41] Daniels, whose story is the basis of *Kat and the Kings,* portrayed the elder Kat. Five younger actor/singer/dancers – four guys and a woman – brought to life Kat's younger self along with his friends.

The group goes from vocalising on the street corner to playing church bazaars, weddings and bar mitzvahs – and all the way to the big time in Cape Town. The guys are fancy dressers and are hot for the girls, whom they attract with their newfound fame. But in apartheid South Africa, they can't use the front door in a whites-only club. When they perform in a big hotel in Durban, they're required to work as bellhops during the day. Soon the group breaks up. The woman and the group's white agent leave South Africa; so does one of the guys; another gets married; and Kat succumbs to a weakness for gambling.

When I was in London briefly in 2004, not yet really familiar with the Tricycle or Kilburn, I telephoned to get a Saturday matinee ticket for *Kat and the Kings*, but there were no tickets left. I have since found the album from 1998, recorded live at the Vaudeville Theatre. It's hard not to get carried away by the joyful singing and the compelling beat. On *Kat's* first visit to the Tricycle, Nick Curtis in the *Evening Standard* gave full credit to the cast: 'Their voices are beautiful, especially when harmonising, and their personalities irresistibly infectious.'[42]

A number of the Tricycle staff named *Kat and the Kings* as a highlight. Mary Lauder recalls that it was 'lovely, and with a bit of a message, quite subtly in there. And beautifully done. One of the reviews said it was like drinking champagne, and it was. Everybody would come out on a high.' Lucy Freeman, education officer in the mid-2000s, was at the Vaudeville Theatre the night Nelson Mandela was in the audience, which was an 'amazing' experience for her. (David Kramer wrote that Mandela went onstage to congratulate Kramer and Petersen. Mandela embraced them and spoke about his memories of District Six.)[43]

What the Tricycle's technical director Shaz McGee remembers is the set. She says *Kat and the Kings* is one of her favourites.

Shaz McGee: It was the most beautiful set I've ever had on that stage. It was designed by Saul Radomsky and built by the guys in Nottingham. Saul and I had it built 200 miles away. And we'd go up every now and then, and I kept saying, Oh, it's beautiful. The floor is beautiful. It's blue, and it's shiny. All the boys were going, Shaz is taking a turn. It had this red velvet proscenium with little pea lights in it. It was a very camp set. As the crew were unloading it and all these elements were coming off, they were going, Wow! At one point on a Sunday night, two of the boys had little brushes, and they were brushing stuff off the pros. I've never seen that before. And then one of them got the hoover out and started hoovering, because there was a little bit of cotton or something on it. It was a sensational set.

After the successful return of *Kat* in 2003–4, the next Kramer-Petersen collaboration at the Tricycle, which arrived in 2006, was followed by tragedy. Petersen was musical director of Kramer's *Spice Drum Beat – Ghoema*, the Tricycle's holiday season show. Taliep Petersen was in London for the December opening night. But then less than a week later, having gone back to Cape Town, Petersen was murdered in his home.

Black theatre productions (1980–2009)

1980

Samba by Michael Abbensetts

1982

Love in Vain by Bob Mason

Sink or Swim by Tunde Ikoli and the company (Foco Novo)

1983

Beyond the 'A' Penny Steps by Tony Dennis

Smile Orange by Trevor Rhone

1984

Playboy of the West Indies by Mustapha Matura (Oxford Playhouse Company) (two runs)

The Boot Dance by Edgar White (Temba Theatre Company)

Two Can Play by Trevor Rhone

1985

A Raisin in the Sun by Lorraine Hansberry (Black Theatre Co-operative)

Lonely Cowboy by Alfred Fagon

Pantomime by Derek Walcott (Temba Theatre Company/Leicester Haymarket)

The Great White Hope by Howard Sackler

1986

The Lower Depths: An East End Story by Tunde Ikoli (Foco Novo/ Birmingham Repertory Studio Theatre)

1987

The Amen Corner by James Baldwin (Carib Theatre) + West End transfer

1988

Trinidad Sisters by Mustapha Matura, after Chekhov (at the Donmar)

1989

All or Nothing at All

1990

Joe Turner's Come and Gone by August Wilson

Remembrance by Derek Walcott (Carib Theatre)

1991

Meetings by Mustapha Matura (Black Theatre Co-operative)

A Long Way from Home by Yemi Ajibade

Pecong by Steve Carter

1992

Viva Detroit by Derek Walcott (Black Theatre Co-operative)

Trouble in Mind by Alice Childress

Pinchy Kobi and the Seven Duppies, devised by the Posse, music by Felix Cross (The Posse)

1993

Pinchy Kobi and the Seven Duppies (cont'd)

The Piano Lesson by August Wilson

Playboy of the West Indies by Mustapha Matura (Tricycle/Nuffield Theatre, Southampton)

1994

Playboy of the West Indies (cont'd)

The Day the Bronx Died by Michael Henry Brown

Come Good Rain, written and performed by George Seremba (Tricycle/BBC World Service/Canadian High Commission)

Ain't Misbehavin': The Fats Waller Musical Show, based on an idea by Murray Horwitz and Richard Maltby Jr

1995

Ain't Misbehavin' (cont'd) + West End transfer

Victor and the Ladies by Jenny McLeod

1996

Two Trains Running by August Wilson

3 Ms Behaving, devised by Gillian Gregory (Infamous Five)

Beef, No Chicken by Derek Walcott (Talawa Theatre)

1997

Beef, No Chicken (cont'd)

1998

Iced by Ray Shell (Black Theatre Co-operative/Nottingham Playhouse)

Sitting in Limbo by Dawn Penso and Judy Hepburn (Carib Theatre)

Starstruck by Roy Williams

1999

Up Against the Wall by Felix Cross and Paulette Randall (Black Theatre Co-operative)

The Amen Corner by James Baldwin (Tricycle/Nottingham Playhouse)

2000

The Amen Corner (cont'd)

The Gift by Roy Williams (Birmingham Repertory Theatre)

Water by Winsome Pinnock and *Wine in the Wilderness* by Alice Childress

2001

Water and *Wine in the Wilderness* (remount)

The Far Side by Courttia Newland (Riggs O'Hara Theatre Company)

Brixton Stories or the Short & Happy Life of Ossie Jones by Biyi Bandele (RSC/Tricycle)

2002

Catwalk by Malika Booker (Nitro/New Wolsey Theatre, Ipswich)

King Hedley II by August Wilson (Tricycle/Birmingham Repertory Theatre)

2003

King Hedley II (cont'd)

2004

Blues for Mr. Charlie by James Baldwin (New Wolsey Theatre, Ipswich/Talawa/Tricycle)

Playboy of the West Indies by Mustapha Matura (Tricycle/Nottingham Playhouse)

2005

Playboy of the West Indies (cont'd)

One Under by Winsome Pinnock

African American season: *Walk Hard – Talk Loud* by Abram Hill
2006
African American season: *Gem of the Ocean* by August Wilson
African American season: *Fabulation or The Re-Education of Undine* by Lynn Nottage (two runs)
2008
Let There Be Love by Kwame Kwei-Armah (two runs)
Radio Golf by August Wilson
2009
Not Black & White: Category B by Roy Williams; *Seize the Day* by Kwame Kwei-Armah; *Detaining Justice* by Bola Agbaje

Productions from South Africa (1980–2009)

1984
Pula and *Imbumba* by Matsemela Manaka (Soyikwa African Theatre)
Black Dog – Inj'emnyama, created by Barney Simon and the Company (Market Theatre, Johannesburg)
1986
Born in the R.S.A., created by Barney Simon and cast (Market Theatre, Johannesburg)
1990
Curl Up and Dye by Susan Pam (Market Theatre, Johannesburg/ Michael's Company)
1991
Starbrites, created by Barney Simon, Fats Dibeco and Arthur Molepo, and Basil Jones and Adrian Kohler of Handspring Puppet Company (Market Theatre, Johannesburg/LIFT)
1995
You ANC Nothing Yet, written and performed by Pieter-Dirk Uys (two runs)

The Suit, adapted by Mothobi Mutloatse from Can Themba's story (Market Theatre, Johannesburg/LIFT)

1996

Truth Omissions, written and performed by Pieter-Dirk Uys

1997

Live from Boerassic Park, written and performed by Pieter-Dirk Uys

David Kramer and Taliep Petersen's *Kat and the Kings* (Tricycle/ Renaye Kramer)

1998

Kat and the Kings (remount) + West End transfer

Europeans Only: An African Audition for Europe, written and performed by Pieter-Dirk Uys

1999

Ubu and the Truth Commission by Jane Taylor (William Kentridge and Handspring Puppet Company); *The Story I'm About to Tell* by Lesego Rampolokeng with cast (Mehlo Players/Khulumani Support Group) and *Phakama: Be Yourself* (Project Phakama) (LIFT)

Dekaffirnated, or Calling a Spade a Spade, written and performed by Pieter-Dirk Uys

2001

Suip! by Heinrich Reisenhofer and Oscar Petersen (Baxter Theatre Centre, Cape Town)

Boy Called Rubbish and *Squawk,* written and performed by Ellis Pearson and Bheki Mkhwane (Sue Clarence Promotions)

Foreign Aids, written and performed by Pieter-Dirk Uys

2002

Sorrows & Rejoicings by Athol Fugard (Tricycle/Baxter Theatre Centre, Cape Town)

2003

David Kramer and Taliep Petersen's *Kat and the Kings* (return) (Tricycle/Renaye Kramer)

2004

Kat and the Kings (cont'd)

2006

Spice Drum Beat – Ghoema by David Kramer (Tricycle/Renaye Kramer)

2007

Spice Drum Beat – Ghoema (cont'd)

Evita for President, written and performed by Pieter-Dirk Uys

2009

Karoo Moose by Lara Foot Newton (Baxter Theatre Centre, Cape Town)

Koos Sas: Last Bushman of Montagu by David Kramer (David Kramer Productions)

3

Irish theatre at the Tricycle

By 1985, the new artistic director turned his attention to his Irish constituency. Kent was always 'very acutely aware of his theatrical hinterland in Kilburn, so he served his community', says actor Dermot Crowley, who starred in an early Irish play at the Tricycle. 'He served the Irish community, and he served the black community in a fantastic way, by doing work that would not only appeal to them and bring them inside the door but also have a broader appeal, so it would move out into the larger community.'

And there was just the right mix of audience in the mid-eighties that I heard about. Kent attributes that 'wonderful cross-section' to the 'climate of the times'.

Nicolas Kent: We were putting on very good black plays, which had a large interest . . . And we were doing Irish work at a time when this area was known as County Kilburn. There were a lot of Irish people here. Because of what was going on in Northern Ireland, there was also a feeling of racism against the Irish. Black people were suffering racism in this country – also by the government's apparent support for the apartheid regime in South Africa. And the Irish were encountering the same situation; the government seemed to support the Unionist establishment in Northern Ireland.

I think people regarded this as a melting pot of those two cultures, and they felt at home here. (During all the bombing, for instance, this was the safest place to be in many ways because the IRA were not about to let off a bomb on their own doorstep.)

The Tricycle tapped into a lively, loyal audience for the Irish plays, relying not so much on the Irish canon and entertainment (although there was plenty of that) but also bringing over new works from Irish companies about such subjects as deprivation in the inner city and the tensions between Catholics and Protestants. By the 2000s, the theatre was presenting Billy Roche's affecting portrayals of small-town life. 'I suppose the Tricycle has a history of stories being told', Roche says, 'and the audience that will listen to that story'.

Flann O'Brien's Hard Life by Kerry Crabbe (1985, 1986)

Robin Glendinning's *Stuffing It* (1982), set at Christmas time in Belfast, featuring a very young Adrian Dunbar and an equally young Robert Glenister, was an early Irish production at the Tricycle. But in 1985, a local paper ran the headline 'At Last Tricycle Goes Irish'[1] with its announcement of the opening of *Flann O'Brien's Hard Life or Na Gopaleens Wake,* a play based on the writings of Flann O'Brien (the assumed name of Brian O'Nolan, who was also known as Myles na Gopaleen, columnist for the *Irish Times*). The play was written by Kerry Crabbe (now known as Kerry Lee Crabbe), who says he'd been a 'very great Flann O'Brien aficionado'.

Kerry Lee Crabbe: Given the nature of the catchment of that theatre, Irish plays were needed. I think the only one [of O'Brien's novels] that hadn't been dramatised was *The Hard Life*, not the most satisfactory of the books. I got permission to use his brilliant newspaper columns to change the shape of it and beef it up a lot.

Crabbe created a metatheatrical work, described in the programme with a delightful come-on: 'In a derelict [theatre] stands a bar. In the bar is a Dublin kitchen. In the kitchen all hell breaks loose as Flann O'Brien tries to drink his way out of a play, within a play, within his head.'[2] The premise is that Flann, played by Dermot Crowley, enters the theatre, voices a protest, but winds up watching a play about his younger self based on his novel. However Flann O'Brien is not called upon to bear the play-within-a-play cold sober. Along with a fellow tippler, the Plain Man (John Joyce), Flann is at a bar raised above the action, looking down on the story of his younger self and his brother (see Figure 3.1). The boys are orphaned and come to live with their half-uncle. The cast of characters include the uncle's drinking pal, Father Fahrt, and Annie (Heather Tobias), the uncle's daughter from a previous marriage, currently acting as his unpaid servant.

Mike Bradwell directed the production, which Crabbe characterises as 'rough theatre'. He remembers that Bradwell asked

FIGURE 3.1 *John Joyce as the Plain Man and Dermot Crowley as Flann in Kerry Crabbe's* Flann O'Brien's Hard Life, *1985.*

Source: Photograph by Douglas H. Jeffery © Victoria and Albert Museum, London.

designer Rodney Ford for a set that looked like '*Star Wars* for tuppence ha'penny'. Dermot Crowley agrees that the production was rough-and-ready, and says that sometimes the director's methods were bewildering.

> **Dermot Crowley:** I suppose having not experienced that way of working before, I was probably a little bit taken aback at the beginning. But Mike Bradwell, as it turned out, was absolutely right because his style of direction was perfect for the material. It was anarchic, it was loose, it was rough, but it had a kind of grace about it that I thought served the material brilliantly. We hadn't a clue what Mike was doing for the first week. He would say something off the top of his head, and you would do it and think, That's a really stupid idea. But then suddenly it would work, and you'd think, Hey, yeah. I was full of admiration for him.

Towards the end of the play, Flann is raised up high above the stage in a fantasy scene in which he is playing the 'Pope/God'. Crowley says, it 'was absolutely terrifying'.

> **Dermot Crowley:** It was brilliant once I was secure, but you see that's the kind of thing about Bradwell. He will suddenly say, 'And of course, this is the bit where you get hoisted up'. And you kind of go, 'Excuse me?' And he'll say, 'Yes, yes, you're going to be like 30 feet up there looking down on the action at the end of the play'. And you think, How am I going to get up there? And he'll say, 'We'll put you up in a swing or something. It doesn't matter.' And you say, 'It *does* fucking matter! If I fall, it matters.' But of course I didn't fall, because it was all very carefully done. And it was wonderful every night. And it was such a surprise for the audience because I would go around backstage and sit in this little swing, literally, which had a little safety harness to keep me from falling out. And then I would be heaved way up above the stage. Audiences love seeing spectacular things like that, and it was a long time ago, as well, so I think it wasn't that common.

The play was filled with 'highly entertaining' moments and scenes, Crowley told me. There was the high-wire walking by Kilian McKenna in the role of young Flann's entrepreneurial brother, who offers to teach other people that acrobatic feat through a correspondence course.

Like Crabbe, Crowley was a Flann O'Brien/Myles na Gopaleen fan.

Dermot Crowley: I grew up reading his columns in the *Irish Times*. They were amazingly tongue-in-cheek, intellectual black humour and sort of captured the Ireland of the time he was writing in rather brilliantly . . . And then I read Kerry's play, which I felt was a wonderful meeting of Flann O'Brien and Myles and Kerry Crabbe. It was a sort of collision between how to make a stage play out of a novel and the wonderful device of Flann himself arriving at the theatre and complaining and moaning about the fact that his book is going to be made into a play, which would be exactly what he would have done.

Although reviewers noted the difficulties of adapting and staging O'Brien's 'quirky', surrealistic work, most agreed that the acting, in particular that of Dermot Crowley, was grand, and that there was fun to be had at the theatre.[3] Audiences flocked to the Tricycle – fans of Flann O'Brien, London Irish, lots of students, Crabbe told me. The play was revived the following year for a second run, with some cast changes and was directed by Deborah Bestwick.

After more than 20 years, one night from that first run remains vivid for Crowley.

Dermot Crowley: The play used to open every night with the audience coming in and sitting down, and before the lights went down, Flann O'Brien used to come in from the bar, through the doors at the back of the theatre, and start haranguing the audience and whoever he could find for actually having the cheek to take his novel and to turn it into a play. He's got this two-and-a-half page speech saying, how dare you come, and he tells the audience to go home, basically, that they've come to the wrong event, that he's going to do everything he can to try and prevent it from taking place, that they were sold their tickets under a misapprehension and that if he'd wanted to write a play, he'd have written a play, but instead he chose to write a novel. It kind of sets the tone for the evening. Eventually Flann makes his way up onto the stage and ends up deciding that he's going to sit down and have a drink behind the bar and watch the action, and that's how the play starts.

One evening – it was well into the run of the first production, and I was reasonably confident about doing it (the first few performances were very scary, to just stay in the body of the theatre and talk to people) – I started my opening speech to the audience, and I started getting heckled from somebody up in the balcony that I couldn't see because of the light, and he went, '*Aaaaaah, fuck off!*' And I got really shaky, and I thought, What if I can't shut him up? What's going to happen to the show? In one sense, it was totally in tune with the kind of rough-edged evening that we were in for. Anyway, he made a couple of remarks and whatever grace I found from somewhere, I managed to say something that shut him up, and I just got on with the piece and did the play. And that was that.

And when it was over, I went into the bar in the Tricycle. I had some friends in, and they said, 'Oh, we had a good time. We liked the evening', la-di-da and all of that. And I said, 'Oh, god, I was so nervous after that guy, the heckling and everything'. And they said, 'Oh, yeah. He was up in the balcony.' They were up in the balcony as well. And I said, 'What happened? What happened?' And they said, 'Well, after you made the remark, he fell asleep on the steps upstairs in the balcony. And he slept all the way through the first half.' There's a very downbeat ending to the play in the first half, so generally speaking the audience didn't applaud at the interval. And after the first half, everybody got up and went to the bar, and when they came back, he was still asleep on the steps. And the second half of the play happened, and then at the very end, at the curtain, when the audience started applauding, this guy woke up and looked around, and he said, 'Oh, Jesus, I missed the interval!' Which I thought was so fantastic. The meaning of it was he missed the opportunity to have a drink, and he wasn't remotely concerned about the play.

More Flann O'Brien

In 1991, Eamon Morrissey first brought his adaptation of Flann O'Brien/Myles na Gopaleen's work to the Tricycle, with *The Brother*, a one-man show he had been performing since 1974. Morrissey portrayed Our Friend, a man of many stories, drinking at a Dublin pub. While the show was enjoyable, Morrissey wrote in a programme that Our Friend is a bore who in real life would actually ruin your night at the pub.[4] According to Tessa Topolski, the Tricycle's literary advisor during Kent's leadership, *The Brother* was 'magical'.

> **Tessa Topolski:** I remember . . . walking in with an Irish friend of mine, and seeing the set of a pub and him sitting on the bar. And he goes and puts one glass down and the hand of the barman puts the other down, 'cause you don't see the barman . . . We were in hysterics, and so was the entire audience.

Joyriders by Christina Reid (1986)

When I first met Nicolas Kent to talk about the Tricycle's tribunals and their contribution to political theatre, he told me that the Tricycle had been political all along. And I discovered an early example of that in Christina Reid's *Joyriders* presented in 1986 by Paines Plough, staged by the company's artistic director Pip Broughton. The play's four teenagers are in a government work-training programme in West Belfast. But, as one trainee says, with an address in Divis Flats they have no chance of getting work. Divis Flats was an actual housing estate known as 'the worst housing development in Western Europe'.[5] To punctuate the scenes, the playwright used songs that had been written by residents of the estate (with Clair Chapman).[6] The songs comment on the awful living conditions – the damp, the mould, the asbestos, the rats – and the desire for real work. Michelle Fairley, in her London stage debut, and Gerard O'Hare played two of the youths, the first of numerous appearances at the Tricycle for both actors.

The Hostage by Brendan Behan (1986)

Towards the end of 1986, Kent staged Brendan Behan's *The Hostage,* touted as the first London production of the play in 14 years.[7] The cast included returnees to the Trike: Eileen Pollock (Bloomers, 1981); Michelle Fairley; Shane Connaughton (whose play *I Do Like to Be* had a run at the Tricycle a few months earlier); and Heather Tobias. In *The Hostage,* Tobias played Miss Gilchrist, the 'sociable worker' who offers spiritual inspiration and indulges in temporal pleasures, and, according to *Time Out*'s Mark Sanderson, she was magnificently portrayed by Tobias who 'has a wonderful way with a bottle of Guinness'.[8] Miss Gilchrist joins the group of prostitutes, Irish patriots, and assorted oddballs who variously burst into song and generally add to the mayhem at the lodging house in Dublin where a British soldier is being held hostage. It's an IRA ploy to obtain a reprieve for a young IRA man imprisoned in Belfast and sentenced to be hanged; both prisoner and hostage are in their late teens.

Apparently the action began well before the start of the play. One critic reported being accosted in the bar by Michelle Fairley and Nora Connolly in their roles as a pair of whores.[9] And *Time Out's* Sanderson wrote about the lively production that 'spills over into the auditorium before and during the performance', with a warning to 'watch out for the collecting tin'.[10] Tobias as Miss Gilchrist would wield that tin before the show, making the rounds of the theatre with another member of the cast.

Heather Tobias: We actually raised quite a lot of money. I can't remember how much. A couple of times I was questioned about what I was doing there because you wouldn't really give money to that particular character, but people were incredibly generous. The collection then went onto the stage. This same tin. I remember one woman was questioning where it was going, was I registered, and had I got the right certificate, which I blew aside and moved on quickly. In the play, the idea was that I was collecting for St Vincent de Paul . . .

We were doing the auditorium up and down, round about. We got a bit overconfident with it. It was amazing. Each night, we'd go backstage and count: 'We've got this much tonight!' Nothing underhand went on . . . It's all meant to be sealed these days. But this thing just unscrewed at the bottom. Sometimes you'd find £5 notes in it. Obviously, we were very persuasive.

A week before the end of the run, the *Hampstead and Highgate Express* reported that *The Hostage* cast members had already raised more than £560 to donate to a United Nations fund for refugees.[11]

Shane Connaughton says he played 'the very strict, puritanical IRA man . . . We used to come out on the stage before the play started and the whores would sit around, and I think I'd come in and look daggers at them and go off again.' He remembers the production as a great success. ('We could have run and run and run. I think we ran for about nine weeks.') 'It was a wonderful show to do because it is such a wonderful piece of theatre. That is real theatre.'

I asked him what he thought about a critic's statement that 'after all the carnage in Ulster and on the mainland', the play was not 'the laughing matter it once was'.[12] Connaughton took exception to that point of view.

Shane Connaughton: I don't agree with it at all. The play was written in 1958 originally, in Gaelic, and was done by Joan Littlewood [at Stratford East], and that was during an IRA campaign, the campaign from 1956 to '62. So the conditions that were going on when we did it were going on when it was done originally . . . The play *is* a laughing matter. That's the whole point of the bloody play.

Pentecost by Stewart Parker (1989)

During the reconstruction of the Tricycle, Kent directed Stewart Parker's *Pentecost* at the Lyric Studio, Hammersmith, with Dearbhla Molloy, Adrian Dunbar, and Michelle Fairley in the cast. The play, commissioned by Field Day, had premiered in Derry in 1987. Kent wrote in his programme essay that Parker had sent him the script in 1988, hoping for a production at the Tricycle when it reopened. But with the delay in the rebuilding and the news that Parker was seriously ill, Kent went ahead with the production at the Lyric Hammersmith: 'We were able to let Stewart know that we would be opening the play this January, and he was looking forward to attending rehearsals. Sadly his illness became worse suddenly and he died on 2nd November 1988.'[13]

Pentecost opens in Belfast some months before the 1974 Ulster Workers Strike. Four people, two Protestants and two Catholics, find their way to the house of a recently deceased Protestant woman. Lenny (Adrian Dunbar as the trombone player) has just inherited the rundown house from his great-aunt, the owner of the property. His wife Marian (Dearbhla Molloy), from whom he is separated, comes to the house and decides she wants to buy it and begins to settle in. She's in the process of getting rid of the trappings of her former life. Friends soon follow – one is a young woman fleeing an abusive husband; another is a transplant to Birmingham who returns for a visit during the Loyalist uprising. When Marian tries to piece together the life of the former tenant named Lily Matthews, the woman's ghost appears to her. Marian discovers that she and Lily have both lost a baby. Lily had given hers away because it was the product of an extramarital affair. Marian and Lenny's son had died at five months, and the two are still deeply affected by that loss. In the end, on Pentecost Sunday, Marian expresses hope for the future in moving beyond loss and hate by embracing the Christ within oneself.

In light of Parker's untimely death, his partner, also a playwright, attended rehearsals in his stead.

Dearbhla Molloy: That was a great help, because she kept me, particularly, on course. It's a slightly nonrealistic play. To get the balance between the real and the mystical – I found quite tricky in rehearsal to hit it right. And one of the key things she said to me, which I assumed was Stewart's intention, was that this woman that I played, Marian, didn't care whether anybody liked her or not. It's a sort of obvious thing, but it was a good pointer at the time. It's not just the pointer of itself. It's that she was there representing Stewart, so she felt like a touchstone for what he would have wanted, and we all trusted her, and Nick obviously had agreed to have her there for all of rehearsal, which was a generous thing for him to do . . . I loved the play. It was terrifically successful. You couldn't get into it; it was jammed (which I think is probably why we did it on television, the same production for the BBC). We did it in a studio theatre, which was quite small. It was very powerful, and probably all the better for being in a studio theatre where we were on the same level as the audience.

Boots for the Footless by Brian Behan (1990)

Mike Bradwell returned to the Tricycle to direct Brian Behan's *Boots for the Footless*. The comedy with songs (which Behan freely admitted was autobiographical)[14] takes place in the 1950s and begins in Dublin with the carryings-on of Padser Sosage, work averse and staying in his brother's home. Padser keeps to his bedroom, where he has stashed his £5,000 inheritance, receiving a variety of favors on its account, especially from the house-helper Bridie, who pursues him, hoping to wed him and share his wealth. The second act moves to the Festival of Britain building site on London's South Bank. Padser (newly parted from his money) and his politically minded nephews are now in London and are members of the crew – and are responsible for the chaos that ensues. Heather Tobias, who played Bridie, recalls that the play 'was really workshopped and crocheted together . . . It was a lot of cobbling, but it was very successful'.

While the play was in development, Shane Connaughton helped Behan (who was 63 when *Boots* opened) shape his first work for the theatre. Connaughton speaks fondly about the author.

Shane Connaughton: Brian Behan was Brendan Behan's brother. And Brian Behan himself had a huge history here. He was the shop steward on the Festival of Britain site, where all those buildings are along the south of the river: the National Theatre, the National Film Theatre, and the Festival Hall. Brian Behan in the 1950s was the shop steward there, and he was Public Enemy No. 1 in all the newspapers because he always brought the men out on strike, looking for more money. He was a wonderful character . . . very much a Behan, part of that famous Behan family. In fact, his subject matter was more or less the same as Brendan's. It was all about the famous mother, Kathleen Behan, and his uncle who used to go to bed every night still wearing his cap. He wouldn't get up in the morning until a late hour, and he used to say, 'I'll get up now that the streets have been aired'.

Connaughton told me about Behan's own eccentricities, describing the time they went to meet with Kent about *Boots for the Footless*.

Shane Connaughton: Nick said he was going to buy us a meal. I met Brian near Kilburn, and we walked up Kilburn High Road. Brian told me he was a vegetarian; he was a very strict vegetarian, a vegan. And on the way up – he was pushing his bicycle (he road a bike everywhere) – he found an apple, a shilling and a monkey wrench, and he was thrilled. And when we got to the restaurant, Nick sat down with us, then Nick went to the gents, and Brian said (he used to call Nick Nicodemus): 'Is Nicodemus paying for this meal?' And I said, 'Of course he is'. And he said, 'Right. I'm having a steak.' He was that kind of a character.

Behan's play had been commissioned by the Tricycle in 1986, but in May the following year, the theatre was engulfed in its own drama.

Shane Connaughton: I remember when I phoned him up . . . I said, 'Brian, very bad news. The Tricycle burnt down last night.' And the first thing he said, 'WHAT ABOUT MY PLAY?' Then Mike Bradwell got involved in it. It was material we'd seen before, and people would argue that Brendan Behan had handled it much better, but anyway Brian did it. It was good. I think Mike Bradwell did a great job on it.

The Factory Girls by Frank McGuinness (1990) and *Once a Catholic* by Mary O'Malley (1991–2)

In autumn 1990, Kent directed *The Factory Girls* by Frank McGuinness, which had premiered in Dublin in the early eighties. Eileen Pollock, Heather Tobias, Michelle Fairley, Kathy-Kiera Clarke, and Val Lilley played the girls of the title, a group of workers in a

Donegal shirt factory who decide to take over the office of the manager (Gerard O'Hare) rather than meekly accept threats of layoffs and higher quotas. And in time for Christmas 1991, Kent directed what Charles Spencer called an 'enjoyably irreverent offering' for the season: a revival of Mary O'Malley's *Once a Catholic*.[15] The comedy is located in Kilburn's environs, at a convent school in the 1950s. In a fifth-form class filled with girls named Mary, Dervla Kirwan was Mary Mooney, a girl who, despite the nuns' incessant disapproval of her, longs to become a nun herself.

A Love Song for Ulster: An Irish Trilogy with Music by Bill Morrison (1993)

Nicolas Kent: *A Love Song for Ulster* was just to do something ambitious and interesting about Ireland and to give a history of Ireland and project forward. It went right through to the peace process, which wasn't even a glimmer in anyone's eye at that time. And I found the writer, Bill Morrison, who wanted to do it. It was a wonderful experience. I think it was one of the best things we ever did here. I'm very fond of that production. It's one of the best things I ever did, anyway. And we had an excellent actors company.

A Love Song for Ulster (The Marriage, The Son, The Daughter), directed by Kent, starred Brendan Coyle, Orla Brady and John Keegan, with a band under the direction of Terry Mortimer and a set by Bunny Christie.

The trilogy is a symbolic treatment of the inflamed Irish struggles after the partitioning of Ireland. It is represented by one extended family and the battle for the rights to the land in the north – manifesting in violence between Protestants and Catholics, cycles of vengeance, interference by religious leaders, and British occupation.

Framed by ghost characters who alternately theorise about biblical lore, provide comic relief, and assume roles to move the events along, the primal drama is set in motion with the division of the island. A Catholic family leaves for the south while the daughter is made to stay behind to marry a Protestant man to ensure their claim on the land. (Morrison told the *Guardian* that he was struck with the idea that the situation in Northern Ireland 'was like an arranged marriage'.[16]) Although she's bitter that she's been abandoned and taken forcibly as a wife, the young woman begins to adapt, coming to love her husband. But he is ambushed in a raid while on border patrol and killed by her brother. She is again raped and taken as wife, this time by her dead husband's harsher brother. Their son, encouraged by his father, eventually wreaks vengeance with bloodlust, murdering his mother's brother. Later the guilt-ridden father seeks forgiveness and comes under the influence of a fundamentalist preacher (His Rev) who plots to wrest the land from him.

There's a possibility for reconciliation with the arrival from the south of the wife's nephew. The young man proposes that they find a way to share the land and live together. He and the northern couple's daughter fall in love and have a baby. But reconciliation is foiled by terrorism and His Rev's machinations; the baby is smothered, setting off another cycle of violence and revenge, and leading to military occupation. (A time line for each play in the programme underscored the historical events and parallels to figures like the Protestant minister Ian Paisley and hunger striker Bobby Sands.) After dramatising the years of turmoil, Morrison ends his trilogy on a positive note when the family sit down for a feast, and the couple's daughter voices her dream that her newborn, second son will be able to understand the dangers of the violent history and make choices instead for love and salvation.

The music was integral to the production, setting the mood, reflecting the action onstage, and serving as sound effects. Terry Mortimer says 'the numbers were historical pegs musically', signposts for the trilogy, which covers some 70 years. But Bill Morrison didn't want Irish music, adds the musical director. He wanted popular music, especially from America.

Terry Mortimer: [Bill] said, 'When I was growing up, we weren't listening to Irish music. We went down to the harbour to see what was the latest thing coming from America. And we all got hooked on swing, got hooked on jazz and then rock 'n' roll.' So this is what he was more interested in doing. He said, also, it's a reminder of what's happening in the outside world. Yes, there is this internal strife going on, but there is a much bigger picture outside of this. And that's what he was keen to bring in. I think at one point the British officer [played by Mortimer] says, This is a blip on the world stage. And after all, we're all Europeans now. [Bill] wanted the music to perform that function, and knowing that, for me, that was much clearer.

The plays were done separately and also all together on trilogy days, with tea and supper breaks.

Nicolas Kent: You don't often get a chance to do six hours of something and look at something in that detail. We've always been good at that. And I can only say this in retrospect, but you could link it together with all the tribunal plays. All that work is asking an audience to concentrate on a subject and look at it very hard. And the trilogy days were quite extraordinary. It was very demanding of an audience. [I talked to Kent about *Love Song* in 2008, a year before he produced *The Great Game* plays in three parts.]

The press was invited to a trilogy day, and there were dramatic reactions to the day's viewing. The *Financial Times*'s Malcolm Rutherford found the production so exciting that he urged people to telephone the Tricycle for tickets immediately. The *Evening Standard*'s Nicholas de Jongh wrote after seeing the plays, that 'sated with feudings, fanaticism and bigotry, I stumbled into the relief of a bloodless London evening, depressed and impressed'. Benedict Nightingale a few years later recalled the trilogy as 'a weird and wonderful blend of soap opera and political allegory'.[17]

Kent relishes feedback he heard long after the production had closed from an audience member who had been at the Tricycle for a *Love Song* trilogy day.

Nicolas Kent: The best thing that happened to me about that was the conversation with an American who came up to me about two years later and said he'd seen the show and loved it. And he said what was more fantastic than seeing the show – he had come on a Sunday and sat through the three plays – he got onto the Jubilee line with his orange, white, and green programme (the colours of the Irish flag), and he sat on the Tube, and he suddenly realised that all along the carriage were people who had the same programme. He said, we sat and debated the play on the Tube on our way into central London . . . We talked about the issues, and people got to know each other.

A Night in November (An Afternoon in June) by Marie Jones (1995, 2002, 2003)

The Belfast-based company DubbelJoint made its first appearance at the Tricycle in 1994, with Marie Jones's adaptation of Nikolai Gogol's *The Government Inspector* in a production staged by the company's cofounder Pam Brighton. The company visited the Tricycle the following year, with actor Dan Gordon in a solo performance of Jones's *A Night in November*. Mary Lauder singled out this play as one of her favourites, calling it killingly funny, expressing so much through humour. It begins in Belfast about seven months before the 1994 World Cup. Acting out all the characters in his tale, dole clerk Kenneth McCallister tells the story of how he awakened to the embedded prejudices that governed all aspects of his life as a Protestant man in Northern Ireland, one who was expected to identify more with the British than with his fellow Irishmen. He begins to examine a lifetime of hate and prejudice after a football match between Northern Ireland and the Republic, where the chanting from the crowd refers to a recent murderous attack by two Ulster Freedom Fighters at a bar in Greysteel, Co. Derry. Kenneth's story ends in a surreptitious trip to America for the World Cup match between the Republic of Ireland and Italy, and a hilarious scene of drunken revelry with his compatriots in New York, where he finds his identity as an Irishman. The revival of *A Night in November* at the Tricycle in 2002 and 2003 featured Marty Maguire as Kenneth.

In 1999, the Tricycle presented Jones's *Stones in His Pockets,* starring Conleth Hill and Sean Campion as extras (as well as all the other characters) working on a Hollywood movie that's filming near a Co. Kerry village, with the Irish folk as background. This provides a source of income and excitement for them, but also has the downside of intruding on their lives and their dreams. *Stones* was remounted in 2000, prior to its West End transfer. And in 2011, Indhu Rubasingham directed a new production of *Stones* at the Tricycle with actors Jamie Beamish and Owen McDonnell.

Dance of Death, a new Irish version by Carlo Gébler (1998)

Carlo Gébler, who is 'mad for Strindberg', says it was Kent's 'inspired idea' to do an Irish version of August Strindberg's *Dance of Death*, Parts 1 and 2. Gébler relocated the Swedish fortress to a British Army garrison off the west coast of Ireland. He set Part 1 in 1913 and Part 2 at Easter 1916.

Carlo Gébler: For an Irish audience it takes place on just about the single most important day in modern Ireland's history, Easter

Monday, 1916. Easter Monday was when the Irish Republican movement (or the part of it that believed in physical force) took over the GPO in O'Connell Street in Dublin and various strategic buildings associated with the British state . . . You don't need to know that to appreciate the play. If you do know it, it's so much better.

Part 1 revolves around the battle between man and wife, bound together for 25 years, living in a remote place and isolated from the other people stationed on the island because of their enmity towards them. Bitter and anger, Edgar, a captain in the artillery, and Alice, a former actress, are ever on the attack, even though the captain is now ailing. The vicious nature of their relationship intensifies with the arrival of Alice's cousin Conor who is to be the new Quarantine Master of the garrison island. Conor is sexually attracted to Alice and gets drawn into the couple's games, but at the end of Part 1, lacking their grit, he is worn down by them both. Gébler decided to add a political layer to the couple, making Edgar a Protestant and Alice a Catholic.

In Part 2, two and a half years later, in the middle of World War I, the domestic hostilities are still going on, and the children, Conor's son and Edgar and Alice's daughter, become implicated in the family drama. The two young people, whose relationship has its own games, declare their love and leave the island, the son about to go off to the army. In the final scene, the captain dies, and Alice is gathered up in Conor's embrace. Michael Cochrane played Captain Edgar Dawson; Marion Bailey, his wife Alice; and Tim Woodward, her cousin Conor Coyne.

Gébler lives in Ireland and didn't attend the rehearsals. When he arrived for the dress rehearsal, it was quite unnerving, says Marion Bailey, because she was worried about what might happen if he didn't like it. But when I asked the playwright what he thought about the production, he said, the word 'stunned is on the nail, on the money. Yes, it was extraordinary to see something that one had been imagining in one's head, reconfigured, recapitulated, reanimated onstage.'

Bailey says that although it might sound strange, given the darkness of the play, they had 'some serious fun in the rehearsal room' for Part 1.

> **Marion Bailey:** My main memory . . . was rehearsing Part 1 with the three of us [Bailey, Cochrane and Woodward] and Nick in the rehearsal room, and we had such a good time. And of course it's a lot of stuff to learn. I can remember Michael and I walking up and down outside the rehearsal room going over and over the opening of the play, which was just the two of us. Every morning we'd spend hours walking up and down, both fearing that it might not go in, neither of us being as young as we were, and it's so frightening. And I do remember when we opened, just getting the lines right was scary.

She sees her character as a 'watery and wild' Irishwoman; Cochrane calls his a 'lonely, bigoted man washed up on a tide of loathing'. Because the play is set in a town miles from anywhere, Bailey says, she remembers feeling it was a 'very bleak and cold and icy world . . . They had to act out this passionate, dramatic terrible fire between them because that was the only thing to keep them warm in this world of bleak damp.'

Alice and Edgar might have been fierce sparring partners, but the actors themselves provided emotional support for each other.

> **Marion Bailey:** We were so profoundly nervous for the first week (one always is), but especially so for that. I have this memory of us both in the wings waiting to go on, and Michael in his braces and me in my corset, absolute terror, just holding hands and doing deep breathing to get ourselves out there. And I always felt that despite my terror, I was in safe hands once I was out there onstage. I knew we would look after each other. All three of us that's true of,

but certainly in that first few minutes, there was never a moment's doubt that whatever went wrong, which actually it didn't, but had it done, we were both in safe hands. Everyone was out there to serve the play and look out for each other, which was lovely.

Reviews were mixed for the four-hour battle royal. However Kate Bassett in the *Daily Telegraph* found a theatre-history connection in the adaptation: 'This Irish version makes one see how Samuel Beckett's tramps are surely descendants of Strindberg's proto-Absurdist couple.'[18] The attendance records show the houses weren't full, and when I mentioned that to Bailey, she agreed: 'I can remember having that feeling of plowing through it for less people than I felt it deserved some nights.'

The Wexford Trilogy: A Handful of Stars, Poor Beast in the Rain, and *Belfry* by Billy Roche (2000–1)

For the end-of-year holiday season in 2000, it was the Oxford Stage Company production of Billy Roche's *The Wexford Trilogy*, directed by Wilson Milam. Located in the small town in Southern Ireland, Roche's three plays take us into a pool hall, a betting shop, and the belfry and vestry of a church. *A Handful of Stars* follows the collision course of a teenage rebel. In *Poor Beast in the Rain*, the return visit of the man who left for England ten years before with a married woman unsettles their friends and her family, reopening wounds and stirring up yearnings. In *Belfry*, a sacristan tells the story of his deeply felt love for someone else's wife and the consequences of their affair. Roche wrote with wonder about the appeal of *A Handful of Stars* for the London audience.[19] The play had opened at the Bush Theatre in 1988.

Billy Roche: Very often on opening night, you're sitting there wondering will anyone care. My stories are on the face of it set in small towns where people don't exactly burst to the top of the mountain, so to speak. They're usually carrying the equipment, and they stay at base camp. So there's always the fear that they won't get it or won't feel for the people . . . My plays are dead in the water if there is no emotion there from the actors to the audience and back and in reverse as well. That's always a worry. I suppose taking things from the small town to the metropolis is always a worry because often metropolitan people don't think there's any life beyond the pale of their own place. So I'm still quite puzzled about why they took to it so well.

For the playwright, seeing the trilogy in its entirety on the weekend meant a day in Kilburn and communion with the audience.

Billy Roche: When you do a trilogy, it's different from your average production, in the sense that on Saturdays and Sundays, people would come for the whole day. And I wasn't in the *Trilogy*, so I was amongst them. That creates an amazing buzz because people are coming to a mini festival of sorts. So they come in and they spend the morning with you, then you find that you're having lunch with some of them or bumping into them again. And the second one is in the afternoon, and then people go off and have a meal. Because it's the Tricycle, they can't go back home again. You're certainly bonded with the audience by the time the day is over. Some of them need a shave, they've been there that long. It was the same thing at the Bush. You get to know the audience; you know whether they're enjoying it or not. Some of them are slacking off, but some of them are getting more and more enthused as it goes along. It's a great compliment to the plays, when people stay the course. That's a lot of stuff to see, three plays in the same day by the same writer.

The Cavalcaders by Billy Roche (2001–2)

The following holiday season, Roche acted in a revival of his play *The Cavalcaders*, directed by Robin Lefèvre. Roche played Josie, a role he had originated, alongside Liam Cunningham, David Ganly and Andrew Scott as members of the Cavalcaders, a barbershop quartet based in a small town in Ireland. Together in a shoemaker's shop run by Cunningham's Terry, the four are cobblers as well as singers, continuing in the tradition of Terry's Uncle Eamon. The play opens seven years after the group has disbanded. The shop has been taken over by Rory, one of the young cobblers. Terry, looking older and in poor health, stops by, and Rory regales him with his plans to modernise the place. In a series of flashbacks, a story unfolds of perfidy and poisonous guilt. Terry's soul is troubled – by his youthful sexual indiscretion with the wife of his beloved uncle, and by the loss of his own wife to his best friend, and by his cruelty towards a young lover who committed suicide. The younger men are not immune to infidelities; David Ganly's Ted eventually sets up house with Rory's wife.

But there's also fellowship and there's music for the Cavalcaders, who rehearse in the shop after hours. In the Tricycle production, Ganly, who 'could sing like an angel', says Roche, also played the piano, albeit by ear. When the piano playing is mimed, 'your heart is always in your mouth because of the technical problems of everybody coming in on time', Roche told me. But when the actor actually plays the piano, he says, it 'gives you so much freedom and reality to it as well. So we were trying to be as good a group as we could possibly be . . . It became much more organic.' Roche wrote three songs for the play in addition to an *Alleluia* from the Mass that was supposed to be the work of Uncle Eamon.

This was Ganly's second time acting in *The Cavalcaders*. In an earlier Cork production, he had been Rory to Roche's Terry. Ganly spoke about working with the playwright/actor, who has the 'ability to step back as an author and allow you to find your way down the path'.

David Ganly: It was just wonderful to have the man himself, the real thing from Wexford in the room, because apart from anything else, the Wexford accent is notoriously tricky . . . If ever we felt ourselves going adrift, we'd just tune into him a little bit. And because he's so musical, you're able to pick up on the musicality of his voice. Even his notes were musical. The way he had to communicate things to you, it was always poetic, never dogmatic, and it put you at ease. So far from its being a pressure, it was helpful to have him there because he also trusted his text. And he could unlock little moments that maybe weren't ringing completely true. He'd tell you why he wrote something, as opposed to what it means, and hope that you'd find the meaning.

The moment the 'crude workmen' began to rehearse their first number, Ganly says, you could feel the 'room change', as if the audience were thinking, What are we in for? What is this?

David Ganly: The very first routine for 'Leaning on the Lamppost', we rush in, one or two people late for this rehearsal. I take the cover off the piano and hit a chord, and we do very ropy warm ups, arpeggios, *lalalala,* and I go, Are yez right? – and we hit that first chord in 'Leaning on the Lamppost'. What Billy wanted was for the other three guys to snap into an almost chorus line and to have an old-fashioned, cheesy routine for 'Leaning on the Lamppost'.

Billy Roche: If we were to go see the Cavalcaders, it would be an old-fashioned vaudeville show that we see. But in a way, they trace the history of pop music, going from barbershop all the way to the Beatles to the Beach Boys songs. The Beach Boys, of course – the sound goes back to the baroque sounds of the church, the sacred music of the church. So that's there too, all that ancient harmony.

On 'Leaning on the Lamppost', you were to fool the audience into thinking that these are four small-town Irish cowboys, really . . . They're small-town workmen. And the audience don't know what they are. They haven't seen the piano yet; they don't know what they're coming down to practise. And when they arrive, they begin to tune up, the audience begin to realise what they're rehearsing, what they're practising, and then suddenly they do this little dance routine, a little vaudeville, Bob Hope–type movement. It's not a choreographed thing. It's a manly, kind of barely get-by routine, from a movement point of view. But the audience just love the sudden surprise of it. First, they sing in unison; suddenly they're in four-part harmony, and the audience have never expected this from this crowd of cowboys. That's what theatre is about, a beautiful surprise for an audience. So in a way, *The Cavalcaders* is everything I know about theatre, from music to movement.

10 Rounds by Carlo Gébler (2002)

Carlo Gébler was commissioned to write a play about the 1998 Omagh bombing in which 29 people were killed and 250 injured – and about the peace process in Northern Ireland. The programme suggests that a source for the play was the report from the police ombudsman's investigation into the intelligence received before the Omagh attack. Gébler found his form in Arthur Schnitzler's *La Ronde*, which came to mind, he says, when Kent commented that 'we're all besmirched and muddied and filthy by the awful compromises and complicities which modern life involves us in'.

10 Rounds, taking place in Belfast and Donegal in the late 1990s, stands for the ten scenes of interconnected sexual pairings as one partner goes on to another. It also happens to be the nickname of a Volunteer, who, the story goes, was shot ten times by British soldiers. In Gébler's play an important piece of information is passed from couple to couple: Ten Rounds Milligan is smelling of fertiliser, which indicates that he is making bombs. But it's the early days of the peace agreement, and people are hesitant to jeopardise the ceasefire. A German au pair is entertained by the IRA man at a Republican club, and she begins spreading the information, which eventually reaches a journalist and also a Republican spokeswoman, but results in inaction. One person did try to inform the authorities and was accused of telling lies that would destroy a hard-fought achievement. When a Northern Ireland official wants to arrest the troublemaker as a preventive measure, he is persuaded to let the Republicans handle him. But the government official is soon bedding the prostitute who first detected the fertiliser on Ten Rounds, and as she confirms the official's worst fears about what Milligan is up to, he runs out of the house – too late to stop the bomb from being detonated.

Seeing the Belfast characters onstage in London, Gébler says, 'is always a bit of a shock, because they're very energetic, but they're also earthy and crude, some of them'. Those characters were made flesh and blood by Des McAleer, Mairead McKinley, Victoria Smurfit, Michael Colgan, Clare Holman, Tim Woodward, Brid Brennan and Stephen Boxer, directed by Nicolas Kent.

> **Carlo Gébler:** The cast were fantastic. It's a very difficult piece to make work because it's a relay race, and if you fumble the baton, the people next in line are going to have a much more difficult time with the race. In your ten minutes, which is what each of the ten scenes take, more or less, you really have to get into your stride and get it right.

When I read the reviews, I became interested in the report of sound effects for the various couplings, which Michael Billington noted had included 'everything from gunshots to operatic blasts'.[20]

> **Carlo Gébler:** There were hilarious things like when the au pair is having a moment of brief intimacy on the kitchen table with the

young man of the house; it's the washing machine at the end of the cycle, when the drum spins so fast that the machine judders on its bearings.

John Bull's Other Island by Bernard Shaw (2003)

Dominic Dromgoole directed Shaw's *John Bull's Other Island* in 2003, with Niall Buggy as the defrocked priest Peter Keegan, David Ganly as mill owner Barney Doran, and Charles Edwards as Thomas Broadbent, an English civil engineer. Broadbent and his Irish business partner travel to the partner's hometown in the Irish countryside with a plan to build a hotel and golf course there, or the Garden city that Broadbent grandly envisions. As Peter Keegan remarks, within 24 hours of Broadbent's arrival in the town, the Englishman has practically won the town's parliamentary seat and has also snatched up the town's heiress. (Broadbent is entranced by the music in her voice, but also quickly realises she would be a great boon to him for electioneering.) Letting nothing stand in his way, he remains optimistic even when Keegan speaks out against the engineer's money-making venture. Broadbent decides that the eloquent Keegan, whatever his views, would be an attraction in the redeveloped village.

David Ganly told me that far from its being a period piece, the 1904 play had 'huge contemporary resonances' in 2003.

David Ganly: This was the beginning of the Celtic Tiger economy in Ireland, and here was Shaw writing about greed, about the ability to own your land, and basically about turning Ireland into a golf course. Meanwhile that was actually happening over in Ireland. Land was being purchased and for the first time corporate Ireland kicked off, and even now [we spoke in 2008, just before the recession] – it's only beginning to slow now – anybody with a smallest plot in Dublin, a corner plot on their house, is building another house beside it. It's what he was saying in this play. You should be careful because Ireland is a nation of people who up until fairly recently couldn't own their land. Now all of a sudden, it's sort of taken over, and if we're not careful – I think it was Brendan Behan who said, 'If you stopped, they'd build a house on your head', when Dublin was thriving. I think it was quite timely for that production, certainly for the Irish people I knew in London because they saw this happening.

The Tricycle's records indicate good houses for *John Bull's Other Island*. Ganly gave me his take on the show's popularity.

David Ganly: There's a huge Shavian audience out there, and there's very little of George Bernard Shaw's work done in London. We found that the first few weeks we were getting the Shavian scholars and members of various societies coming to see the show, and they'd come back and bring people. Then we started getting the Irish audience as well, helped hugely I have to say by the presence of Niall Buggy in it as the priest. There was a certain kudos to getting an actor like Niall for that show. It is quite funny – you put an Irish actor into a play, and you're sort of guaranteed 60 other Irish guys coming to see them. There's a wonderful social network in London between not just the actors but family. People would come over from Dublin to see shows at the Tricycle. The artistic director at the time of the Abbey came over to see the show because it's also a play that rarely gets done in Ireland. People were coming from far and wide.

The Quare Fellow by
Brendan Behan (2004, 2005)

In the same year that the Tricycle mounted its verbatim play about the British detainees at Guantánamo Bay, the theatre hosted Brendan

Behan's *The Quare Fellow*, an Oxford Stage/Liverpool Everyman and Playhouse production, directed by Kathy Burke. In Dublin's Mountjoy Prison, the 'quare fellow' is about to be hanged for the murder and dismemberment of his brother. The three acts cover the day before and the morning of the hanging, during which an array of inmates (some repeat offenders, some youths), keenly aware of the imminent execution, get on with their daily lives, making jokes and doing chores (see Figure 3.2). The young ones come by to get a gander at the women hanging up laundry in the yard. An old-timer sneaks drinks of methylated spirits, the salve for his rheumatism. Two inmates place bets on whether the condemned man will be executed or reprieved at the last moment – and others dig his grave. There is no reprieve. The prisoners howl when the hour arrives, but prison routine resumes with inmates working on the grave, divvying

FIGURE 3.2 *(From left) Gerard Rooney, Ciaran McIntyre, Tom Vaughan-Lawlor, and David Ganly in Brendan Behan's* The Quare Fellow, *2004.*

Source: Photograph by Graham Brandon © Victoria and Albert Museum, London.

up the dead man's discarded letters, which they might be able to sell
to the Sunday papers.

David Ganly played one of the prisoners in what he says was a
memorable production, a cast of 17 men, which Kathy Burke was
'well able' to tame.

David Ganly: It's extraordinary to see that amount of bodies and
in this small space and this metallic structure that is the Tricycle
seating. It just lent itself wonderfully to the claustrophobia of a
1950s Dublin prison...

Everybody on that stage wanted to do good by Kathy. This
was a big thing for her to be directing, and we wanted to make
sure that it went well for her. I'm here 12 years this year [2008],
and some of my closest friends came from that show. It was an
extraordinary bond.

Kathy's final note to us before we opened the show was, 'I'm
going to ask you all to do one thing for me, and that's at the half-
hour call every night, I'd like you all to meet onstage, and I would
like one of you to offer up the show to somebody who can't be
there, but who would have loved what we're doing'. She didn't say
to people who are dead, but that sort of is what happened. And
we ran that show I can't remember how many weeks on that first
run and then on the subsequent second run and on tour. Every
single night we offered up that show. Somebody would stand up,
and they'd talk about a person in their life who wasn't around but
who would have loved this. They'd mention their name, and we
would collectively, 17 of us, all say their name, and we'd sing a
verse of 'The Old Triangle'. It meant that we went out that night at
beginners doing the show for one person. It was a stroke of genius
on her part because it absolutely pulled us together. I was amazed:
we never ran out of people to offer up to ... The oldest actor, Tony
Rohr, started to monopolise, and his stories of how people had
passed on just became darker and darker. We had to stop him. We
had to say, 'Tony, that's it. Come on.'

The production did tremendous business on its first run and had a second run the following year in late spring. Ganly says that first run 'was just breathtaking'. They were getting repeat audiences – and some atypical customers.

David Ganly: I remember one night there was a fairground at the far side of the Kilburn Park. And for some reason – I think it was raining – they closed the fairground this night. It was a travelling fairground. Four or five of the guys who ran this came to see the show that night, and they sat in the first two rows. I don't think they'd ever been to a theatre before. They were Irish travellers, basically, and they had a drink in the bar beforehand and were in good spirits. They were absolutely entranced and glued to this show and found themselves cheering and singing, albeit slightly terrifying to you as actors onstage, not quite being able to gauge them.

I do remember catching myself and going, This is the most eclectic mix of people I think I've ever seen in a theatre. Because word got out on that play. Not only had Kathy Burke got her industry friends to come and see it, many quite high up the ladder, but word had got out about what a great evening it was. So we were getting people from the business who had no Irish connections, no connection to Kathy Burke; we were getting so many directors and designers and actors coming in to see the show. And they were sitting next to locals from Kilburn; they were sitting next to north London Jewish people. It was a wonderful mix.

The Field by John B. Keane (2006)

In Tom Murphy's *A Whistle in the Dark*, a Royal Exchange production at the Tricycle in spring 2006, a family's history of violence leads to the unthinkable when the eldest brother is drawn into a fight and kills the youngest of the clan. Following on that production's heels was Keane's 1960s play *The Field*, in which a struggle for a piece of land results in death and a cover-up that implicates the villagers of Carraigthomond in southwest Ireland. For five years, Bull McCabe has rented a widow's field for grazing his cows. Convinced that his cows' manure and his oversight have enriched the land, he is determined to own the field that adjoins his property and provides passage to water for his land. When the widow puts the field up for sale, he bribes the local publican/auctioneer to make sure that he's the only real bidder. However the day of the auction, a challenger (an Irishman by way of England) arrives, with plans to pave over part of the land for a concrete-block business. McCabe tries to warn the outsider off; failing that, he and his son lie in wait for the man and in a fit of fury kill him. Everyone, even the police, knows who committed the crime, but there's no solid evidence. The villagers, frightened and self-interested, close ranks and let the McCabes get away with murder.

Róisín McBrinn had been assistant director on *The Quare Fellow*, and she was now directing her own production at the Tricycle. Heather Tobias, who played the widow and also doubled as the wife of McCabe's cousin, told me about working with the young director.

Heather Tobias: We had a very short rehearsal period. And Róisín was fantastic. Her one thing was there was no way there were going to be any caricatures. These are real people. So we were all rehearsing, and we didn't actually know what we were in, which made some of the men very unsure. And we had this incredible music we heard from backstage, which was like Doctor Vibes. But it worked. I was saying to people, 'This is really weird. I feel as if I'm in Ibsen.' It was so intense, like with Ibsen, peeling the onion. But it worked.

Lorcan Cranitch was a seething Bull McCabe, frightening Tobias's widow and making her all too aware of her vulnerability as a woman living alone on the side of the road. And David Ganly played the publican whom Bull easily reels in for his price-fixing scheme.

David Ganly: It was interesting even casting someone like Lorcan Cranitch as the Bull. Lorcan's not a big, imposing man, but he has a psychological intensity to him. And I think that's what Róisín was interested in. It was seeing a community closing off and protecting its own. The threat doesn't have to be violent. Some of the great stories – look at *Jean de Florette* – all you have to do is cut off someone's water supply, and you ruin their life. It was that psychological darkness she was going for. She achieved that pretty successfully. It was a rocky old rehearsal process in the end. I think we only had three and a half weeks, and that wasn't quite enough. I'm not quite sure what happened there. I think Nick saw the size of the cast and thought, we need to do this cheaper, so he cut a week. But again, Nick took the risk with an unknown director. And the cast she assembled was top rate.[21] I thought it was extraordinary to get those people to work with a director for the first time.

The Field ran from the end of May through the first of July, coinciding with the World Cup, which might have affected the box office. It 'was OK, but it wasn't great', says Mary Lauder, so the Tricycle didn't take up the option weeks. Tobias thinks the time of year might have been a factor. 'It's just a shame that it was across the summer, and it was baking hot. If it had been on in the autumn, we'd have been sold out.' Even so, she says, as often happens at the Tricycle, towards the end of the run 'word gets out, and then things build up'. Tobias wrote to me about an incident at one performance.

Heather Tobias: There was a man in the front row, when we were performing *The Field*, whose mobile went off, and he proceeded to take the call and have a conversation, with the audience shouting at him to turn it off. We were all onstage and waited for him to finish. He gave us the best applause at the end. Strangely, he had an uncanny resemblance to J. B. Keane.

Doubt: A Parable by John Patrick Shanley (2007–8)

Kent directed *Doubt* at the end of 2007. The 'cheerful number', as Lauder laughingly called it, was in line with the Tricycle's original policy for the holidays: to present something serious when other theatres were doing pantomimes and family shows. Their rationale was that the Tricycle was doing work for families and children year round. Eventually, however, that was amended to alternate years for the serious fare.

So during the 2007 holiday season, the show was *Doubt: A Parable*, the award-winning play by the American dramatist John Patrick Shanley about a priest who is suspected of an improper relationship with a 12-year-old schoolboy. It's set in a New York City Catholic school in 1964, where a struggle begins between the nun who is the school's principal and the alleged abuser who teaches there. Despite the male hierarchy of the church, Sister Aloysius is bent on proving the priest's transgression and getting him removed from his position. She tries to enlist the mother of the boy – the first black student at the school. But the mother (Nikki Amuka-Bird) wants no part of the nun's crusade. In a final confrontation with Father Flynn (Pádraic Delaney), who has maintained his innocence, Sister Aloysius insinuates that she knows about his misbehaviour in previous assignments, after which the priest does leave her school. To her dismay, however, he is relocated and gets a promotion.

Dearbhla Molloy played the principal, in a 'superb performance as the fearsome Sister Aloysius', wrote Charles Spencer.[22] Molloy told me she knows about nuns. There's a nun in her family, and she went to a convent school herself, where there were 'various terrifying headmistresses'. She liked the 'whodunnit aspect' of the play but found it limiting that her character was all on one note. 'It's just that absolute, not allowing any other. She's got to be adamant the whole way through. She's got to be absolutely convinced from the beginning right until the last page.' And, Molloy says, there's very little time to develop the doubts that she expresses in her last line.

Dearbhla Molloy: There isn't the space because you just have that very little last scene, and time has elapsed between the second last and the last scene. And I assumed, I thought that during that time, she'd gone over absolutely everything. So I have doubts is not something that she's thinking now for the first time. It's an awful conclusion that she's arrived at, and it's a kind of hellish place to be. Because if she's wrong, she's destroyed a whole lot of lives. . .

The doubts are about the institution of the church and all those things that bother us, how the church can tacitly condone such behaviour.

On the day of the official opening, critic Matt Wolf blogged in the *Guardian* about the usual 'mixed-to-negative' reception in London for productions of American plays that had won 'acclaim back home'. His headline: 'Feted in New York, Trashed in London.'[23] Indeed a number of the London critics were not entirely sold on the play, and one even expressed disdain that it had won the Pulitzer Prize. (It also won the Tony Award for Best Play.) Molloy has a theory about the response in England, with regard to the audience. She thinks the English audience is not as sentimental as the American audience and not 'as intrigued as the American audiences were by the sort of underpinnings of Catholicism that run through that play, that that play is dependent on'.

The year 2010 began with the world premiere of Frank McGuinness's *Greta Garbo Came to Donegal*. In a role specially written for her, Michelle Fairley was once again at the Tricycle, where she had made her London debut 24 years earlier.

Irish theatre productions (1982–May 2012)

1982

Stuffing It by Robin Glendinning

1985

Flann O'Brien's Hard Life or Na Gopaleens Wake by Kerry Crabbe

1986

Flann O'Brien's Hard Life (remount)

Joyriders by Christina Reid (Paines Plough) (two runs)

I Do Like to Be by Shane Connaughton (Irish Company/Tricycle)

The Hostage by Brendan Behan

1989

Pentecost by Stewart Parker (at the Lyric Studio, Hammersmith)

1990

Boots for the Footless by Brian Behan

The Factory Girls by Frank McGuinness

1991

The Cure at Troy by Seamus Heaney, after *Philoctetes* by Sophocles (Field Day)

The Brother, adapted from the works of Myles na Gopaleen (and performed) by Eamon Morrissey (Dublin Comedy Theatre)

Once a Catholic by Mary O'Malley (Tricycle/Bill Kenwright for Liverpool Playhouse)

1992

Once a Catholic (cont'd)

Just the One, written and performed by Eamon Morrissey (Dublin Comedy Theatre)

Love and a Bottle by George Farquhar, adapted by Declan Hughes (Rough Magic)

Una Pooka by Michael Harding

1993

The Ash Fire by Gavin Kostick (Pigsback)

A Love Song for Ulster (The Marriage, The Son, The Daughter) by Bill Morrison

Studs by Paul Mercier (Passion Machine)

At the Black Pig's Dyke by Vincent Woods (Druid Theatre/LIFT)

'One Hell of a Do', Jon Kenny and Pat Shortt (D'Unbelievables)

1994

The Government Inspector by Nikolai Gogol, adapted by Marie Jones (DubbelJoint)

'One Hell of a Do' (remount)

Lady Windermere's Fan by Oscar Wilde (Rough Magic)

1995

A Night in November (An Afternoon in June) by Marie Jones (DubbelJoint)

Uncle Vanya by Anton Chekhov, in a version by Frank McGuinness (Field Day)

Red Roses and Petrol by Joseph O'Connor (Pigsback)

1996

Byrne and *The Brother*, solo pieces by Eamon Morrissey

The Gay Detective by Gerard Stembridge (Project Arts Centre)

1997

Kitchensink by Paul Mercier (Passion Machine)

'I Doubt It', says Pauline, Jon Kenny and Pat Shortt (D'Unbelievables) (Southern Comedy Theatre)

The Mai by Marina Carr

Sive by John B. Keane (Tricycle/Palace Theatre Watford)

1998

Sive (cont'd)

Dance of Death, Parts 1 and 2, a new Irish version by Carlo Gébler (an adaptation of August Strindberg's play)

1999

And the Brother Too . . ., devised and performed by Eamon Morrissey, based on the writings of Flann O'Brien

Paddy Irishman, Paddy Englishman, and Paddy . . .? by Declan Croghan (Birmingham Repertory Theatre)

Catalpa, written and performed by Donal O'Kelly (Red Kettle Theatre Company/Andrews Lane Theatre, Dublin)

True Believers by Joseph O'Connor (Fishamble)
Stones in His Pockets by Marie Jones (Lyric Theatre, Belfast)
2000
Stones in His Pockets (remount) + West End transfer
The Wexford Trilogy: A Handful of Stars, Poor Beast in the Rain, and
Belfry by Billy Roche (Tricycle/Oxford Stage Company)
2001
The Wexford Trilogy (cont'd)
The Kings of the Kilburn High Road by Jimmy Murphy (Red Kettle
Theatre Company)
As the Beast Sleeps by Gary Mitchell (Lyric Theatre, Belfast/
Tricycle)
The Cavalcaders by Billy Roche
2002
The Cavalcaders (cont'd)
The Clearing by Helen Edmundson (Shared Experience)
A Night in November by Marie Jones
I Dreamt I Dwelt in Marble Halls, adapted by Ade Morris (Watermill
Theatre)
10 Rounds by Carlo Gébler
2003
A Night in November (remount)
The History of the Troubles (accordin' to my Da) by Martin Lynch and
Grimes & McKee (Mac Productions)
John Bull's Other Island by Bernard Shaw
2004
The Quare Fellow by Brendan Behan (Oxford Stage Company/
Liverpool Everyman and Playhouse)
Waiting for Godot by Samuel Beckett (John Calder's The Godot
Company)
The Shadow of a Gunman by Sean O'Casey
2005
The Quare Fellow (remount)

2006

A Whistle in the Dark by Tom Murphy (Royal Exchange Theatre, Manchester)

The Field by John B. Keane

2007

The Pride of Parnell Street by Sebastian Barry (Fishamble)

Doubt: A Parable by John Patrick Shanley

2008

Doubt (cont'd)

I'll Be the Devil by Leo Butler (RSC)

Rank by Robert Massey (Fishamble)

2010

Greta Garbo Came to Donegal by Frank McGuinness

The Dead School by Pat McCabe (Nomad Theatre Network/Livin' Dred)

Chronicles of Long Kesh by Martin Lynch (Green Shoot Productions)

2011

Lay Me Down Softly by Billy Roche (Wexford Arts Centre/Mosshouse)

The Absence of Women by Owen McCafferty (Lyric Theatre, Belfast)

Stones in His Pockets by Marie Jones

2012 (till May)

Stones in His Pockets (cont'd)

4

The verbatim and political plays

Kent says the verbatim work was for 'getting across a political message'. With the tribunal plays (most of them edited versions of inquiries) and the Tricycle's own investigations, he addressed illegal exports of tools for making arms to Iraq and, later, the invasion of Iraq – as well as racism in the police force, war crimes, human-rights abuses, and torture. The plays aimed to be balanced and accurate, and to open up discussion and 'debate', a word I frequently heard with regard to the Tricycle's political work. In Kent's final years at the Tricycle, that work extended to cycles of dramatic plays about the history of Afghanistan from the nineteenth century forward and a 'partial history' of the atom bomb. Both the verbatim plays and the play cycles earned the Tricycle the reputation as a vital force in London's political theatre.

The Tricycle's foray into verbatim theatre started in 1994 with its tribunal play *Half the Picture*. When I met Kent in 2005, I told him I had read articles that seemed to say the theatrical presentation of the inquiries could be more relevant than the journalistic coverage. The tribunal play, he said, isn't necessarily more relevant, but it gives a different perspective. It's an alternative to the sound bites on television and in the print media. 'On television, you see it in one minute, and people don't grapple with issues.'[1]

Because public inquiries are usually conducted over months or even years, he added, theatre can be useful to 'get an overview of an issue'. Thus Kent undertook the staging of tribunal plays for which his longtime collaborator, journalist Richard Norton-Taylor, with a touch of genius, edited testimony from inquiries that lasted anywhere from months to years for a two-hour-plus play.

Half the Picture: The Scott "Arms to Iraq" Inquiry, adapted and redacted by Richard Norton-Taylor, with additional material by John McGrath (1994)

Richard Norton-Taylor: It was [Nick Kent's] idea. It all started because I had a group of thespian friends, including Nick, theatre people, who lived near me in north London. And Nick knew I was writing in the *Guardian* these regular articles about this inquiry, which we called the Scott 'Arms to Iraq' inquiry – which was a consequence of a rather embarrassing court case [the Matrix Churchill trial, 1992] that collapsed – into arms-related weapons and machinery that Britain sent [to Iraq] without telling Parliament, when Saddam was a friend of the West. Nick had been reading my articles, five hundred words one day, a big article, a couple of days later a small article. This went on for weeks, months, actually, and he said, 'Why can't we bring it all together for the theatre and do a piece?' And I was full of trepidation, actually. Anyway, I edited from the transcripts what I thought were the highlights and the most interesting pieces, as well as humour – the kind of dissembling of civil servants and officials which happens in every government, I suppose.

The Matrix Churchill trial fell apart because it came out that ministers knew about the firm's illegal exports to Iraq of machine tools that could be used to manufacture arms – and that one of the defendants, Paul Henderson, former managing director of the company (an Iraqi-controlled firm based in Coventry), was in fact an informant for MI6.[2] The inquiry that followed, led by Lord Justice Richard Scott, examined whether the government's policy on arms exports to Iraq had been changed without Parliament's knowledge and whether ministers had misused Public Interest Immunity Certificates at the Matrix Churchill trial, in an attempt to keep sensitive documents secret. The play – culled from 70 hours of evidence given by ministers, government officials, and civil servants – was staged with just two weeks' rehearsal. Its title refers to testimony from a former Foreign Office official (then ambassador) who said that answers to Parliament 'might be half the picture'.[3]

When I was first looking for a script of the play, what I found was individual faxed pages in the Tricycle's archives. Norton-Taylor told me that was how the process had begun.

> **Richard Norton-Taylor:** I was faxing pages. Initially, I was doing drafts for a character at a time, or a scene with one main witness. Obviously, I was happy to do much more than we needed. I was happy to get the advice of Nick, the director. I got impatient with him afterwards as I got more confident and knew more of the director's task and the view of a director. But then, I was modest about it and would send these things in, and we'd cut them all down and we'd talk to the actors quite a bit. I was quite relaxed about it. I wasn't like a sort of playwright where you're very protective of your own words in a traditional writer's sense. I was more a journalist, allowing myself to be 'subbed'.

This first tribunal is distinct from the ones that followed, says actor Thomas Wheatley, in that it was the only one that was at all funny.[4]

Thomas Wheatley: It became known as a Whitehall farce . . . Not only was it entertaining because you had all these Tory ministers weaving their way in and out – the semantics, the language – but also once the audience were able to engage with the material, this dry material suddenly came alive.

Richard Norton-Taylor: This is a kind of Whitehall farce but an almost unintentional humour. People who are speaking, not realising that they actually can be laughed at and are making a fool of themselves. Senior civil servants and Cabinet Secretaries who very rarely if ever talk in public. They live in a secret world, and when they're talking, they're talking amongst peers who would never embarrass them; they're always having private discussions. And even though they were rehearsed for this public inquiry, the Scott inquiry, they didn't realise the effect of what they were saying because they were so used to talking in in-jokes, or in a rather arrogant way, or euphemisms, and dissembling, playing on words, being dishonest in different degrees, that they couldn't stop that practice in an open inquiry . . . A lot of people in the audience who hadn't appreciated that this is how British civil servants and ministers talk were laughing a lot. And it had the added character of Alan Clark, who was a very arrogant and kind of Olympian character. [Clark had been trade minister from 1986 to 1989 and defence minister from 1989 to 1992.] . . . There was Thatcher, there was John Major, mumbling around, saying, OK, I may have been prime minister and I was Chancellor of the Exchequer and foreign [secretary], but I had all these papers coming in – I didn't know anything about it.

The play's hearings opened with William Hoyland as Prime Minister John Major. Hoyland says he spent hours studying tapes of the man.

William Hoyland: There were certain things I did replicate. Like he has a very unmoving upper lip. He talks by moving his tongue and his lower lip. It's just an odd way of talking, and if you get that right, you're halfway there. That sort of thing, and I would wear a pair of glasses that were similar to his. And he parts his hair on this side, and so on. So you do those kinds of things. But I wouldn't try to absolutely imitate him because I found that – and I think we all did – very restricting. And I didn't see John Major at the inquiry, but Nick did, and I would go very much on his notes – by what sort of mood Major was in, whether he was shifty, whether he was confident.

Wheatley and Hoyland are both 'tribunal players', Wheatley having appeared in all the inquiry plays and Hoyland in all but one. The roles for the staged inquiries generally required 'this unusually large collection of older men', as described by Wheatley, who says he was cast as 'a more-or-less credible look-alike or seem-alike' for William Waldegrave, a minister at the Foreign Office from 1988 to 1990, and thereafter a cabinet minister. Most of the actors played more than one role, and Wheatley doubled as Assistant Treasury Solicitor Andrew Leithead. The solicitor was questioned about his editing of a witness statement for the trial. Wheatley remembers that Leithead used to get 'one of the biggest laughs in the evening about photocopying the Public Interest Immunity certificates' – implying that his office was churning them out. The actor says he never got to see a photograph of Leithead, but there was documentation of Waldegrave, who was very well known.

Thomas Wheatley: I did get a tape and tried – as we subsequently have tried to do – to get some of the body language. And I watched that and looked for the hand mannerisms and to some extent the way they speak. [Waldegrave] was a clever man, brilliantly clever, and his mind was always further ahead than his mouth. He talked very fast and incredibly fluently and eloquently, but it was all tumbling out and sometimes it didn't make any sense at all. So I tried to get that. Very long sentences, and gobbledygook in some cases . . . He was the one who agonised most about the issue, and he was the one in most danger, probably.

A reviewer called Waldegrave 'impish', but the actor didn't quite agree with that characterisation.[5]

Thomas Wheatley: Impish. I'm not sure. He was sort of youthful and sprightly – and the rapid speech. But impish implies something evil, which he wasn't. I think he was an honourable man. He did come up with these rather circular arguments, but I think people regard him as one of the more honourable people in that story because he did worry about it.

This tribunal is also different from the others in that it is not strictly verbatim. While the dialogue from the hearings is word for word, with minor exceptions, there are monologues written by playwright John McGrath, representing actual and fictional people: a Matrix Churchill office worker who tried to blow the whistle on the firm's exports; Matrix Churchill's Paul Henderson; economist John Kenneth Galbraith on the connection between government and the military industry; a Kurd on Saddam's atrocities; and a Palestinian supporter of Saddam's. The play closes with a reprise of statements from the inquiry. I asked Norton-Taylor about the theatrical additions.

Richard Norton-Taylor: Nick wanted to spruce it up a bit, if you like, or make it more creative and more exciting and interesting, and break it up from the rather static, by definition, piece that I did . . . It's all rather static and wordy, so we wanted a bit of more imaginative, creative stuff from McGrath, which probably is [because] – I think it's a good thing – we didn't have the confidence on just having the edited transcripts and nothing else.

Yet early in the run, says Hoyland, it was clear that the 'verbatim bits were actually far more riveting than the created bits'. I spoke with Norton-Taylor about whether the fictional additions might have undermined the credibility of a verbatim project.

Richard Norton-Taylor: It certainly detracted, in the sense it diluted the specific point about having the edited transcripts of what actually was said by real people in the real inquiry . . . which needed concentration on the part of the audience too. So I think maybe we needn't have had it, to be honest. At the time, I thought it was quite effective. But if we started all over again, we wouldn't have that extra stuff, I don't think.

That's in retrospect. Before the production opened, there were concerns about how it would all work as theatre.

Richard Norton-Taylor: I remember going to the first rehearsal, [thinking] this is boring, this will never ever work in the theatre, with people coming to the theatre and paying money. Maybe I'd been too close to it, and I didn't also appreciate the full skills of actors and of Nick Kent, the director.

The witnesses, one of whom was Lady Thatcher (Sylvia Syms), faced questions posed by a very savvy, skilled female lawyer. Jan Chappell in the role of Presiley Baxendale QC 'traps her victims', wrote John Peter in the *Sunday Times*, 'by deploying the manner of a bright and helpful girl guide'.[6] Chappell says Baxendale's 'extraordinarily beguiling manner . . . disarmed people she was interrogating because her delivery gave the impression that she was asking questions of her own curiosity'.

Jan Chappell: I was lucky enough that I actually caught her on one of the very last days of the inquiry. It was just sheer luck. And I don't know how I would otherwise have approached it. I assume that Nick and Richard would have given me a description of the woman, and I would have tried to relate to that. And I would have researched as much about her as I could. But to actually see her working, especially as she had such a vivid personality – it was absolutely perfect to have caught her. I think I might otherwise have made some rather less interesting decisions about her character and style.

Any lingering doubts the team might have had about the reception of the play evaporated when the audiences arrived and the reviews hit the stands.

> **William Hoyland:** I can remember quite clearly there was terrible trouble at the dress rehearsal of a technical nature, and it was quite tense, but I think we all felt this really is very, very interesting. And as soon as the reviews came out, we realised we would be playing to full houses. Preview audiences in a small theatre like the Tricycle can be on your side in a way that the general public might not be, so you have to take that with a slight reservation. But once we got such good reviews from a spectrum of political points of view, we realised that we were on to something good.

The critics responded for the most part with a great appreciation for the clarity that the presentation brought to a complex situation, both in the editing and in the performances. Irving Wardle in the *Independent on Sunday* considered that 'the act of framing the event on a stage, with actors re-creating the speech habits and body-language of our leaders, puts it under a piercing light and renews the original sense of shock'.[7]

> **William Hoyland:** It did take off immediately. People were very excited to see these people, Mrs Thatcher, John Major, Alan Clark [played by Jeremy Clyde], but also fascinated to see people like John Kenneth Galbraith and some of the civil servants involved in it whom one never sees publicly. We don't have in our country a system whereby things like the Hutton inquiry and indeed the arms-to-Iraq inquiry are televised[8] . . . So people were fascinated to see how these things function, what sort of relationship the chairman has, whether there's representation and how indeed our elected representatives and civil servants, whose wages we pay, behave. It's all very well reading what they say, but seeing them shift in their chairs and cough and stumble or seeing them answer very positively – that's a whole revelation to British people.

Following the four-week run, *Half the Picture* was performed for Parliament on 11 July in the Grand Committee Room of the House of Commons, hosted by MPs Menzies Campbell, Michael Meacher and Richard Shepherd.

> **Jan Chappell:** When you think of it, the idea of it was surreal. There was a bit of me that wanted to laugh. We were taking Sylvia Syms who was pretending to be Mrs Thatcher, the ex–prime minister, into the Houses of Parliament to act Mrs Thatcher in front of whatever MPs who worked there would come along. We were fascinated to know who would turn up. And of course those cabinet ministers did not turn up.
>
> **William Hoyland:** Some of the Labour politicians just wanted to see John Major make a fool of himself. Actually the issues were more important than that. It was a strange occasion, that one. It wasn't so much a poke in the eye to them as we thought we might be. I think a lot of the more interested MPs, the MPs who cared about the issue, had come to the Tricycle. In fact, as we always do, we had question-and-answer sessions once a week. And a lot of members of the shadow cabinet, as it was then, had come to those to engage in the issues with different people. So the House of Parliament was in some ways disappointing and in other ways fascinating.

A filmed version of *Half the Picture* (somewhat pared down) aired on BBC Two in February 1996 at the time of the Scott Report.

> **Jan Chappell:** When I think back, it makes me laugh. I think it was so sweet how we thought when we did *Half the Picture* it was going to have more impact. Somehow we were going to help bring the government down. The government remained completely immune to anything. The scandals that came out, and the ministers stayed. And being a child of the fifties and sixties, I thought, I can't believe they're just riding this. They're just staying there. How can they?

Nuremberg War Crimes Trial, edited by Richard Norton-Taylor (1996)

Norton-Taylor says he was uncertain about doing *Nuremberg.*

Richard Norton-Taylor: I didn't know how it was going to play and what the response was going to be in '96, the 50 years anniversary. I had no idea, really, because it had been done. They'd done plays about it and films about it, and so people had known a lot. And people had read about it, and there are many books about it. But Nick again was the driving force, optimistic about that, and I think there was enough audience around, especially in north London, and again it got tremendous acclaim.

His first task was to read the transcripts. (There are 23 volumes in the HMSO edition.) But he says he had 'a bit of luck'.

Richard Norton-Taylor: The first bit of luck was a friend of mine, a secondhand bookseller . . . found a secondhand edition of all the official British transcripts in some warehouse somewhere. I bought them for about £20. So I could keep them in my hand. I could mark them with a pencil on my bus journeys to work every day or over a coffee, and that made a lot of difference.

Once you've chosen the characters, there are obvious scenes which one did – [Hitler's designated successor Hermann] Goering, for example. But there are other scenes too, and there's an extra element of the British interest, which was how [Sir David] Maxwell Fyfe took over from Robert Jackson, the American chief prosecutor who really couldn't control Goering. Goering was almost controlling him in the interrogation. That intrigued me. And you choose people. I remember choosing Alfred Rosenberg [Reich minister for the Occupied Eastern Territories]. Why did I choose Alfred Rosenberg? He was a minor figure in a way, but he was the intellectual defender of Nazism and anti-Semitism, even though he had Jewish blood himself. But partly because he was active as a proselytiser of the Nazi doctrine. And at one stage, he's playing on words as well, *Ausrottung*, the meaning in German of extermination. He says it doesn't really mean it. That's a thread of some of the tribunal plays – some people say the more boring thread, but I think actually quite interesting thread of playing on language, how language can mean a lot of different things, how you can lie and people in civil service say that's not a direct lie, or the ambiguity, which interests me a lot too.

Norton-Taylor chose four of the trial's 22 defendants. In addition to Goering and Rosenberg (Jeremy Clyde), there was Field Marshal Wilhelm Keitel, chief of staff of the armed forces, and Albert Speer (Michael Culver), armaments minister. He also included Rudolf Hoess, the commandant of Auschwitz, who was called to the stand as a witness.

Goering (Michael Cochrane, sporting dark glasses) is the first defendant up. He testifies that the Gestapo was for state security, and that the concentration camps were for their enemies. However, an unrepentant Goering insists that when he was in charge he had no knowledge of the mass murder at the camps. Cochrane says he read extensively and watched film of the Nazi, before and during Goering's incarceration. 'Whether right or wrong', he says, 'I decided that of all the Nazi leaders, Goering was probably the only one with a huge sense of humour'. Cochrane's assured, smiling Goering would lean into the microphone at times, lowering his voice to give his answer with a thick layer of condescension. Charles Spencer called his performance 'tremendous . . . exuding arrogance like a rank scent' and reminding 'us that evil can also exert a hateful hypnotic glamour'.[9]

A tightly wound Keitel, played by William Hoyland, defends his soldiers with the now familiar claim for the atrocities of the war: they were following orders. He considers that he was a loyal officer who was serving the führer, and says it was as a soldier acting on orders that he signed a document calling for political hostages to be shot.

William Hoyland: I found out as much as I could about Wilhelm Keitel. Obviously he's in encyclopedias and histories of the Second World War. One of the things I found out about him, which is well documented, was that he was really pleased to overcome the love for his son and send him to certain death on the eastern front for the sake of his country. He wrestled with it and decided it was a wonderful thing that he'd managed to overcome this weakness, this sentimentality that made him attached to his son. [His three sons all went to war.] The fatherland was more important, and he was pleased with that. Now I found that quite difficult to understand. And the other thing I found out about him was, he was terribly upset that Eisenhower wouldn't let him keep his swagger stick, his badge of generalship. He even wrote to Eisenhower and said, Look, I behaved like a gentleman, why can't you? And his last request before he was killed was for a brush and dustpan so that he could leave his cell clean.

Understanding that man was quite difficult. But a friend of mine said, I think that I can help you. Keitel was a Prussian. That's German as well, but a separate identity. In the early days of the invasion of Poland, when the Poles had cavalry and the Germans had tanks, some of the Prussians found that difficult. And Hitler got rid of quite a lot of them, but not Keitel.

Thomas Wheatley as Hoess painstakingly detailed the setup at the camp as the victims went to the gas chambers, discussing the time it took for them to lose consciousness. I asked Wheatley whether there was a difference in his acting approach for the historical trial as compared with a contemporary inquiry.

Thomas Wheatley: It was still verbatim, transcripted material. I'm not sure because it was historical that that made any difference to the approach. Certainly I don't think any of us came in trying to create a character. We did do research. I went to the Imperial War Museum and saw footage of Hoess in the witness box. So I did see him and hear him a little bit. But he was famously normal. The banality of evil. There really wasn't anything at all to pick up on. I did try to get inside the man. And how on earth do you do that with somebody who's murdered, at his own calculation, two and a half million people and is absolutely OK about it?

The reason he was selected by Richard was that his testimony was unique in that he told the truth because he didn't have any problem with the truth. Everybody else was weaving their way around the truth. He was brought in in a very strange way by German counsel for Ernst Kaltenbrunner [chief of Reich security] who was in the dock as a defence witness, partly I think because he would look so bad that the people in the dock would look less bad. But also most importantly because he was going to give testimony that the decision about the Final Solution was so secret that none of them could have known. And in our piece that's largely what he's talking about. So that's why he was brought in, and once he got there, as you see from the piece, he just doesn't have any difficulty with the truth. And so he gives this extraordinary dispassionate account of it all. Anyway how I got into it was perceiving that this was a man who quite simply wanted to do everything absolutely right. And so all I did really was determinedly answer the questions absolutely correctly. I remember I'd listen very carefully to the question and then answer to the best of my ability.

Wheatley told me he loves the 'precision of the designs each time', creating the life of the court. For *Nuremberg*, in the forties courtroom evoked by designer Saul Radomsky, a 'fantastic atmosphere' was built up, he says. 'The richness of having a couple of American soldiers, always one black, one white, with the white helmets [as sentries], and people speaking French and German as interpreters in the back.'

William Hoyland: Those of us who have been in nearly all of them – well, this is my view, but it is shared – think that in purely theatrical terms, taking as it were the content away, *Nuremberg* was the most successful. It was a massive cast, as well as the four defendants that were chosen, very well chosen . . . They represented all the different strands of Nazism and German patriotism. And the translators, a number of different lawyers, the GIs – Nick created a wonderful room. Theatrically, it was probably the best of them.

Kent commissioned one-act contemporary response plays as openers to *Nuremberg* – *Ex-Yu* by Goran Stefanovski; *Haiti* by Keith Reddin; and *Reel, Rwanda* by Femi Osofisan. (Alternating on Mondays through Thursdays, the three were performed together on Fridays and Saturdays.) The response plays got mixed reviews.

Thomas Wheatley: I know they were difficult and rather long. And with *Nuremberg* tacked on, the press night went on for hours. They were difficult pieces and were perhaps a bit under-rehearsed. *Ex-Yu* did work. It was rather a nice piece. When we brought *Nuremberg* back in the autumn of that year, the other two were ditched, and *Ex-Yu* continued with *Nuremberg*, and *Srebrenica* came in as well.

Srebrenica, edited by Nicolas Kent (1996, 1997)

The prologue to *Nuremberg* had been a speech by Justice Richard Goldstone, chief prosecutor of the UN International Criminal Tribunals for the former Yugoslavia and Rwanda. When Goldstone came to see *Nuremberg*, says Kent, 'he was very impressed with the place and the work we were doing'. Kent in turn went to the Hague in summer 1996, to attend the Rule 61 hearings on Radovan Karadzic and Ratko Mladic.[10] Testimony from three days of the hearings about

Srebrenica were formed into a tribunal play by Kent from transcripts of audio recordings.[11]

The play's witnesses recount the terrible events that led to genocide: the Bosnian-Serb army's blockade of the UN safe area during the war in Bosnia; the invasion of the enclave by the Bosnian-Serbs in July 1995; the Muslim refugees fleeing to the town of Potocari and the UN compound there; the deportation evacuations (in which Muslim men were separated from the women and children) – overseen by General Mladic, and followed by the wholesale murder of the males at the hands of the Bosnian-Serb army. (News reports have estimated that from 7,000 to 8,000 Muslim men and boys were killed with the fall of Srebrenica.)

Drazen Erdemovic, the last of the four people who give testimony in the play, had pleaded guilty. The play's Erdemovic is a Croat in his twenties, who as a married man with a pregnant wife joined the Bosnian-Serb army out of necessity. Jay Simpson portrayed the traumatised soldier who says he tried to protest but was forced to participate in the executions or be killed himself. He relates how civilian Muslim men transported in buses from Srebrenica to a farm were lined up and shot, more than one thousand by the end of that day, 16 July 1995.

Critics valued Kent's restrained approach to staging the hearings. He 'recreates the business-like, subdued atmosphere in which the most ghastly of crimes are described', wrote *Time Out*'s Jane Edwardes. And from the *Sunday Times*'s John Peter: 'Nicolas Kent's edited presentation of these hearings is among the most shattering hours I have spent in the theatre.'[12]

William Hoyland was Colonel Karremans, the commander of the Dutch peacekeeping forces (see Figure 4.1). Crippled by the blockade, the commander and his men were unable to protect the enclave.

William Hoyland: *Srebrenica* was for me one of the most shocking of them . . . It was incredibly powerful. Playing Colonel Karremans was an extraordinary experience because he was such

FIGURE 4.1 *William Hoyland as Colonel Karremans in* Srebrenica, *edited by Nicolas Kent, 1997 (remount).*

Source: Photograph by Douglas H. Jeffery © Victoria and Albert Museum, London.

a weak man – and yet probably a decent man, not a bad man, not an evil man, a man who was just out of his depth. And Mladic was so much cleverer, out of Karremans's league in terms of cunning and guile. When the report came out, the entire Dutch government resigned. They were reappointed the next day, but it was a pretty wonderful gesture. Our country was partly responsible for this, and we must take that responsibility.

The year after *Srebrenica* played with *Nuremberg*, it was produced on its own at the Royal National Theatre in November as platform performances, and it also travelled to the Belfast Festival.

William Hoyland: We took *Srebrenica* to Northern Ireland, which was a very bold thing to have done. You'll probably get viciously attacked for reporting this, but some people consider there to be some parallels between the situation in Northern

Ireland and Srebrenica . . . And one of the journalists, Maggie O'Kane, who works for the *Guardian* and who helped us with *Srebrenica*, was from Northern Ireland. She was very keen to take it there. The after-show discussions in Northern Ireland were extremely heated.

The Colour of Justice: The Stephen Lawrence Inquiry, edited by Richard Norton-Taylor (1999)

The Colour of Justice – considered their best tribunal, says Norton-Taylor – stemmed from a racist murder in southeast London. Stephen Lawrence, a black teenager, was waiting for a bus in April 1993 when he was assaulted and fatally stabbed by a gang of white youths. Owing to a faulty police investigation, no one was convicted for that crime despite common knowledge of the identity of the attackers. After years of activism by the Lawrences, including an unsuccessful private prosecution, Home Secretary Jack Straw of the newly elected Labour government called for a public inquiry, chaired by Sir William Macpherson.

Norton-Taylor's play lays out the extent to which entrenched racism in the police force affected its investigation, beginning with one of the first police responders at the crime scene who neither looked for Lawrence's wounds nor attempted first aid. There were false assumptions about the victim and his friend, Duwayne Brooks, who was with him on the night of the attack. There was the insensitive treatment of the victim's parents. And missing records and disregarded leads and delay in arrests. But 'it wasn't all about police incompetence and racism', says Norton-Taylor. 'We had this character called [Conor] Taaffe.' The Irishman, who was on his way home from church with his wife, came upon Stephen Lawrence and Duwayne Brooks after the stabbing and saw Lawrence fall to the ground. Taaffe bent down by the boy and prayed over him. He told the inquiry 'in a poetic way, an emotional way', says Norton-Taylor, that when he went home he poured water mixed with Lawrence's blood that had gotten on his hands on a rose tree in his garden.

A number of the actors in *The Colour of Justice* were tribunal veterans: Michael Culver as Macpherson; Jeremy Clyde as the Lawrences' counsel Michael Mansfield; Jan Chappell as a family-liaison officer; William Hoyland as a belligerent former detective named John Davidson; Thomas Wheatley as an inspector at the crime scene who testifies that he no longer has notes of the incident but does have the clipboard; and James Woolley as counsel to the inquiry. Kent directed the play with Surian Fletcher-Jones.

'A most magnificent production', says Kwame Kwei-Armah, about this tribunal. 'Even as an enterprise, it was amazing.' And very special, I was told by others, was the moment when Macpherson would ask the inquiry's attendees to stand for a minute of silence in honour of Stephen Lawrence and his courageous parents. Then everybody in the audience would stand along with the actors. Mary Lauder says, 'Everybody did it, including my own brother. I thought he would be, What is this about? That really meant something to me.' Architect Tim Foster talked about how moving it was that the audience stood, adding, 'It seems to me that's exactly what that kind of theatre ought to be about'. Jenny Jules, who portrayed two different lawyers in the play, remembers how the audience were caught up with the piece, as if they were at the actual inquiry.

Jenny Jules: Sometimes the boy who was playing Jamie Acourt, one of the accused, would feel threatened. People wouldn't speak to him in the bar. People would think he was the actual guy. His name was Christopher Fox. He had a tough time. And I said, 'It's because you're such a good actor. Your portrayal of this horrible, evil young man is so powerful, is so real, so genuine that the audience believe you're him.'

Fox's Jamie Acourt appeared near the end of the play. An obdu-
rate witness, he claims to have no connection to the many knives
that were found in his home and denies that he and his friends
carry knives. Asked if he, his brother and his friends are racists, his
answer is no. When confronted with his gang's ugly racist threats
captured by a surveillance video he had seen, and asked whether
he is 'shocked' by them, he says he isn't, then refuses further comment. The actor got a special mention from Charles Spencer: 'Fox is
flesh-creepingly repellent as one of the racist yobs suspected of the
murder'[13] (see Figure 4.2).

Acting choices, I was told, must fairly represent what occurred at
the inquiry.

William Hoyland: Paul Foot, who's unfortunately dead now
and who was a very good journalist, went to every single session

FIGURE 4.2 *Michael Culver as Sir William Macpherson and
Christopher Fox as Jamie Acourt in* The Colour of Justice, *edited by
Richard Norton-Taylor, 1999.*

Source: Photograph by Douglas H. Jeffery © Victoria and Albert Museum,
London.

of the Stephen Lawrence inquiry, and he was very helpful to me because if you remember I become very aggressive, and there was actually something that he wanted us to put in. When John Davidson finished giving his evidence – there was a section in the public gallery for police – he looked up and winked at them. We didn't put it in because that wasn't on record. Only Paul Foot had seen it, and although we're absolute believers, we didn't feel there was enough evidence. If five or six people had seen it, we might have put it in. We have to be absolutely scrupulous in those areas to not do anything that would be considered untrue, or people could question, even question. We don't want anyone to in any way question anything we do as not being truthful. Because once you do that, you've lost the battle. What we say is, This is what happens. Make your own mind up as to whether people are behaving well or badly.

The accurate re-creation extends to the mise-en-scène: the computers, the rows of desks, the ring binders, lawyers whispering to each other, and people walking in and out. The hearings had been in Hannibal House at Elephant and Castle, south London. Designer Bunny Christie apparently captured the room exactly.

James Woolley: I understand that one of the journalists who came to the first night – that was a very long inquiry, and he'd slogged through the whole inquiry – said, 'Just for an awful moment, I thought I was back in that room at the Elephant and Castle', because it had replicated it so well.

Stephen's parents, Doreen and Neville Lawrence, and their lawyers were at the January press night for *The Colour of Justice*. Neville Lawrence joined the postshow discussion chaired by Channel 4's Jon Snow, who encouraged the audience to write to the BBC about broadcasting the play.[14] (In fact it was filmed and televised on BBC Two the following month.) The production 'just blew up', says Jenny Jules. 'It became this whole newsworthy event.'

Thomas Wheatley: The reason it did happen so successfully, I suppose, was that we absolutely coincided with the publication of the report. The report came out while we were performing it, and we immediately became part of the headline news, which rolled for much of that period. So there were television news teams up at the Tricycle, and extracts were played, I think, from the play in the news programmes. And the Lawrence lobby, Doreen Lawrence, solicitor Imran Khan, and Duwayne Brooks as well, spent quite a lot of time up there.

The report, published on 24 February 1999, found that 'the investigation was marred by a combination of professional incompetence, institutional racism and a failure of leadership by senior officers'.[15] That was during the run at Theatre Royal Stratford East, where the production had transferred in mid-February.

Thomas Wheatley: We first went to Stratford East, and it was packed. The audience was younger, and there were more black people than at the Tricycle. They were very responsive, and they were not a theatre audience. More than any other piece, the Stephen Lawrence piece brought in people who didn't go to the theatre. And at Stratford East, that meant they participated. Those of us who were playing dodgy policemen were heckled, which is very exciting.

Then we went to the Victoria Palace, which was vast. They didn't use the upper levels, just the stalls. But hundreds and hundreds of people came. We were a long way from them, but it worked. And that was a whole lot of different people.

In the autumn, *The Colour of Justice* toured England with a stop at the Royal National Theatre in London and a trip to Belfast.

Jenny Jules: We toured the play around the country. If there's one thing I've learnt about the British people, they hate to be called racist. You can call them anything, you can call them any name you can find, but to call them a racist makes them absolutely furious. This is one thing they never want to be associated with. I didn't know that. And I was happy – I was proud to know that people, whether they were racist or not in their attitudes and their actions, didn't want to be a racist. That was important for me.

One of the many accolades for the play came from Stephen Lawrence's father.

Nicolas Kent: Neville Lawrence was asked on *Newsnight*, 'What's the best thing to have come out of the inquiry? What's the most educative thing that can be done now?' He said, 'Everyone should see the Tricycle Theatre play'.

The Colour of Justice won the *Time Out* Live award for outstanding achievement for theatre; the production was included in the 'Calendar of Notable Events' for 1999 in Richard Eyre and Nicholas Wright's *Changing Stages*; Michael Billington wrote about the play's significance in his book *State of the Nation*.[16] (Norton-Taylor told me that it's a textbook in some police colleges.)

In 2008, Kent attended an unusual production of *The Colour of Justice* in Madrid.

Nicolas Kent: I spoke at the beginning of the play, gave a talk about verbatim theatre and how we had reconstituted the inquiry room, and it was all very austere, exactly like it was in the inquiry, with a great attention to detail. It was a big mistake because I should have talked about this after I'd seen the play, but they put me on before I saw it. I went to see the play, and instead of the inquiry room in a government building in Elephant and Castle, I walked into a sand pit, with tailors' dummies strung diagonally from the ceiling and one chair painted green stuck in the middle. Then a cast of six came on, three men and three women, none of whom were black – the whole point of the play is that it's about racism. And they stripped off to black lacy underwear, and then they put on these neo-Nazi uniforms.

And they did the play for two and a half hours without an interval, which is a long time to sit through this entire play. All playing all the parts. It was staggeringly interesting, but hardly anything to do with the play. And this audience sat in rapt attention.

Postscript: In January 2012, two of Stephen Lawrence's attackers, Gary Dobson and David Norris, were found guilty of his murder at the end of a trial in which new evidence incriminated them.

Justifying War: Scenes from the Hutton Inquiry, edited by Richard Norton-Taylor (2003)

Six months before the March 2003 invasion of Iraq by US and UK forces, the British government published the dossier with the claim that Iraq could deploy some weapons of mass destruction within 45 minutes. In late May, a couple of months after the unpopular war began, Andrew Gilligan, then correspondent for Radio 4's *Today* programme, reported that a senior official had told him the 45-minute claim was inserted in the week before publication because Downing Street ordered that the dossier be 'sexed up'.[17] That precipitated a heated conflict between the government and the BBC. By July, chemical- and biological-weapons expert David Kelly was named as the source for the broadcast. On 15 July, Dr Kelly answered questions at a televised hearing of a parliamentary foreign-affairs committee. The following day, he appeared before the intelligence and security committee, and on 18 July, he was found dead, having committed suicide. An inquiry into the 'circumstances surrounding the death of Dr Kelly' opened in August at the Royal Courts of Justice, with Lord Hutton presiding.

Hutton ruled that while his opening statement and lawyers' addresses could be televised, evidence of witnesses would not be filmed for TV or broadcast on radio.[18] That was a cue for the Tricycle, which mounted its next tribunal play, *Justifying War: Scenes from the Hutton Inquiry*, for an autumn 2003 opening.

Richard Norton-Taylor: I was very reluctant to do this partly because it was so soon after the inquiry itself . . . It was only a couple of months after the end of the hearing, which people had seen, and the television had picked up by then. The daily television had done a lot of the reports, which they hadn't done on the Macpherson inquiry into Stephen Lawrence's death, and they certainly hadn't done on the Scott inquiry beforehand. And it was quite difficult, because apart from one or two scenes, where you had his widow at the end, a lot of it was rather too much going backwards into the depths of Whitehall and the machinations. And some of the best, more colourful language and more striking omissions in the inquiry had come out of e-mails rather than people talking, which made it more difficult.

In preparation for the production, Kent attended the inquiry, as did some of the actors. With a limited number of seats – ten in the public gallery – James Woolley, who played Lord Hutton, says he queued as early as five o'clock in the morning to gain admittance so that he could watch Hutton and get a feel for the way he ran the court. Charlotte Westenra, Kent's co-director, also arrived early to get one of the coveted seats.

Charlotte Westenra: I'd join what we began to call the Hutton junkies, and we'd kind of meet up about seven, swap coffee, get breakfast. The only day I didn't get in was when Tony Blair was speaking because people were queuing up overnight to hear him. You'd have to come quite early when Alastair Campbell was speaking or when different people were speaking.

Designer Claire Spooner, who went to the hearings on the day of Campbell's testimony, says she got there 'very, very early and managed to get a seat in the adjoining room', where there was a video link. 'Lots of people were being turned away.'

> **Charlotte Westenra:** I think the other thing to put in there was that the court case became like a piece of theatre, which sounds horrifically callous. I don't mean to be disrespectful to Dr Kelly, but what I mean is that it became a public event. The first three days would be quite boring because you wouldn't know who everyone was. But then after that you'd start to see the different themes, as if you were watching a play. And you began to see the links. You began to see different stories coming to the surface and then you wouldn't hear of them for two weeks, and then suddenly you would hear of them. And then at the end, I remember, James Dingemans, who was the QC for the inquiry, said, 'Somewhere along the way we lost a summer. I hope we exchange it for understanding.' And he got a lump in his throat because obviously this was so personal to him. Then I got a lump in my throat, and I realised that it was a massive process to go through. Because that was just the beginning. That was the research bit done. Now we were going to start working on the play.

Although broadcasters were barred from filming the evidence of witnesses, the inquiry set up a website to give open access to written evidence and the transcripts of daily testimony.

> **Charlotte Westenra:** We had copies of all the transcripts because they [were] made available to the public. Every night they would appear on the website. So you would have personal e-mails from Alastair Campbell made available, and something like four weeks later they would be quoted in the inquiry. For me, that was the most significant part of the whole inquiry. Because it was really about freedom of information. We could download day by day what all the witnesses said, but obviously it was thousands and thousands of pages. What I would then do once Richard had edited it down was print up anything that the witnesses he

included said. So we still had a lot of transcripts, and they were available in rehearsals.

The play focuses on reporters' contacts with Dr Kelly; the friction between the government and the BBC over the broadcaster's accusations; the naming of Dr Kelly as the source for the BBC news story; and the tragic outcome for him and his family. Among those on view are journalists, the BBC's chairman, the defence secretary, and civil servants.

Andrew Gilligan (played by William Chubb) admits that his language had not been 'perfect' in his first unscripted broadcast when he stated that the government probably knew the 45-minute figure in the dossier was 'wrong'. He subsequently used the word 'questionable' instead.[19] At the end of June, Kelly wrote a letter to his manager saying he had spoken with Gilligan, but he did not believe he was the 'single source' cited in that story. (Excerpts of that letter are reprinted in the programme.)[20] The Ministry of Defence (MoD) soon issued a release suggesting that 'an individual had come forward', after which the MoD adopted a policy to confirm Kelly's name to 'any journalist who offered it' – as James Blitz of the *Financial Times* (Thomas Wheatley) found out.[21] Blitz relates how his colleague came up with Kelly's name through an internet search using information about the source that had been given in a press briefing.

Twelve witnesses from the first phase of the inquiry are in the play, but Prime Minister Tony Blair's testimony was left out. Reviewers noted his absence, some using the analogy of *Hamlet* without the prince.[22]

Richard Norton-Taylor: I would have rather liked Tony Blair in a way, but I was persuaded by Nick. Nick said, If you have Tony Blair, it would overshadow the rest . . . And Blair did not add anything in terms of revelation to the sum of knowledge. I think Nick thinks it tends to caricaturisation. Everyone is going to look at Blair and see how he's played because he's been played so many times on television, and plays by David Hare, and so on, and the film *The Queen*. I think we could have had him, probably, very briefly.

Blair's director of communications, Alastair Campbell, was on view, however, acted by David Michaels. Campbell strongly denies he was responsible for including the 45-minute claim in the dossier. The play also features a very theatrical appearance by Andrew Mackinlay, a Labour MP on the foreign-affairs committee that had questioned Dr Kelly. The MP's aggressive style and his likening Kelly to chaff in a diversionary tactic by the government had caused a backlash against Mackinlay. During the run of *Justifying War*, the MP went to Kilburn more than once, I was told – and saw himself interpreted onstage by Roland Oliver.

Charlotte Westenra: He completely adored Roland Oliver, who was playing him. I remember the two of them sitting in the Tricycle bar, and they were identical. Roland had got his mannerisms . . . Mackinlay was such a lovely man. And I think it was very important for him because he got a really rough time. He was on the select committee, and he was videoed pointing a finger at David Kelly just before David Kelly committed suicide. And Mackinlay got quite animated, but that's the way he talks. And actually what he was doing was trying to get at the truth of what happened. It's a very complicated issue, the whole Dr Kelly affair. I think Mackinlay felt very upset, because after Dr David Kelly died, they would play this video again and again. At the inquiry Mackinlay got up in the courtroom, and he gave this passionate defence about the meaning of Parliament and how people should be held accountable. And you just wanted to stand up and applaud him there and then.

Mrs Kelly is the last witness, which is the one liberty taken with the actual chronology of the inquiry hearings. Because Mrs Kelly had given evidence remotely, her photographic image was shown on-screen, and her testimony was transmitted over an audio link. Mrs Kelly (played by Sally Giles) talks about her husband's withdrawal and his utter distress, giving a portrait of the modest man embroiled in a public controversy. Her testimony concludes with an account of her husband's final moments at home before he left for what she thought was just a walk. Paul Taylor wrote in the *Independent*: 'I shall never forget the brief, harrowing silence at the other end of the line before Mrs Kelly, hitherto steady and stoic, confirms that the painkiller her husband used [in his suicide] was the medication that she takes for arthritis.'[23]

Installing the audio link for that testimony got just a bit complicated.

Shaz McGee: The Hutton inquiry was very simple until Nick decided that David Kelly's wife would give evidence from the upstairs dressing room by a live link every night – instead of just having . . . the testimony on minidisc with the answers recorded, which would be absolutely foolproof. But Nick was, No, no, no. It's got to be live every night. So we ran cable (when we took all the cable out, we coiled up about three kilometres of it!) from the control room, under the stage, up the back stairway into the dressing room. And Nick wanted two of everything, in case one system failed. So she'd have two headsets in case one headset broke. She'd have two microphones, in case one microphone didn't work. She'd have two cue lights, in case one of the cue lights didn't work. She had an infrared monitor of what was happening onstage. She had an audio monitor which was run in separately, because there's one on the wall for the actors to know when to go downstairs for their cues, but Nick wanted another one in case that one failed. That was a really easy production, except – but we were all laughing about it.

Justifying War was broadcast on BBC Four in early January 2004, some weeks before the report was published. The BBC took several hits in Hutton's report for its story with 'unfounded' allegations regarding the dossier, for a 'defective' 'editorial system' that hadn't vetted the story, and for the management's failure to follow up after the government complained about Gilligan's broadcast.[24] The BBC's chairman Gavyn Davies, director-general Greg Dyke, and Andrew Gilligan all resigned. The government for the most part was found to have acted properly – leading to cries of whitewash. But the Tricycle wasn't finished with looking into the Blair government's involvement in the Iraq war. First, however, the theatre turned its attention to Guantánamo Bay.

Guantanamo: 'Honor Bound to Defend Freedom' by Victoria Brittain and Gillian Slovo, from spoken evidence (2004)

In the post–9/11 war on terrorism, the US naval base in Guantánamo Bay, Cuba, became a repository for 'unlawful combatants' – or terrorist suspects. There were British citizens among the detainees, who were being held 'indefinitely without trial' by Britain's 'closest ally', Kent says, and the 'government was not protesting to get them out'. Kent decided to do something about that. In January 2004, he commissioned journalist Victoria Brittain and novelist Gillian Slovo to create a verbatim play based on interviews 'with detainees, their families, their lawyers, and also to use any public statements made by government officials in the United States or in Great Britain'.

Then in February, Foreign Secretary Jack Straw announced that five British detainees would shortly be returning to the United Kingdom. Victoria Brittain told Matt Foot for the *Socialist Review* that when the detainees were released, 'we suddenly thought, have we still got a play, or will they have said so much that everybody will know everything? In fact this didn't turn out to be the case at all.'[25] The interviews plus correspondence, statements to the press, and a law lord's speech make up Guantanamo: 'Honor Bound to Defend Freedom', which opened in May 2004.[26] Verbatim accounts tell the story of Muslim British citizens and a resident who were branded as terrorist suspects through guilt by association and unproven accusations and simply by being in the wrong place. The Iraqi-born al-Rawi brothers whose family had emigrated to Britain were picked up in Gambia where the elder brother was intending to open a mobile peanut-oil processing plant. Jamal al-Harith, from Manchester, set out on a religious journey to Pakistan, landed in a Taliban prison in Afghanistan after a truck he was travelling in was hijacked – and later was transported by the Americans to Kandahar airbase and detained there. Moazzam Begg had left Birmingham with his wife and children for Afghanistan hoping to set up a school. He had trouble getting the Taliban's approval for his plans, came up with another project, and started installing water pumps in Afghan villages. But when Afghanistan was under attack, he took his family to Pakistan, where he was arrested by Pakistani and American soldiers.[27]

Wahab al-Rawi was released in Gambia after almost a month of detention and interrogation. His brother Bisher (a British resident), Jamal al-Harith and Moazzam Begg were eventually sent to Guantánamo Bay. Al-Harith talks about being put in chains, interrogated, and confined to solitary in freezing conditions. Begg writes home that after a year in custody, he still doesn't know what crime he had committed (see Figure 4.3). And lawyers make the case against detention without trial at Guantánamo. An American military lawyer brings up the corrosion of the justice system with regard to the US military commissions, as does Lord Justice Johan Steyn, whose excerpted lecture 'Guantánamo Bay: The Legal Black Hole' frames the play.

FIGURE 4.3 *Paul Bhattacharjee as Moazzam Begg and Jan Chappell as Gareth Peirce in* Guantanamo: 'Honor Bound to Defend Freedom' *by Victoria Brittain and Gillian Slovo, 2004.*

Source: Photograph by John Haynes, courtesy of the Tricycle Theatre and John Haynes.

There were the two writers and also two directors, Nicolas Kent and Sacha Wares – and many ideas about the script, the casting, the design and the staging. Jan Chappell, who played human-rights lawyer Gareth Peirce, says that when there were differences of opinion between the directors, 'I remember we would laugh. She'd be jumping in and he'd be jumping in, and then they'd end up having a discussion while we hung around. But it wasn't a big thing, not for us.'

Rehearsals were in progress when Tariq Jordan auditioned for the role of Ruhel Ahmed, one of the young men from the Midlands known as the 'Tipton Three', who had been detained at Guantánamo.[28] 'The character I went up for was literally just added into the piece', says Jordan. Ahmed had been released in March, and 'the writers got some letters at quite a late stage'. Most of the play was performed in direct address out front, Ruhel Ahmed's speeches taken from his correspondence to his family.

Tariq Jordan: I remember my rehearsals because I'd never experienced working with two directors before. It was fine when they were both working together, but sometimes when they were working with you at separate stages, one thought one thing would work better and another thought another thing. But generally it came together quite well. Because the play was static in the sense of movement, it was literally just sitting down, talking about what these people are saying, and there was always this thing of not trying to act it. With the letters that I had, I remember Nick would always say to me, they kind of speak for themselves. You don't need to try and force anything onto them. The power of what is going on there is in these letters.

Jordan says that because of the developing political situation, script changes continued into production.

Tariq Jordan: I remember one of the first previews, I got five more lines from another letter. So it was constantly going on, and occasionally we had to change some of the lines. While we were doing the play, one of the prisoners was released. We had to change something there. We were watching the news every day thinking it was going to change the play.

According to the programme, members of the British government did not agree to be interviewed – but Jack Straw does appear onstage to make his February 2004 announcement. Earlier, US defence secretary Donald Rumsfeld takes the stage in a press conference. He gives the impression, despite denials to the contrary, that there might be less rigid standards for the treatment of the detainees, who, he says, are unlawful combatants and thus not considered prisoners of war. William Hoyland 'spookily dons the mantle and manner' of Rumsfeld, wrote Nicholas de Jongh.[29]

The tribunal plays typically end without a curtain call, which was also true for *Guantanamo*. Tariq Jordan says, 'We'd finish the play, the lawyers would pack up and leave, and the prisoners would finish their prayers and stay in their cells', or cages, as re-created by designer Miriam Buether.

Tariq Jordan: And the audience didn't know, one, Is the play over? Are they going to do something else? And after a bit, they realised it was over and started clapping. Then with the etiquette in theatre, we're expected to come onstage and bow, but didn't. They'd clap. They'd finish clapping, and then they'd sit there and wouldn't know what to do. Then it got to a point where they'd just sit there watching [the prisoners]. And in a way, they had to think about what they'd seen. Because they were seeing it as they were leaving as well. And the illusion wasn't broken. In reality, it's not been broken, because there were, there are prisons still in Guantánamo Bay.

When the reviews came out, there were leading sentences that were a publicist's dream. Alastair Macaulay in the *Financial Times* began his review with, 'The Tricycle Theatre is the most valuable home of political theatre in Britain today'. Charles Spencer led with, 'There is no theatre in Britain that has told us more in recent years about the way we live now than the Tricycle in Kilburn'. Expounding on the 'lucid, sober' production, Spencer wrote that the play worked 'most powerfully' at the 'human level', for example, Paul Bhattacharjee's portrayal of Moazzam Begg and his increasing despair as the detention wore on.[30]

Benedict Nightingale (*Times*), however, raised the fact that the evidence presented in the play had not been tested.[31] In my 2005 interview with Kent, we talked about sources and fact checking for this journalistic form of theatre.

Nicolas Kent: I've never yet done a play where I've made an allegation and it's me making the allegation. It's always other people making the allegation, whom I report accurately, who don't remain anonymous. So in *Guantanamo*, the fact Jamal al-Harith says, 'We were tortured', I don't have to question that. He said that. So you can take it and believe it or disbelieve it. It's up to you as an audience to do that.

After the scheduled run at the Tricycle, the production moved in June to the New Ambassadors in the West End for 12 weeks.

Tariq Jordan: The run at the Tricycle was about three weeks. It was quite a short run. I think I only rehearsed for about ten days at the most. Then we were on. It all happened so quick. And then we heard the play was to be taken to the West End. There was a plan for it to open in New York. We heard there was going to be one in Australia. And we didn't have a clue where this was going to go. It felt huge. And everyone knew about it. You could go to meet people, you'd say you were in this play called *Guantanamo*, and they'd say, Yeah, I've heard of that. A lot of the time people had seen it and seen the poster in the Tube as they went down the escalator – and huge writing, *Guantanamo*. You'd never seen that sort of topic of a play before in the Tube. The poster for the West End, you've got Paul Bhattacharjee in an orange boiler suit sitting on his bed with [the title] *Guantanamo* over his head.

During the West End run, there were no planned postshow talks as there had been at the Tricycle, but that didn't stop theatregoers from engaging in impromptu discussions.

William Hoyland: At the New Ambassadors, there's a sort of corridor to the side. Well, every night there would be people in that corridor arguing, and one would come out the stage door and unless you were in a violent hurry, you'd still be there 20 minutes later. It was wonderful.

The production was exciting international interest. Kent told the *Evening Standard* just after the play transferred to the West End that 'emails have been pouring in from all over the world . . . Today we're selling the rights to Sweden, and we've just had enquiries from Belgium.'[32] Kent and Wares went to New York to direct a production at the Culture Project in lower Manhattan, which opened in August 2004. (In the autumn, Archbishop Desmond Tutu appeared as Lord Steyn for two performances.)

The Tricycle took the play to the House of Commons in February 2006. Moazzam Begg had been released in January 2005, and now he was able to attend the reading of the play that so movingly portrayed his incarceration. In April 2006, *Guantanamo* went to Capitol Hill with a reading for the US Congress. Continuing the afterlife for the play, the Center for Constitutional Rights and the Bill of Rights Defense Committee (BORDC) sponsor a Guantánamo Reading Project. A BORDC web page offers a downloadable script and how-to suggestions.[33]

Just after the announcement in January 2005 about the release of the last of the British citizens from Guantánamo, I asked Kent whether he felt his production had a connection to that development, by stirring up interest and getting people more passionate about the issue. He said 'it's a little bit', and he shared a tangible outcome of the production. Kathleen Mubanga, the sister of detainee Martin Mubanga, 'didn't give a single press interview, wouldn't cooperate with us on the play, came to see the play four times, found it intensely moving', Kent said. She was then 'in touch a lot, and suddenly started coming on demonstrations and suddenly started giving interviews to the press'.

After almost three years' imprisonment at Guantánamo Bay, Martin Mubanga was one of the four released in January 2005. Jan Chappell had met his sister Kathleen at the Tricycle.

Jan Chappell: When we did *Guantanamo*, one day I was in the foyer, and this Asian guy came up to me and said, 'Uh, Gareth Peirce. Gareth Peirce.' I said, 'Yeah, I played Gareth Peirce'. He said, 'I'm a taxi driver, but I'm a friend of Katie Mubanga. She's here. I want to do something about this.' And I said, 'Katie Mubanga is here!' She hadn't at that point made any contribution. I said, 'Oh, really. Please introduce me.' So I met Katie, and as you know, after that she became more and more active.

When the Tricycle was nominated for an Olivier Award [2005] for its work on *Guantanamo*, I thought this is the nearest to any acting award Jan Chappell is likely to get – I'm going. By this time, Martin Mubanga was out; he'd been released. And so I phoned up Katie Mubanga, and I said, 'Would you like to come with me to the Olivier awards?' And she said yes. We didn't win. Some actor for the Royal Court did, and it was disappointing. And in the taxi going back, I was going, 'Oh, how could we not win?' She said, 'We did win. Martin's out.'

Postscript: British resident Bisher al-Rawi was finally released in 2007.

Bloody Sunday: Scenes from the Saville Inquiry, edited by Richard Norton-Taylor (2005)

In January 1998, Prime Minister Tony Blair announced that there would be a 're-examination' of Bloody Sunday, which was warranted by new evidence. More than two decades earlier, on 30 January 1972, in Londonderry, the British army had killed 13 civilians at the time of a civil-rights march. (A fourteenth person, who had been wounded, later died.) The inquiry held immediately afterwards, led by Lord Widgery, was completed by mid-April. Widgery's report had cast suspicion on people who had been killed. Because of the inquiry's timescale, Blair said in his statement, Widgery 'did not receive any evidence from the wounded who were still in hospital, and he did not consider individually substantial numbers of eye-witness accounts provided to his inquiry in the early part of March 1972'.[34] Thus as a result of the new evidence that had been presented to the British government by the families of the victims and by the Irish government, an inquiry into Bloody Sunday, chaired by Lord Saville, was established.

Considering the Tricycle's Irish community and the theatre's past successes in staging the public inquiries, the Saville inquiry would have seemed a natural for the Tricycle. But Richard Norton-Taylor said that 'curiously enough, Nick didn't think it would work. He was quite reluctant to do it.' Norton-Taylor urged him to go ahead with the project.

Nicolas Kent: Bloody Sunday does figure quite large in the British psyche. It's a major, major thing. Troops opened up fire, killed 13 people. That's a lot of people to kill. So we decided to do it. It was quite obvious we were accredited, and quite a few people were interested in us doing it.

Bloody Sunday: Scenes from the Saville Inquiry, directed by Kent with Charlotte Westenra, opened at the Tricycle in April 2005 and was remounted that autumn. The play begins with the March 2000 address by counsel to the inquiry, then covers the hearings from February 2001 through January 2004. The testimony brings into sharp focus the battleground of an occupied Northern Ireland. The British army had anticipated trouble from the Derry Young Hooligans on the day of the civil-rights march, which had been organised to protest internment. (A programme glossary defines the Derry Young Hooligans as a group of 'hard-core youths' who waged a daily assault on the British troops, throwing 'stones and missiles'.)[35] The army called in the 1st Battalion of the Parachute Regiment to carry out an 'arrest operation' in the event that the hooligans attacked the soldiers.[36] That operation went way beyond its purview when the troops entered into the Catholic area known as the Bogside and indiscriminately shot unarmed civilians.

In the first section of the play, eyewitnesses (one of whom had been shot in the leg) go over some of the horrors of the day. When Bishop Daly (played by Michael O'Hagan) takes the stand, the counsel reviews his statements with him. The hostilities in the Rossville Street area between some people in the crowd and the army had begun to accelerate, the army responding first with water cannon and CS gas and then live bullets. Panic set in, people were running, and Daly began running with them trying to get out of range of the advancing soldiers and armoured personnel carriers. He reached the area of the Rossville Flats in the Bogside. A shot felled a teen who had been running beside Daly. He tried to help the teen (who died), and he administered last rites to some of the others who were killed. One of the dead was Barney McGuigan, a man in his forties, whose murder is discussed in later testimony. He had been holding out a white handkerchief and was trying to go to the aid of someone wounded when he was struck by a bullet to the back of his head.

Bernadette Devlin McAliskey was MP for Mid Ulster in 1972. She had just begun a speech to the marchers when shots broke out, she says. McAliskey (Sorcha Cusack) makes it clear that she does not hold the British government's inquiry in high regard and says she's there only out of respect for the relatives (of the victims). In her view, the 'British Army declared war on the people seeking justice in this country on that day'.[37]

In the latter section of the play, we hear from the officers in charge and two of the Paras. One soldier tells the inquiry that at the time of the incident he was 18 years old and frightened. That was his attempt to explain why the statements he made to the Royal Military Police – about acid bombs and nail bombs being thrown at his unit and about his company being fired on – contained inaccuracies.

Richard Norton-Taylor: You had the victims, the families and the soldiers, and you got admissions by soldiers and even the generals, the senior army, officers, [then Brigadier] MacLellan, for example, admitting for the first time his orders were disobeyed.

And you got the questioning about who may have fired the first shots. Even though a lot of people knew that . . . people wanted to know more about it and hear the actual evidence over two-plus hours.

The play concludes with the testimony of Reg Tester, who was a quartermaster of the Official IRA. Tester had given evidence that three weapons were out that day, and that after the army opened fire, he did try to retaliate, but his rifle jammed. At which point, he says at the inquiry, he realised that firing was too dangerous because civilians could be hit. But when prodded, he concurs that the IRA had fired shots that day.

> **Richard Norton-Taylor:** We talk about whether the soldiers were shot at, and at the end, a member of the Official IRA admits [it] – we had to put that in . . . We had to put that at the end because of chronology, even though I was very unhappy with that at the end. But I think the rest of it was strong enough. We had to be fair. We were a bit criticised, of course. We had to put as much evidence from both sides as we possibly could because it was anyway so obvious that the soldiers had done something wrong.

Some actors were able to meet the people they were portraying, before and after the production. Michael Cochrane played General Sir Robert Ford, British commander of land forces in Northern Ireland at the time of Bloody Sunday. Ford had written in a memo that shooting selected ringleaders of the Derry Young Hooligans (after a warning) would be the way to restore order in the area. And for the other side, the actor doubled as the IRA's Reg Tester. Cochrane went to a couple of the inquiry sessions, but he didn't see either of his characters giving testimony. However, he watched film of the general and went to Derry to meet Reg Tester.

> **Michael Cochrane:** He couldn't have been kinder to me, and I learnt things from him and about him that I could never have

found out from books or film . . . When Reg came to see *Bloody Sunday*, one of the actors said to him, 'What was it like seeing Michael being you?' Reg replied, 'When the lights went up, I thought he looked just like me, with his hair slicked back and wearing the same jacket, but then, when he opened his mouth, well, I had to laugh'.

Perhaps I ought to explain that Reg and I have become good friends, and we met all his family including his formidable wife Bridie. One of his sons told me that I'd captured his father's sincerity, candour, and honesty.

Claire Spooner's set in *Justifying War* had replicated the 'rather empty' courtroom, but for *Bloody Sunday*, she re-created 'the feel of the chaos'. ('There was paper piled up to the ceiling', she says.) The Saville hearings took place in the Guildhall in Londonderry and also at Central Hall, Westminster, in London, where they moved as a protective measure for the soldiers who testified. The *Bloody Sunday* set was an abstraction of the two courtrooms, says the designer.

They used plasma screens in the production to display maps, photographs, and documents.

Claire Spooner: It looked wonderful lit just by the screens. You had a dark set with the screens glowing out at you to begin with, and it was a great design feature. There was something about the barrage of information coming at you [during the performance] – media accounts, witness statements, army documents, maps, or blank screens – that was very profound.

Tribunal player James Woolley took over the role of lawyer Edwin Glasgow for the remount. He had not been in the original production, and that gave him the chance to experience a tribunal as an audience member.

James Woolley: I went to *Bloody Sunday*, which I was in latterly. When it first was on, Nick did ask me if I would be in it, but I was doing another play, so I couldn't. I didn't know they were going to do it again. I don't think that they did at the time. I'd never seen a tribunal play, and there I was seeing it, and it was wondrous. I was completely sucked in . . . It gradually built up, and you thought, My God, this was awful . . . Then I got to be part of it after that. And we went to Northern Ireland and Dublin, which was fantastic.

In Northern Ireland, they played in Belfast and then went to Derry.

Charlotte Westenra: Moving to Derry was of course much more profound. First of all, you literally looked at this map of Derry day in, day out. I was preparing for *Bloody Sunday* for months before we went into rehearsal. So you began to know all of the streets. As you walked into the auditorium, there was a massive map of Derry. So you felt like you knew it really well. And you turned up, and it's a tiny little place, Derry. And it was slightly depressing being there because you felt the sense of Bloody Sunday all around you. Now I don't know if we were supersensitive because we knew so much about it. There were the famous pictures. You saw those pictures everywhere you went. Then there was the first night, and you could have heard a pin drop.

William Hoyland says the Derry audience members were also outspoken. He played two roles, one of which was Colonel Derek Wilford, then commanding officer of the Paras charged with scooping up 'as many hooligans and rioters as possible'.[38] Wilford admits that his original statement about witnessing sniper fire was false, but he maintains he saw only one of his soldiers firing – despite a log showing that more than one hundred rounds had been fired by his troops in the Rossville Street area.

William Hoyland: Playing Wilford in London, it seemed like an ordinary theatre audience. Playing it in Derry, people were vocalising in the way that they had when they were in the gallery at the actual tribunal. Even the day I went, which was a very boring day at Westminster, there were members of families there who would shout out: Rubbish! Liar! Nonsense! And so you got that response in Derry; although not quite that response because they were reliving it, you still got certain things. Not just me, but the other army people. There would be muttering in the audience . . . Sometimes it did feel like they were watching it for the first time in the public gallery. It is very exciting. And one can respond to it, by looking up or shrugging your shoulders, as they would have done. One's not inventing things here.

Thomas Wheatley first played lawyer Glasgow in the spring run, then took over as counsel to the inquiry Christopher Clarke in the remount. Wheatley told me when I interviewed him in 2006 that this tribunal was one of his favourites. ('*Nuremberg* and *Bloody Sunday* are the tops for me.')

Thomas Wheatley: I wanted to say something about *Bloody Sunday*, and one or two other reasons why it's my favourite. The material looked as if it was going to be very dry. Richard Norton-Taylor, with his great flair for pulling out what's important and who's important and what is dramatically effective, on this occasion, more than any other, has also managed to construct an amazingly coherent story through the whole piece. He's chosen particular people and moments in the very short space of time that we're talking about, and the threads are drawn all the way through the two and a half hours of it. That's brilliantly successful on his part.

And the other thing I wanted to say about it is, I've already suggested that the Irish question is kind of box-office poison in this country. Everybody's sick and tired of Ireland. And I think it did OK in the spring, but by the time we did it three more weeks in the Tricycle in the autumn, the audience was very thin. Anybody who had wanted to come had been. And not many people wanted to come. In Ireland, of course, especially in Dublin, absolutely packed; it found its own audience, and we went to them, as it were. And a lot of us, and I was guilty of this too, went into the piece originally with the prejudices that we've collected: that the inquiry was probably a waste of time and money, and why are our boys being victimised? A lot of my friends were quite angry that this was going on at the Tricycle, and they were not going to come. People felt quite strongly that the inquiry should never have been set up.

Well, of course, once you get in there and you have the real people saying authentic things in that important situation, you get drawn in. We the performers get drawn into the story, and I think those who did come would have gone away with those prejudices broken down. I certainly believe that when the report comes out, it will prove to have been worthwhile and crucial to have had the inquiry whatever the expense, not only to give the people of Derry some closure on the situation, but also because the issue is relevant now. The accountability of the military is still an issue. And so more people should have come to *Bloody Sunday*, and the BBC should certainly have televised it.[39] The radio version will be very useful when the report comes out. I'm sure it will prove to have been worthwhile and very proper of the new Labour government of 1997 to have grasped the nettle and decided that they should do it.

Bloody Sunday won an Olivier Award in 2006 for outstanding achievement in an affiliate theatre. The play was broadcast on Radio 4 in two parts in January 2008 and was re-aired in June 2010 just before the report was published. The Saville inquiry spanned 12 years and cost more than £190 million. The report – 5,000-plus pages – found that none of the dead or injured 'was posing a threat of causing death or serious injury'.[40] The newly elected Prime Minister David Cameron pronounced in the House of Commons, 'What happened on Bloody Sunday was both unjustified and unjustifiable. It was wrong.'[41]

Called to Account: The Indictment of Anthony Charles Lynton Blair for the Crime of Aggression Against Iraq – A Hearing, edited by Richard Norton-Taylor; devised by Nicolas Kent (2007)

The hearings for the Tony Blair indictment were set up by Kent to mould into a tribunal play.

Richard Norton-Taylor: That was more Nick and a lawyer friend, Philippe Sands. That wasn't really mine. I bit immediately because it was a great idea. But really Nick devised that. We were talking about how frustrated we were there was no inquiry; there was no parliamentary inquiry. The inquiries they had [Hutton, 2003, following the death of Dr Kelly, and Butler, 2004, looking at the intelligence on weapons of mass destruction] weren't followed up . . . So let's do our own thing.

Kent and Norton-Taylor teamed up with Sands, leading for the prosecution, and Julian Knowles, for the defence (both lawyers from Matrix Chambers), to determine whether Prime Minister Tony Blair could be charged with a war crime. The actual cross-examinations began at the Matrix offices, which also happened to be the chambers of the prime minister's wife, Cherie (Booth) Blair. After the venue was published in the press, says Kent's assistant director Philip Honour, reporters started phoning the chambers to get in touch with Mrs Blair. The proceedings were then moved to an accountancy firm in the City. The interviews in London were conducted in January and February 2007. Sands, Knowles and lawyers Alison Macdonald and Blinne Ní Ghrálaigh gave their services to the project pro bono.[42]

    With this devised piece, Kent and Norton-Taylor were able to have a bit of input prior to the editing process.

Philip Honour: Philippe and Alison Macdonald and Julian did an amazing job . . . They spent so much time preparing for it. There were times that Richard or Nick would pass a question to Philippe or Julian saying, Why don't you ask about this? . . . But mainly they left it up to them.

Defence counsel Knowles states that the evidence for the prosecution is from 'peripheral figures'.[43] Because of the nature of the project, the 11 people who gave testimony at the proceedings were voluntary witnesses. Some reviews commented on the absence of the major players – Tony Blair, for one. The lineup for *Called to Account* included witnesses who had formerly held such positions as UN weapons inspector, commissioner for the Intelligence Services, and permanent under-secretary in the Ministry of Defence. James Woolley (who played Juan Gabriel Valdés, Chilean ambassador on the UN Security Council in 2003) feels it's interesting to hear firsthand testimony from figures 'you don't read about and see so much', to get the 'backroom chat'. Norton-Taylor was surprised by how many people agreed to participate: 'We got Richard Perle, for heaven's sake. He was a very good catch.' (From 2001 to 2003, Perle was chair of the Pentagon's Defense Policy Board.)

They also got Clare Short, who had served in Blair's cabinet. As a Labour MP, Short voted for the war, but two months later resigned from the cabinet. She gives a cutting description of Blair's informal management style and accuses the prime minister of having been dishonest, notably about his commitment to the invasion of Iraq.

Michael Mates was a Conservative MP. He had voted for the war, and he had been on the committee of the Butler inquiry. In his testimony, he talks about that committee's findings, saying the government's claims for Iraq's weapons capabilities were owing to a 'cock-up'.[44] Mates struggles somewhat during his testimony, consulting a copy of the Butler report (provided to him by one of the lawyers) before answering certain questions. Honour says the MP was concerned about sticking 'close to the book' because he hadn't realised the Tricycle's interview was going to be on the record: 'So there's a part on the tape where you can see he's very confused and anxious' – which was caught by Roland Oliver in performance.

> **Philip Honour:** A lot of people were a bit shocked that we portrayed him as this bumbling character when he is a very accomplished politician. That was why, because he was absolutely thrown, but he still wanted to do it.

The prosecution examines Blair's reason for going to war, the timing of his commitment to the war, and the measures he might have taken to ensure that outcome. Sands considers the advice given by Attorney General Lord Goldsmith about the legality of going to war. The attorney general's judgement changed over a ten-day period in March 2003 and paved the way for Britain's military action. At first, Lord Goldsmith contended they needed 'hard evidence' that Iraq was not disarming. However, on 17 March, a day before the House of Commons vote on the war, Goldsmith stated that Iraq was clearly 'in breach' of UN Security Council Resolutions, leaving himself open to accusations of giving legal advice that was influenced by the prime minister.[45]

The cast of *Called to Account* featured familiar names like Jeremy Clyde and William Hoyland. David Michaels was defence counsel Knowles, and Thomas Wheatley, prosecutor Sands. Both actors had observed the actual lawyers in action, and cast members were given a copy of their character's tape to study. The real Clare Short looked 'quite pale' watching Diane Fletcher portray her, Honour told me, relating what her parents had said the night they all saw the show.

While much of the press was positive regarding the project itself, some of the response was cooler for this invented tribunal. Charles Spencer objected to the 'worryingly partisan' construction, and Jane Edwardes wrote that 'nobody who appears has anything to hide and consequently there isn't much drama'.[46]

As an actor, David Michaels found the defence lacking.

David Michaels: I would often say in rehearsals, Why didn't I ask more questions? I didn't think Knowles defended Blair particularly well. (Maybe he didn't feel like defending the indefensible.) It was his job to have done it better. I felt unarmed slightly.

Norton-Taylor gave me his own critique of the piece when we spoke in 2008.

Richard Norton-Taylor: On *Called to Account*, the most unsatisfactory thing was you don't indict people for such a war crime. Looking back on it, I would have had a lesser crime alleged. At the end of the day, everyone agrees, even in the play, that you can't do it in the current state of international law with war crimes like that given the evidence, accepted by the prosecution as well as the defence . . .

So there is this residual feeling that Blair got away with a lot and maybe when the British troops come back, there will be another inquiry. It's a live issue . . . Obviously no one expects him to be indicted for anything, of course not. But people haven't forgotten about the invasion of Iraq and his role in it. It's still being discussed, especially the lack of planning post invasion. And it's discussed in the context of Afghanistan . . .

[The play] worked. It had an extended run. People came to see *Called to Account*. I think they wanted to get some of the arguments rehashed again too, a particular kind of audience.

Called to Account ran from mid-April through early June 2007, and that July, it played on Radio 4. During the run of the production, the prime minister announced his resignation. Blair left office towards the end of June. In 2010 and again in 2011, Blair was called before the Chilcot inquiry to account for taking Britain to war in Iraq.

THE VERBATIM AND POLITICAL PLAYS   181

Tactical Questioning: Scenes from the Baha Mousa Inquiry, edited by Richard Norton-Taylor (2011)

Britain's involvement in the Iraq war was once again centre stage at the Tricycle – and this time the subject was torture. During a British operation in Basra in September 2003 to uncover Saddam loyalists and insurgents, members of the 1st Battalion The Queen's Lancashire Regiment (1QLR) arrested seven men at a hotel where weapons were found on the premises.[47] One of the seven was Baha Mousa, the hotel's night receptionist. The Iraqis (ten in all by the end of the day) were placed in a temporary detention facility (TDF) and subjected to conditioning techniques, a strategy for tactical questioning. They were hooded, plasticuffed, shouted at – and in this case physically abused. After 36 hours of detention, Baha Mousa was dead. At a court-martial a few years later of seven soldiers from 1QLR, only Corporal Donald Payne was convicted. He pleaded guilty to inhuman treatment (his actions had been captured on video) and served a year in prison. In 2008, following a successful appeal to the Law Lords by the Mousa family, the secretary of defence called for a public inquiry, which was chaired by Sir William Gage, to look into the death of Baha Mousa and into the treatment of the other men held at the TDF.

Tactical Questioning draws on the hearings from July 2009 to June 2010. Counsel to the inquiry Gerard Elias (Thomas Wheatley, see Figure 4.4) acknowledges the difficulties the British soldiers faced: the extreme heat, the long days, the insurgency. When he introduces the case, he shows the video in which Corporal Payne screams and curses at the hooded, plasticuffed detainees, physically forcing two men to stand in a stress position at the wall with their knees bent. These techniques, Elias emphasises, 'had been prohibited in 1972'.[48]

FIGURE 4.4 *Thomas Wheatley as Counsel to the Inquiry Gerard Elias in* Tactical Questioning, *edited by Richard Norton-Taylor, 2011.*

Source: Photograph by Tristram Kenton, courtesy of Tristram Kenton.

Former private Aaron Cooper (Luke Harris) is first up in a progression of soldiers who were involved in the incident. He names the men who took part in punching the detainees, a list with his name on it for the initial go-round. The men were riled up, according to his evidence, because an esteemed captain had been killed in an insurgent attack. (At the time of the hotel raid, the multiple's Lieutenant Rodgers told them the Iraqis they were picking up might have been responsible for that attack.) Cooper gives an account of the struggle that led to Baha Mousa's death. He helped Corporal Payne restrain the man so that Payne could reapply the plasticuffs that Mousa had managed to get free of. Having to replace the cuffs a second time unleashed excessive violence in the corporal, who waged a full-out assault on Baha Mousa. Donald Payne (Dean Ashton) later gives his version of what happened in terse, staccato-like answers to counsel.

There are conflicting stories of who meted out the abuse and who knew about it. Rodgers (Christopher Fox) denies having participated in the punch-fest and says he was not aware of the assaults, despite testimony to the contrary.

Christopher Fox: Rodgers, from my point of view, had his story, and he was sticking to it. They all contradict each other. In that respect, he doesn't have a lot to worry about. No one knows who's telling the truth here because everyone is telling a slightly different story.

Major Peebles (Rick Warden) was the Battlegroup Internment Review Officer, whose job involved oversight of detentions and tactical questioning. However, it's possible he stoked the fires when he let the guards know that the Iraqis in custody might have been responsible for the recent deaths of three Royal Military Police. And while Peebles visited the TDF, he insists he didn't see over-the-top mistreatment of the detainees. (Baha Mousa had 93 injuries on his body.)

Yet there is a 'shining light' in the tribunal, as actor David Michaels calls the man he portrayed: Lieutenant Colonel Nicholas Mercer, legal adviser for the army in 2003.[49] Not long after the invasion of Iraq, Mercer saw hooded detainees in stress positions and sent a memo to the general firmly stating that these practices were in violation of international law. But his complaints, he says, were not welcomed.

In the preparation phase of rehearsals, the actors learned about the dark side of the British occupation in Iraq. Rick Warden says Baha Mousa was the 'tip of the iceberg'.

Rick Warden: We met one of the lawyers in question. I think he said there are hundreds of cases – British custody deaths – that are, in his opinion, brushed under the carpet as casualties-of-war deaths. What does get raised slightly in the piece, but that's not that overt, is the shift in policy since 9/11, that with terrorism and in fighting an enemy we don't fully understand – faceless insurgents we're understandably nervous about and scared of and don't know their language – all sorts of rules, in particular the Geneva Convention rules, go out the window in those interrogation rooms, and unfortunately that means collateral damage, that means people like Baha Mousa getting killed.

David Michaels: We had an army person come in, a Marine actually, who had been in Basra. He said they didn't know anything about Iraq before they went. They weren't told about the history or the religion. This wouldn't have happened with Baha Mousa if anybody had questioned him and found out his religious stance. He was a Shia. It's very unlikely he'd be pro–Saddam Hussein.

At one and three-quarter hours without an interval, says actor Alan Parnaby, the production might have tested the audience's concentration. Parnaby in the role of chairman Sir William Gage was onstage for the entire time. He says, 'Thankfully, there was no coughing or shuffling'. There was, however, some visceral response. Warden's Major Peebles was hissed one night at the end of the scene, when he tells Elias that the reason they placed a hooded detainee next to a hot, noisy generator was that 'it was convenient'.[50] In contrast, after Mercer's speech about a 'moral compass', in which he stresses the importance of training soldiers to intervene when they see abuses 'rather than turn a blind eye', Michaels thought he heard a couple of people clapping as he left the stage.[51] But, he adds, he didn't try to elicit that response.

> **David Michaels:** I probably could get applause if I decided to make that last speech kind of impassioned. People don't do that in an inquiry. It's that fine line. You have to give it the weight it would get in an inquiry. But I really felt there were a couple of people in front who wanted to clap. Because as you say, it's four unremittingly bleak soldiers, followed by an incompetent major, and you are despairing. And then at least I come on and go, it's not all bad.

There were four-star reviews from the *Times*, the *Guardian*, and the *Telegraph*. But I was told by a few cast members that the houses were disappointing. Parnaby thought people might be unfamiliar with the subject matter ('Who's Baha Mousa? I've never heard of him. What's this all about? What's tactical questioning?'). And Michaels felt the media weren't interested in the actual inquiry.

> **David Michaels:** I think if the media had picked it up, if the papers had reported it the way the play reports it, we'd be having a lot of people coming through the doors. Because it is our Abu Ghraib. It is appalling what happened, really, but without that oxygen of publicity – and I think it would have helped if the report had come out. The report was meant to have come out . . . in the middle of June. That would have created something.

Rick Warden says he values the 'quality' of the houses, which were very strong. The show ran from early June through the beginning of July. The report was published in September. It denounced the 'gratuitous violence on civilians' and made recommendations (73 of them) towards the proper treatment of prisoners of war.[52]

The Riots by Gillian Slovo, from spoken evidence (2011, 2012)

Just been to see "Riots" play at Tricycle. Really incisive and stimulating piece, especially on day we now know Mark Duggan was unarmed. – 19 Nov [2011]

twitter.com/#!/johnmcdonnellMP

Went to Tricycle Theatre to see THE RIOTS, wanted to hate it, especially as I am played by ex cop from the Bill. It's wicked tho! MUST see – 29 Nov [2011]

twitter.com/#!/StaffordScott_

Kent's penultimate project as the Tricycle's director was an examination of the UK riots of August 2011, which began in Tottenham, quickly spread to other sections of London and Britain, gave rise to looting, arson, and destruction of property, and resulted in five deaths. By the end of August, the government appointed a Riots Communities and Victims Panel to do an exploration of what happened and why, but it did not establish an official public inquiry.

Nicolas Kent: There isn't a public inquiry, but there has been on such occasions in the past. With the Brixton riots [1981], there was a public inquiry. When something goes severely wrong in this country, then you normally have a public inquiry. In Brixton there were riots which were confined to one area, and they were probably as violent as these riots, but these riots were all over the country, and the police lost control, and there should have been a public inquiry. It's really bad there wasn't a public inquiry.

The Tricycle organised its own investigation. Gillian Slovo (co-author of *Guantanamo*) collected testimony from politicians, police, community leaders, and residents of affected areas. *The Riots*, directed by Nicolas Kent, was up and running by mid-November 2011.

Cabinet ministers and MPs lent their voices to the play, which meant there were perspectives from the three major parties. As the programme notes, some politicians refused. Those who said no were Home Secretary Theresa May, Justice Secretary Kenneth Clarke, Labour leader Ed Miliband, and London Mayor Boris Johnson.[53] Still the real difficulty was to get testimony from the rioters. To that end, the Tricycle advertised a free-phone number, and associate producer Zoe Ingenhaag placed a notice in the prison newspaper *Inside Time*, appealing to those who had been 'caught up' in the riots to write or telephone.[54] Two of the letters the Tricycle received were used in the play, and additional testimony from rioters came from documentary footage.

Act 1 presents the story of how the riots started in Tottenham on the night of 6 August. Family and friends of the slain Mark Duggan, who had been shot by police two days before, held a demonstration at the local police station in the late afternoon. The police were unwilling to speak with members of the group, says community member and activist Stafford Scott (Steve Toussaint), stating it was a complaints-commission issue. The demonstrators asked to meet with a high-ranking officer and waited for one to show up. As night approached, they gave up and went home. By then the crowd had greatly increased, and the trouble began. Kids attacked two unmanned police cars, first hurling vegetables, then setting fire to the vehicles.

The police noticeably did not intervene, which was surprising, Scott says, when kids are 'used to getting stopped before they do something'.[55] (The play takes up the resentment caused by police targeting blacks with stop-and-search.) As the riots 'kick off', observers and looters talk about an almost festive spirit in the air. In a nod to the role that social media and text messages had played in the riots' spread, tweets from the riots were scrolling on screens in the Tricycle's auditorium prior to the show.

The police speak of being understaffed, unprepared and out-numbered by the rioters, and worried about their own safety – still remembering the murder of a policeman in a riot 26 years earlier on Tottenham's Broadwater Farm housing estate. A traffic diversion by the police had been bungled – and is shown on a *London A-Z* map of the area, with moving arrows indicating the routes. Kate Bassett on TheatreVOICE talked about how well the story was told with 'really choice, spare use of video and projections', and testimony from people who were pointing out the missteps in the roadblocks: 'It's just absolutely crystal clear what happened.'[56]

Central to act 1 is the heart-rending story told by Mohamed Hammoudan (Selva Rasalingam), a father of two boys. The three were sleeping in their flat above Carpetright on the High Road when the shop was set on fire. After he was awakened by one of his sons, Hammoudan and the boys made their way down the stairs of the smoked-filled building and out into the street. Although some rioters were trying to warn tenants to leave their flats, others threw tyres to stoke the fire, and Hammoudan watched the building and his home being destroyed.

Selva Rasalingam, who played Mohamed Hammoudan, listened to the original hour-long interview in which he got a feel for 'the nature of that man'.

Selva Rasalingam: He seems terribly stoical about the whole event, surprisingly – a sense of humour about it, often chuckling about one thing or another. His mind gets drawn to the ironies of these little ironic things that happen, some of which appear in the play – and then the kind of madness of speaking to the banks and people trying to get all his ID back and organise his bank account and all those sorts of things, and he's just told them he's lost everything in the fire and they will not stop going through the process of: 'OK, can you give me your passport number, please?' 'I've just told you that everything was lost in the fire.' It wouldn't stop. The way he was telling these things – the frustration's there, obviously, but the fact that he can find the comic irony in it all runs throughout the whole thing. Funnily enough, the material that's in the play is the most seriously delivered stuff, so I did find myself trying to capture some of the other material, so some of that could come through what's actually in the play. Because if I just kept it as it was in the original, it would have been a bit drier than I was able to make it, and he's not dry like that. He's stoical, but he's positive.

The two spoke on the phone just before performances began, and Hammoudan assured the actor he was fine about being portrayed onstage. Rasalingam says that when Hammoudan came to see the play at the Tricycle, and they chatted after the show, he 'seemed more serious than he had been in the interview'.

Selva Rasalingam: He was lighter before. Maybe because time's passed, things have sunk in. Maybe it's that the ripples of the event had been going on for however many weeks and months since then. So of course, he's in a different place; it was hardly surprising. I did feel he had a different demeanour to what he'd sounded like on the disc.

The second act moves on to a riots postmortem by politicians and community activists, among others, offering reasons for the unrest – and possible solutions. Camila Batmanghelidjh (Dona Croll), who founded Kids Company, a charity for disadvantaged youths, points to the disrespect shown to the poor in the inner city as an underlying cause of the uprising. Diane Abbott, Labour MP for Hackney North and Stoke Newington, proposes giving young people 'some sort of ownership' as a first step towards a solution.[57] Her example is the rioters' texting one another not to touch the Hackney Empire. That theatre, she says, has a history of doing arts programmes with black youths.

Croll played Diane Abbott as well as Batmanghelidjh.

Dona Croll: I feel very privileged to have been able to play them in a play like that because the play felt like a living, breathing thing because it's happening now. And, yes, slightly protective. What these women had to say, I really wanted the audience to get it.

The letters that the Tricycle had received from the rioters are in a section about the sentences handed down. One is from an 18-year-old Londoner, who wishes to correct the false media reports depicting her as a 'disruptive low-life teenager'.[58] She is concerned that she be held responsible for her actions alone, and she ends her letter with an apology. The other is from a 26-year-old Manchester man, who describes seeing shops with windows smashed and doors missing, then going into one of them, and being caught stealing. He received a two-year sentence for burglary. (He took '£25 worth of Oil of Olay', according to the BBC.)[59]

There was a great deal of preproduction publicity in the print media and on the BBC. Excellent reviews and a hot topic led to sold-out houses at the Tricycle. In January 2012, the production moved to the Bernie Grant Arts Centre in Tottenham for a ten-day run. The real-life counterparts of the 'characters' Stafford Scott, Leroy Logan, and Pastor Nims Obunge participated in after-show discussions. Alan Parnaby portrayed solicitor Greg Powell (also a character in *Guantanamo*) and Labour MP John McDonnell. Parnaby told me that although advance sales seemed to indicate they wouldn't be playing to full houses at the arts centre, the run soon sold out there. We talked about who came to see the production in Tottenham and how those audiences compared with the ones at the Tricycle.

Alan Parnaby: It was a bit disappointing there weren't more people from the black community to the Bernie Grant Arts Centre. They were there, but not as big a majority that was hoped for. The audiences were very different to the Tricycle, though. The Tricycle audiences were extremely engaged, obviously, and I would say the

Tottenham audiences were even more engaged, and I've tried to analyse that. I can only think the audience was comprised of a lot of people who had firsthand experience of the riots, might have been affected by them if they'd been shop owners or lived in the area and their houses had been subject to arson. Parents of children who had been dragged up into the courts. And obviously the local dignitaries. But the engagement was very different. It sounds slightly pretentious, but you could actually feel it from the stage. They really wanted to be there . . .

And sometimes we had people standing throughout the whole show. They allowed people to stand in the upper side galleries, and they allowed people to sit on the gangways as well. I don't think our Health and Safety would have liked that. They probably took the audience from 260 up to past the 300 mark. That's a commitment, isn't it? Those people really wanted to see it, if they were willing to stand.

At the play's end, Hammoudan talks about what it felt like to see bystanders taking photos of his burnt-out home, capturing a piece of history, when he had just lost all the records of his personal history. Pictures of the Carpetright building being consumed by fire appeared in news stories and on the internet; a version of it, a photograph of police in riot gear watching the fire, was used for the programme and the script cover of *The Riots*.

As it happens, Hammoudan's portrayer was born in Tottenham and has his own connection to the building.

Selva Rasalingam: That building is a landmark from my childhood. Every time I walked to the supermarket or the shops in the high street with my mum, we turned that corner and we passed that building. Or if we were driving home from anywhere, my dad would turn the corner and he'd see that building and you'd know you're just about home. It's a landmark, and it's gone.

So it had an impact all by itself before any sense of there being riots. Just seeing that burning building had a personal impact.

The political play cycles

The Great Game: Afghanistan (2009, 2010)

Part 1 (1842–1930) 'Invasions and Independence': *Bugles at the Gates of Jalalabad* by Stephen Jeffreys; *Durand's Line* by Ron Hutchinson; *Campaign* by Amit Gupta; *Now Is the Time* by Joy Wilkinson.

Part 2 (1979–96) 'Communism, the Mujahideen and the Taliban': *Black Tulips* by David Edgar; *Blood and Gifts* by J. T. Rogers (in 2009); *Wood for the Fire* by Lee Blessing (in 2010);[60] *Miniskirts of Kabul* by David Greig; *The Lion of Kabul* by Colin Teevan.

Part 3 (1996–2009, –2010): 'Enduring Freedom': *Honey* by Ben Ockrent; *The Night Is Darkest Before the Dawn* by Abi Morgan; *On the Side of the Angels* by Richard Bean; *Canopy of Stars* by Simon Stephens; monologues and duologues by Siba Shakib; verbatims edited by Richard Norton-Taylor.

In October 2006, Kent had produced a weeklong run of short plays about the genocide and devastation in Darfur titled *How Long Is Never? Darfur – A Response*. Using that programme as a model, Kent commissioned a series of short dramatic pieces for a project about Afghanistan, which, he wrote, was 'surely going to be the main focus of British, European, and American policy for at least the next decade'.[61] The result was 12 half-hour plays by as many writers, accompanied by additional pieces about historical figures and contemporary verbatim interviews. The play cycle looks at the history of Afghanistan from the mid-nineteenth century to the present:

war, imperialist aggressions, attempts to modernise the country and reform its system, fundamentalist takeover, tribal culture, the poppy-growing economy. *The Great Game* festival also featured films, ceramics and photography exhibits, play readings, talks, and discussions.[62]

Directed by Kent and Indhu Rubasingham (assisted by Rachel Grunwald), the three-part play cycle could be viewed separately on weekday evenings or all in one day on marathon weekends in spring 2009. The following summer, *The Great Game* was remounted at the Tricycle prior to a four-city US tour. An ensemble of 15 actors in 2009 (14 in 2010) played some 90 roles.[63] The characters ran the gamut from British and Soviet soldiers to mujahideen, CIA operatives, Taliban, tribesmen, and NGO workers – not to mention an amir, a king, and two queens.

Before any of the plays were written, project designer Pamela Howard worked on an overall design concept. Howard says, 'Nick had decided on the writers and the dates, and the challenge was to create a framework, and then respond quickly to each individual play as they came in'.[64] (Miriam Nabarro was the associate designer.)

Pamela Howard: I had a clear idea in the very beginning, which was about Afghanistan – death. Nick showed me a piece in the newspaper about the painter Mashal, who'd been painting this picture of 500 years of Afghanistan in the bazaar at Herat. He was a famous fine-art painter, and he had taken his inspiration from the early Persian miniatures, known as the school of Behzad. But the Taliban came and forced him to watch while they whitewashed it out. Nick said to me, 'Do you think we could try and stage that, and show the actual whitewashing of the wall?' That was really how it started.

Howard created a magnificent mural, 5 m wide by 4.30 m high (approx. 16.4 ft by 14 ft), with images and people from Afghanistan's history. (Two iconic females – Malalai of the battle of Maiwand in

1880 and the fifteenth-century Queen Gohar Shad – are depicted in Shakib's pieces.) When the production opens, the artist is working on the mural, which hadn't been completed. 'That's because I had to try and not make too much detail above and behind the actors', says Howard. 'And I think that worked, particularly because lighting designer James Farncombe manages to light it in such a way that it just becomes a landscape behind them.' As envisioned by Kent, the mural was ultimately obliterated by the stage Taliban.

But when Kent told Howard that he wanted to somehow show the Twin Towers (on 11 September), she says, 'we didn't really know how to do it. And suddenly I thought if the mural wall is painted white, but you could still see the picture underneath, you could project the Twin Towers.' Ben Ockrent's *Honey*, the opening play of Part 3, begins in 1996 when the CIA is trying to get back the Stinger missiles that it supplied to the mujahideen during the Soviet occupation. The play ends in 2001, when the Taliban have taken over most of Afghanistan, and Northern Alliance leader Ahmad Shah Massoud, who's been battling them, is assassinated by two 'journalists' connected to al-Qaeda. The sound of a bomb exploding was followed by footage of the attack on the Twin Towers projected onto the mural wall; the mural fell back, and a field of poppies dropped in from either side for Abi Morgan's *The Night Is Darkest Before the Dawn*. That play's setting is 2002 in the countryside, where the poppy is being farmed. The Taliban are gone, and an American from an aid organisation has arrived to help fund schooling for girls.

Pamela Howard: I thought with all these plays, one of the things I need to do is clear out the sides, clear out the back and really look at what space is available. And as soon as I did that and measured up what the back is, I saw that the mural could go all the way back. And I think that was the beginning of the whole story of this. Because as soon as we saw it could go back, I saw that something could fall in from the sides that might look like the Twin Towers, but I wanted it to turn into a poppy field. I wanted to associate opium, poppies, and death with the bombing of the Twin Towers and death. So that one results in the other because the events were connected. The killing of Ahmad Shah Massoud was two days before 9/11 and the bombing of the Twin Towers. Then it goes to Afghanistan and becomes a field of poppies. I didn't know then that Abi Morgan's play would come in and actually be the perfect play. I was just overall thinking of the big images because at the time I had no idea of the sequence of events.

Part 1's *Bugles at the Gates of Jalalabad* by Stephen Jeffreys goes back to 1842 and the first Anglo-Afghan war, when thousands of retreating troops from the British army and their camp followers have just been killed. In the cycle's final play, *Canopy of Stars*, by Simon Stephens, it's 2009/10, and British soldiers are once more in Afghanistan. There are three scenes. The first is near the Kajaki Dam in Helmand Province. A sergeant and a private are at a sandbag bunker waiting to go on a mission to root out insurgents. The second scene, in blackout, is the battle at a village. And the third is in the sergeant's home in Manchester. It's late at night, and he's sitting on his sofa watching TV. Howard told me that she and Kent both thought that rather than a great finale, 'it's just got to be one man on a sofa – that's all'. She added, 'Because that's the awfulness of it'.

Kent had asked for a dramaturgical change to that final play.

Nicolas Kent: Simon Stephens's play arrived and was exactly as you see it, except the last scene, which was about the soldier recounting a dream he'd had to his wife. It seemed rather discursive and more to do with his own post-traumatic stress disorder. I said to Simon, I couldn't quite see the point of it, and I didn't think that was the right way to end the trilogy. 'What I need at the end of this trilogy is a debate. I need the wife to be totally against him going back to Afghanistan and him totally for going back. I want to leave the audience uncertain as to which side we should be on because that's the whole idea of the trilogy – to open up a debate.'

And he said, 'Well, that sort of political polemic is not really the sort of thing I write'. And I said, 'Well, that's what I'd like you to write'. And with enormous grace, he wrote the scene, which I think is one of the strongest scenes in the whole trilogy. I'm a terrific admirer of his work.

The 14 writers brought a variety of styles and tones to the cycle. Early in Part 1, Ron Hutchinson's *Durand's Line* provides comic moments in a scene of jousting between British India's foreign secretary Sir Henry Mortimer Durand and the amir of Afghanistan over the imperialist mapping of the country.

Rick Warden's numerous roles in *The Great Game* included Thomas Salter Pyne, an actual person who was the amir's engineer (see Figure 4.5). Pyne plays the piano and sings to defuse the tensions between the amir and Durand.

> **Rick Warden:** I think it's in *Butcher & Bolt*, David Loyn's book; there's a hilarious description of Pyne and his entrapment between these two great historical figures Abdur Rahman, amir of Afghanistan, and Sir Henry Mortimer Durand. There's even mention of [Pyne's] atrocious piano playing . . . He kept both of them entertained, Loyn suggested, in quite a comedic way. He worked for the amir, you see . . . The hook for me was the idea of this little Cockney man, many, many miles from home, who's made this place his own home and who entertains people of that stature on a plinky plonk piano while key negotiations are going on at a very high level.

The amir warns the foreign secretary, who's pushing for a permanent border, that 'to impose such a thing on a land as vast as this, which has never had them, is to invite endless trouble'.[65] That's just one of the themes in the trilogy: the problems that arise when other nations and organisations insert themselves in Afghanistan, whether driven by imperialist motives or even humanitarian impulses. (In Richard Bean's *On the Side of the Angels*, British NGO workers brokering

FIGURE 4.5   *(From left) Rick Warden, Danny Rahim, Paul Bhattacharjee, and Michael Cochrane in Ron Hutchinson's* Durand's Line (The Great Game: Afghanistan), *2009.*

Source: Photograph by John Haynes, courtesy of the Tricycle Theatre and John Haynes.

land rights in the tribal culture get embroiled in an unsavoury deal, which leads to a tragic outcome for them.)

The Tricycle was again nominated for an Olivier Award for outstanding achievement in an affiliate theatre. (The Royal Court won the Olivier for *Cock*. Kent, Rubasingham and the Tricycle won a Liberty Human Rights Arts Award).[66] Michael Billington called *The Great Game* a 'mind-blowing achievement'.[67] But with the expanse of subject matter and multiple playwrights' voices, there were conflicting opinions about the individual plays: one critic's 'superbly eloquent and chilling' play was discussed by another in unflattering terms.[68]

Rick Warden: In a strange way, we feel a little bit critic-proof on *Great Game*, and the reason I think we feel that is not just because we rate the work very highly and we're very confident in its power, but it's also because our press is real and it's happening every day. We're not fabricating something mythical or fantastical. People are drawn to *The Great Game* because they're interested in Afghanistan and what's happening.

Warden played General Sir David Richards in verbatim sections. (He summed up some of the general's points: 'We will need to talk to the Taliban and maintain great pressure on them simultaneously to help the people of Afghanistan that we've made great promises to, that we can't abandon. We can't abandon the people of Afghanistan is really the gist of General Sir David's verbatim.') When the general saw the play in 2009, the actor met him.

Rick Warden: We got on very well. He was a bit dismayed that I had a moustache. You might have read this. And I tried to explain to him that I had big sideburns, for obvious period reasons [for Warden's role as Pyne] . . . He's very affable, really gregarious, ultra friendly. I have to say not dissimilar looking to me, but about 20 years my senior. And he immediately started ribbing me about being too small (even though he's pretty small himself), not good looking enough to play him, which is his favorite joke, and this stupid moustache that had to go.

The next time the general saw him, Warden had dropped the period moustache, but, says the actor, that was 'because my wife told me to'. Richards, newly named chief of the defence staff, had returned to the theatre in July 2010 to attend a special marathon for the military, bringing with him Sandhurst officer cadets. Channel 4 News was on the scene.

Rick Warden: Extraordinary day. I would say the highlight of the whole two runs at the Tricycle was the military day. They got all the jokes, they knew all the geography, they knew all of the historical context. These were a mixture of policy makers, decision makers in the army, and officer trainees, so people who knew and had done their homework, and they made for an absolutely fantastic audience . . . The idea of a private performance for people who make decisions, in political-theatre terms, you don't get any better than that.

The first stop on the 2010 US tour was for the Shakespeare Theatre Company in Washington, DC. *The Great Game* moved on to the Guthrie in Minneapolis and Berkeley Repertory Theatre in California, then finished the run in December for the Public Theater in New York City. But in February 2011, the production returned to Washington, for two trilogy days, again for the military and policy makers – this time for the Pentagon.

The Bomb – A Partial History (2012)

> First Blast, Proliferation: *From Elsewhere: The Message . . .* by Zinnie Harris; *Calculated Risk* by Ron Hutchinson; *Seven Joys* by Lee Blessing; *Option* by Amit Gupta; *Little Russians* by John Donnelly.

> Second Blast, Present Dangers: *There Was a Man. There Was No Man.* by Colin Teevan; *Axis* by Diana Son; *Talk Talk Fight Fight* by Ryan Craig; *The Letter of Last Resort* by David Greig; *From Elsewhere: On the Watch . . .* by Zinnie Harris; verbatims edited by Richard Norton-Taylor.

Kent was 'going out with a bang', wrote the journalists.[69] He too used the phrase when we spoke in March 2012 about his final production as director of the Tricycle.

Nicolas Kent: I just couldn't face trying to raise money for my last two years, and all the time thinking – I'm 67 now – and I'll leave when I'm 69, having kept the place afloat for two years and not have done very much in those last two years of what I wanted to do. So I thought may as well go out with a bang and a *Bomb*, and just enjoy it. That seemed to be the best way to do it. I'm certain it's the right decision.

The project was spurred by a conversation he'd had a couple of years earlier, Kent wrote in a programme essay. The decision for the renewal of Trident, Britain's nuclear deterrent, was coming up, and he was asked why the Tricycle wasn't entering the debate on nuclear weapons.[70] The Tricycle did just that when the director took on the assignment. We talked about his choices for the subject matter of the plays.

Nicolas Kent: I wanted to do the Cuban missile crisis from a Russian point of view. I was trying to take the landmarks of the history of the nuclear bomb, the big events like Reykjavík and the end of the cold war – but gradually we got pushed off course a bit. When some of the first scripts came in, many of them didn't really work as well as I'd hoped, and I had trouble getting people to deliver on time. The whole project got a bit behindhand, and as it got behindhand, I decided to decouple it with the Lee Blessing play, which was dealing with the cold war. [Blessing's *A Walk in the Woods* was staged in autumn 2011.] Then sadly the Russian play didn't work well either, and there were various other problems.

So I decided that we would focus more on the beginnings of proliferation and how that happened, and not do a chronological history, although in the end it was somewhat chronological, but not entirely. We dealt primarily with proliferation in the first half and the way that some countries got rid of nuclear arms, like, obviously, Ukraine. And in the second half, we dealt more with the present dangers that we faced, the British Trident fleet and what nuclear missiles were for now, why we were retaining them when there didn't seem to be a cold war enemy anymore. The whole thing evolved and changed.

The Bomb – A Partial History (accompanied by a festival of film, art exhibits, talks, stand-up comedy and music) came together in two 'blasts' of short plays by nine playwrights plus verbatims edited by Richard Norton-Taylor – and added up to five hours of theatre. As with past multiplay productions, each blast ran separately on week-nights, with both parts playing on Saturdays and Sundays, from February through 1 April. *Great Game* writers and actors joined the team for this project. A number of the other actors had worked with Kent before, and all had appeared at least once on the Tricycle stage.[71] Kent and actors alike talked about the hilarity in rehearsals. 'The rehearsal process was a ball. We laughed long and loud because we all know each other. It's very serious subject matter, but that didn't stop us behaving like children', says Rick Warden.

With ten plays in all, the two pieces by Zinnie Harris begin and end the series.

Nicolas Kent: Zinnie Harris was going to do something about the present Iranian negotiations, which is the territory that Ryan Craig finally did. And Zinnie got rather stuck on that. So I asked Zinnie if she would be prepared to do another area. And she said, What? And I suggested the Frisch-Peierls story to her, and she settled for that and then put a new spin on it, bringing it up to date [for the closing companion piece], in what I think is a beautiful play.

The opener, *From Elsewhere: The Message . . .*, takes place in 1940 at Whitehall. It's a two-hander about the Jewish scientists Otto Frisch (Daniel Rabin) and Rudolf Peierls (Rick Warden), one Austrian, one German, both then working at Birmingham University. They're about to inform the wartime British government about the viability of building a bomb. They're nervous and somewhat intimidated by the portraits of the great English figures like Admiral Nelson, shown in video projections on panels that were transformed into different backdrops for most of the plays.

Rabin says the way Zinnie Harris 'places words on the page', in a kind of poetic format, 'instructs you how to do it'.

Daniel Rabin: And there's a lot of freedom within that structure, but it's a structure that's really important to her. And it makes it very interesting to act. I like where she's taken those characters in terms of that waiting room at Whitehall and the conversation they have in the very beginning. It's just nice to have nothing else but two people chatting, who are under pressure, and she's done it very, very well, and realistically, and I think very dramatically . . .

Rick and I discussed the fact that they're kind of clowns, in a way. It's quite Vladimir and Estragon [from *Waiting for Godot*], in a way. And we decided not to play up on that. We thought that's there in the script . . . It's the relationship which really intrigues me, and which I like playing, actually, the relationship between the two guys.

By the second scene of the following play, Ron Hutchinson's *Calculated Risk*, America has dropped atom bombs on Hiroshima and Nagasaki.

Daniel Rabin: There's a play very early on, *Calculated Risk* . . . with Prime Minister Clement Attlee, where they're discussing the pros and cons of developing the nuclear bomb. And there's a line about the cat being out of the bag – that you can't really put it back in. Once the technology is out there for a nuclear bomb, you're not going to forget that technology. Another character in that play, which I love, says, You can't stop science in its tracks.

Attlee is meeting with his foreign secretary, a field marshal, and the physicist William Penney. Rick Warden played the scientist, and to do that, he says, he had to 'flirt with what it would be like to have been Penney, in Penney's head in 1945'.

Rick Warden: He essentially says, We can't go backwards scientifically. And any discussion (I'm talking as Penney now), any discussion I have with people that suggests we can is a discussion with Luddites who don't understand the way the world works, and whose world is actually much smaller than my world. And I know this for a fact, because Ron [Hutchinson] came to see the piece, and I was so pleased that he did because he said, Yeah, it's rats in a cage, which is how he described the rows that go on, with one of the people in the room realising the world has changed forever. And that's Penney, and he's 20 years younger than anybody in that room, and he's far, far brighter in a scientific sense than anyone in that room.

Throughout the production, newsreel and historical clips gave context to the development of the bomb. Images of the devastation in Japan in 1945 were a painful record of the atomic attack on that nation. Footage also charted the politics. Labour leader Hugh Gaitskell's 1960 speech opposing disarmament was projected onto the inside cover of a centre-stage silo. ('I very much liked the idea of the silo coming up', Kent says.) Designer Polly Sullivan and video designer Douglas O'Connell skilfully combined the set pieces and projections to connect the different periods and varied locations.

India in the late sixties is the setting for Amit Gupta's *Option*. The country is on its way to a nuclear weapons option, much to the dismay of the sixtyish professor (Paul Bhattacharjee) whose nuclear research for the government has been dedicated to producing energy for the country. A pacifist guided by Gandhi's principles, the professor opts to resign when India won't sign the Nuclear Non-Proliferation Treaty. A young physicist (Tariq Jordan) stays on without his mentor to see his own formulas turned into a reality. It's an uneasy parting of the two men (see Figure 4.6).

Tariq Jordan: What was nice about that one, you've got this young mind who is very ambitious, and sometimes ambition can make

FIGURE 4.6 *Paul Bhattacharjee, Tariq Jordan, and Shereen Martin in Amit Gupta's* Option (The Bomb – A Partial History), *2012.*

Source: Photograph by John Haynes, courtesy of the Tricycle Theatre and John Haynes.

you very single-minded, and you can forget about everything else that's going around you, especially people who are trying to look out for you, because you're so focused on what you want to achieve ... It's very touching because you've got a young student who has been taught by this professor, and he's now taking over because he's beginning to outwit his professor. And the professor now finds it difficult to keep up with him, so the roles are reversed.

The First Blast finale is a wild and wacky comedy (*Little Russians* by John Donnelly) about the nuclear warheads left in Ukraine after the breakup of the Soviet Union. Kent says he knew he needed a 'theatrical coup' for the production, and a huge nuclear missile upstage was both a spectacular set piece and the focal point of the action in *Little Russians*. A Ukrainian family tries to sell it to an arms dealer. They're quite eccentric, however, and have trouble completing the transaction. Rick Warden describes his character as 'mad as a box of frogs'; his brother, played by Tariq Jordan, has a weak grasp of negotiation tactics. He wants to give back some of the money handed over for the sale. Daniel Rabin was the arms dealer, a Chechen nicknamed Dennis. In the end, the deal is off anyway when Russian and American military arrive with great fanfare to claim the missile.

In the Second Blast's present dangers, the threat that Iran is building nuclear weapons underlies *There Was a Man. There Was No Man.* by Colin Teevan and *Talk Talk Fight Fight* by Ryan Craig. The first is premised on treachery between Israel and Iran in the development of Iran's nuclear capabilities, including a computer virus and an assassination; in the other, an EU delegation rehearses for talks with Iran about whether it's complying with the Non-Proliferation Treaty. Rabin, who acted in both those plays, spoke about the complexities of the Second Blast.

Daniel Rabin: It's become so entangled, world politics. The situation in Iran, the situation in the Middle East. The Israel question. The words that have been used, extermination and being wiped off the map. And the fact that Israel has the bomb unofficially, but no one else is allowed in the Middle East. It's such a complicated political issue, and it's grown. It can be used in so many global issues politically, that it's so complicated . . . The second part is much more complicated than the first, and you really do need to pay attention to that. It's a difficult part to watch, and some of the ideas are quite difficult to grasp.

David Greig's *The Letter of Last Resort* in the Second Blast was the high point of the programme for a number of critics. (That August, Kent restaged the play at the Traverse Theatre in Edinburgh.) Belinda Lang played a newly elected prime minister and Simon Chandler was the civil servant in charge of arrangements in *Letter*, a play based on an actual practice. Lang's prime minister must write a letter of instructions to the commander of the Trident submarine, to be opened only in the event of the nuclear destruction of the United Kingdom. That missive tells the commander whether or not to retaliate. With impeccable timing, the two actors navigated the arguments about the implications of wreaking vengeance on millions of people.

In the Zinnie Harris closer, *From Elsewhere: On the Watch . . .*, it's present-day Iran, 70 years after we first met Peierls and Frisch (and who in actuality were both dead). In *On the Watch*, they're nuclear inspectors clad in radiation suits, outside an Iranian nuclear facility, making notes about what they've just observed (see Figure 4.7). 'They're in this weird purgatory', says Rabin. 'They're in a way paying for, as they see it, the information they passed across, and the implication of that action.'

FIGURE 4.7 *Rick Warden as Rudolf Peierls and Daniel Rabin as Otto Frisch in Zinnie Harris's* From Elsewhere: On the Watch . . . (The Bomb – A Partial History), *2012.*

Source: Photograph by John Haynes, courtesy of the Tricycle Theatre and John Haynes.

Kent made the public announcement of his leave-taking well before mounting *The Bomb*, and the critics paid tribute to him in their reviews.

Rick Warden: You know what I was most happy about with the reviews? I promised myself I wouldn't read any this time. I thought, I'm 40 years old. I do not need to read any of these reviews anymore. I really don't. And of course I failed dismally to not read any of them, and I read them all. And what I was most happy about, regardless of the fact that they were four stars, which is great because that helps with houses, was that nearly every single one picked out something peculiar and special about Nick and his creative, geopolitical contribution to the London stage. And I was really proud for him more than anybody else. They didn't pick out individual performances very much. They picked out Nick.

The Tricycle's homegrown verbatim plays and political play cycles (1994–2012)

1994

Half the Picture: The Scott "Arms to Iraq" Inquiry, adapted and redacted by Richard Norton-Taylor, with additional material by John McGrath

1996

Nuremberg War Crimes Trial, edited by Richard Norton-Taylor (played with one-act responses: *Ex-Yu* by Goran Stefanovski, *Haiti* by Keith Reddin, and *Reel, Rwanda* by Femi Osofisan); *Srebrenica*, edited by Nicolas Kent (with *Nuremberg* and *Ex-Yu* remount)

1997

Srebrenica (remount, prior to tour)

1999

The Colour of Justice: The Stephen Lawrence Inquiry, edited by Richard Norton-Taylor + transfer to Theatre Royal Stratford East and Victoria Palace + autumn tour, including the National Theatre

2003

Justifying War: Scenes from the Hutton Inquiry, edited by Richard Norton-Taylor

2004

Guantanamo: 'Honor Bound to Defend Freedom' by Victoria Brittain and Gillian Slovo + West End transfer

2005

Bloody Sunday: Scenes from the Saville Inquiry, edited by Richard Norton-Taylor (and remount + tour)

2006

How Long Is Never? Darfur – A Response: Many Men's Wife by Amy Evans; *Bilad al-Sudan* by Juliet Gilkes; *Words Words Words* by Jennifer Farmer; *Silhouette* by Carlo Gébler; *Distant Violence* by Michael Bhim; *IDP* by Winsome Pinnock; *Give, Again?* by Lynn Nottage

2007

Called to Account: The Indictment of Anthony Charles Lynton Blair for the Crime of Aggression Against Iraq – A Hearing, edited by Richard Norton-Taylor

2009

The Great Game: Afghanistan. Part 1, Invasions and Independence: *Bugles at the Gates of Jalalabad* by Stephen Jeffreys; *Durand's Line* by Ron Hutchinson; *Campaign* by Amit Gupta; *Now Is the Time* by Joy Wilkinson. Part 2, Communism, the Mujahideen and the Taliban: *Black Tulips* by David Edgar; *Blood and Gifts* by J. T. Rogers (replaced by *Wood for the Fire* by Lee Blessing in 2010 remount); *Miniskirts of Kabul* by David Greig; *The Lion of Kabul* by Colin Teevan. Part 3, Enduring Freedom: *Honey* by Ben Ockrent; *The Night Is Darkest Before the Dawn* by Abi Morgan; *On the Side of the Angels* by Richard

Bean; *Canopy of Stars* by Simon Stephens; monologues and duologues by Siba Shakib; verbatims edited by Richard Norton-Taylor

2010

Women, Power and Politics: Part 1, Then: *The Milliner and the Weaver* by Marie Jones; *Handbagged* by Moira Buffini; *The Lioness* by Rebecca Lenkiewicz; *Bloody Wimmin* by Lucy Kirkwood; verbatim accounts edited by Gillian Slovo. Part 2, Now: *Acting Leader* by Joy Wilkinson; *The Panel* by Zinnie Harris; *Playing the Game* by Bola Agbaje; *Pink* by Sam Holcroft; *You, Me and Wii* by Sue Townsend; verbatim accounts edited by Gillian Slovo

The Great Game: Afghanistan (remount + US tour)

2011

Tactical Questioning: Scenes from the Baha Mousa Inquiry, edited by Richard Norton-Taylor

The Riots by Gillian Slovo

2012

The Riots (at Bernie Grant Arts Centre)

The Bomb – A Partial History: First Blast, Proliferation: *From Elsewhere: The Message . . .* by Zinnie Harris; *Calculated Risk* by Ron Hutchinson; *Seven Joys* by Lee Blessing; *Option* by Amit Gupta; *Little Russians* by John Donnelly; Second Blast, Present Dangers: *There Was a Man. There Was No Man.* by Colin Teevan; *Axis* by Diana Son; *Talk Talk Fight Fight* by Ryan Craig; *The Letter of Last Resort* by David Greig; *From Elsewhere: On the Watch . . .* by Zinnie Harris; verbatim edited by Richard Norton-Taylor

5

Dressing-room stories and encores

Part 1: The Tricycle dressing rooms

The downstairs dressing room is 'practically on the stage', says a director, a sentiment echoed by an actress who calls that proximity 'a scream'. I heard about the wonderful communal atmosphere in the Tricycle's dressing rooms (an upstairs one, a downstairs one, and a 'green room'). But I also learned about tensions that can arise in small quarters: some years ago, a physical fight broke out in the downstairs dressing room between two actors on the last day of the run. For the most part, however, the stories were very good-humoured.

Shaz McGee (McGee gave me a tour of the theatre, then showed me a framed *Guardian* profile of Kent from 2004): There's a quote in there from Sylvia Syms, and she mentions the state of the dressing room. She says it's fantastic working at the Tricycle, except for those bloody dressing rooms . . . For *Bloody Sunday* [2005] and for the Hutton Inquiry [*Justifying War,* 2003] and *The Colour of Justice* [1999], I had to turn the dock area – which is the load-in area – into a dressing room because there were so many people. We tried to make it nice. I put a carpet down on the floor, put a mirror up, some clip lights around it and a little blow heater if it was winter. But it's part and parcel of working here. I really detest it when people come in and they know what they're going to get, but they still complain. And there are some actors, they know the story, it's what's written on the wrapper, if you come and work at the Tricycle. But some people will still come in and they'll have a little moan about, 'My last job, I had my own dressing room'.

Pauline Black (on *Love in Vain*, 1982): It was only the second production I was ever in, at that time anyway. I found the whole thing very exciting. It was quite a small cast. There was only one other female in it. We had our dressing room on one side of the stage, and the guys had their dressing room on the other side of the stage. And we'd swap backwards and forwards during the production, and it was a really lovely atmosphere and my initiation into proper theatre acting.

Terry Mortimer (on *The Great White Hope*, 1985): There was quite a big cast of men, as usual in most plays these days. Hugh [Quarshie] had his own dressing room, obviously. The rest of us shared one of the other dressing rooms. The cast was so big and the dressing room was so small that we couldn't all be in there at the same time unless someone sat on the fridge and used that as a dressing-room desk. We couldn't all be there at the same time and make up, if we needed to make up. It was such a great atmosphere. We all had to get on, and we did.

Anton Phillips: (on the transfer of *The Amen Corner* to the West End, 1987): I think the cast cohesion started to suffer a little bit. You're in the West End; there are 18 dressing rooms; everybody can have their own dressing room. The only time they ever met was onstage at the beginning of the play. Whereas at the Tricycle, all the women were in one and all the men in one dressing room. But once it went into the West End, that cast cohesion, that ensemble, started to break down.

Jenny Jules (on *Pecong*, 1991): There were about eight women. We shared the smallest space in the dressing rooms. There was this one actress – she played Sweet Bella Pandit. Her name is

Sharon Hinds, beautiful looking woman. Gorgeous on the inside and the outside. We ended up calling her Dizzy Hinds. Every day Sharon would come to work and get changed into her costume. We'd do the play, and we'd come back to the dressing room, and she'd be standing up in her knickers, sometimes knickers and bra, but mainly her knickers, and she'd be going, 'Um, does anybody remember what clothes I was wearing to work today?' That happened at least twice a week. She would lose her clothes in the room somewhere because she went and got changed in the loo, or she was doing something else. Or who knows what happened. I remember one story in particular, when she was wearing a bra that day, and she walked onstage as Sweet Bella Pandit – Sweet Bella was a mute, and she had the most beautiful costumes – with a huge ball dress almost, and this multicoloured bra was attached to the hem of her skirt. And she walked across the stage dragging her bra, and she was supposed to be a deaf mute, and I remember her going, 'Bloody hell!' Dizzy Hinds. We laughed so much in that room. There was no space even to have a punch-up. We just had joy. I've mainly had joy in my dressing rooms.

Dona Croll (on *Victor and the Ladies*, 1995): When we did that play, there were six of us women. The Tricycle really only has two dressing rooms. A large one downstairs, stage left, which takes about seven or eight people, and then a little one upstairs just by the wardrobe, which takes about three people at a pinch. And we were working with Rudolph Walker playing the chap. And they gave him the big dressing room downstairs, and put all of us upstairs. And we said, It seems a bit silly. Maybe they thought Rudolph is a bit older and didn't want to go up, because it's a very steep staircase. When he found out, he said, Oh, my goodness, how silly of them. No, no, no. Of course, you must have the big room, he said. He's a lovely gentleman.

Marion Bailey (on *Dance of Death*, 1998): My only memory is being downstairs with the boys. So I think I must have hung out with the two guys [Michael Cochrane and Tim Woodward] downstairs. I do remember I would go down and hang out with them because I felt lonely, I think. And we always used to treat ourselves to a bottle of bubbly afterwards. And as time wore on, and we were running out of money, it sort of moved from the first week where we would be having Bollinger to Sainsbury's – just treat ourselves to that after the show.

Michael Cochrane (on the tribunals): The best dressing room in the world. Ten or so actors of every age, creed, colour, et cetera, all engaged in fascinating dialogue. Not for the fainthearted, perhaps, but the humour is enormous.

Thomas Wheatley (on the tribunals and *Nuremberg*, 1996): It's the funniest dressing room in London. It's got to be, and quite often led by Michael Cochrane, or Cocky, as we know him, who is the funniest actor I know. And it's an absolute delight to get back there each time, with half of us old hands and then newcomers coming in. And with *Nuremberg*, that material was so potent and distressing, you have to find ways of dealing with that. One way which we all dealt with it was that the dressing room was the campest and funniest place. Hysteria. We were frequently asked by the stage management to be a bit quieter.

William Hoyland (on the tribunals and *Bloody Sunday*, 2005): The men's dressing room in the Tricycle is very, very small for a large-cast play. And as I said, there is a kind of repertory of us, and we even have our own places now. And for *Bloody Sunday*, we had an actor who hadn't been in any of them before who was playing one of the soldiers, and he was from Northern Ireland and one of the relatives, and he's much younger than all the rest of us. He said it was the happiest dressing room he had ever been in.

After the second or third, that dressing room was one of the happiest dressing rooms I have ever been in. Normally when you get to be my age, you get your own dressing room or you share with one other, so it's a bit like slumming it. But then one got to look forward to it enormously because actors can be competitive, but there was no competition between any of us. We're all in the same boat. We're all at the same status, more or less, and if we weren't, it didn't matter. And we're all here to do what we think to be good work for not very much money. And there was very little ego, which is quite unusual with actors. So for me that dressing room is really important in my life. It was a wonderful experience being with those friends and colleagues time and time again.

Sharon Duncan-Brewster (on *Blues for Mr. Charlie,* 2004): We were packed in like sardines. In the Tricycle, there's a section that they call the green room, which no offence, Mr Kent, but a green room, it ain't. It's an area where you can heat up food. It's like a kitchen area. There were six women. It was all of us down in this green room. And then they had to make a passway for the guys to come from the upstairs changing room down to the stage. You normally walk down through the green room backstage. You couldn't do that because we were changing. They had a section of the green room cut off, so that they could go through a side door from their staircase onto the stage.

We couldn't make any noise because you could hear us backstage. We would turn the lights quite dim, have a little lamp in the corner, and we would sit and chat about all sorts of things. There was a mouse. I didn't see it. Two of the girls saw it. Now can you imagine girls in a dressing room and a mouse. They were so hysterical, the hysteria got brought onstage. Theatres always have mice; that's cool. But that whole dressing room thing, you'd bend over, you'd be putting your makeup on and someone's backside would be here. A guy's coming through – they're going to get an eyeful.

David Ganly (on *The Quare Fellow,* 2004): The dressing room is tiny on stage left, and for *The Quare Fellow*, there were 12 of us, 12 grown men in that dressing room. And we used to have to take it in turns to get dressed into our prison gear. The largest member of the cast, Ciaran McIntyre, looks like an Irish Santa;

he's a formidable size. Somehow or other, the poor girl laying out these prison uniforms, all of which are identical, managed to swap Ciaran's with Matt Dunphy's, who was the most impish member of the cast. As I said, we'd go out at the half-hour call to offer the show up, so Ciaran was already wearing his trousers. But the play would start with us putting on our shirts and our waistcoats in our cells and waking up and emptying out our slop buckets. There were four cells, and Ciaran was at the beginning with me and another actor. He was there absolutely for beginners. The first image you see is him coming out. Somehow or other, because we had to take it in turns, he hadn't checked his waistcoat and his shirt. And the show started, and this giant of a man was having to get into the equivalent of babyGap clothes. It was just ridiculous. So after that, we did have to dress in shifts. It was like a production line. It was prison conditions. It was definitely life imitating art. The improvements to the theatre – the money was all spent out front. There isn't room back there, but there's a certain pleasure to be had from that level of intimacy. But very definitely we blurred the lines between prison conditions and what our union would expect.

Kobna Holdbrook-Smith (on the African American season, 2005–6): It's small, you share, you go a bit mental. When we did *Fabulation*, Lucian [Msamati], Don [Gilet], Nathan [Osgood], and myself shared a dressing room. The four lads . . . We had the downstairs for *Walk Hard* and *Gem* because there were more of us. And then we had the upstairs for the switcheroo. But we had this game, where we would spin a – Don had this Vaseline tub. How did it start? Don was sitting on his dressing table with a coin, spinning a coin, then it stopped. He spun it to see how long he could spin it for. And so we all got fixated on how long Don could spin this thing. So we started timing him. Then we started betting on what times each spin was going to yield. That evolved into each of us having a spinning competition, seeing who could spin this coin the most. Then that evolved to a Vaseline tub, 'cause it was heavier; it was like the little lip balms. We were spinning this thing. It became a big thing. We were, like, OK, all right, we'll go down in one minute. One more spin.

It's lovely. You get chums. I think it promotes that because it's a bit like a family. Everyone thinks their organisation is like a family, but the Tricycle really is. And it has its ups, and it has its downs, and sometimes you're cross with the woman behind the café or the box office or whatever, and sometimes they're cross with you. But mostly you get on. That's what families do. And because of that, it means that as actors, you get along together. I had a conversation on the way in actually about how some actors are mainly concerned with their role. The comic reference to it is, bullshit, bullshit, my line. And you're not really allowed to get away with that at the Tricycle. Because it's all collective, and it's all collaborative. So even when you're sharing a space, you all end up doing things together. It's good.

Heather Tobias (on *The Field*, 2006): The front of the house now at the Tricycle is really swish; it's really upmarket. And it's a lovely place to work. The only thing that hasn't changed is the dressing room. You have to get fit for the women's dressing room. You've seen that huge great flight of stairs. You kind of know when you're getting fitter 'cause you're not panting by the time you get to the end. It's the charm of it. In fact, this last play, *The Field*, was brilliant because it was just Rita Hamill and I. Just two. And the guys were going berserk because they were all squashed in that little space downstairs.

Rick Warden (on *The Great Game: Afghanistan*, 2009): I'll leave you with this story. I'm not going to shock you. A certain wonderful and esteemed actress from *The Great Game* needed cheering up for all sorts of reasons. And we knew that she had to make an exit through Chicago [the men's dressing room] to get back to the ladies' dressing room, which is called Penang. We knew at a certain point, she had to go through our dressing room.

There was no other way for the poor lady to go. So on two or three different occasions, three young actors, myself, Nabil Elouahabi, and Hugh Skinner, were naked in there. And we were naked in comedic manner. So one day she came in and I was doing a Rubik's Cube on my lap, with nothing on. I think Nabil was checking his eyebrows, probably, in the mirror, and Hugh was bending over the sink. And she had to get through. Just so that she knew it wasn't a fluke, the next day we all were in yoga positions doing a yoga class. She got mightily cheered up. And when she tried to respond in kind, we took the fight to her, and we all went into the ladies' dressing room looking for a certain prop that didn't exist – with no clothes on. It's definitely my fondest memory of the dressing room in four years.

Part 2: Encores

A fiery Scottish king

Nicolas Kent described his production of Macbeth *(1995), starring Lennie James and Helen McCrory.*

Nicolas Kent: We actually set fire to the stage completely. It started with the end of the battle, and then Macbeth and Banquo slew two rebels. They were fighting with torches. We used no artificial light at all until we got to England. And they were fighting with torches, and then they torched the earth on the stage, and it all went up. There was a wall of fire. It was really interesting, because you wouldn't get away with that in any other theatre in this country because of fire regulations. We got away with it because the fire department here looks after two venues. It looks after us and Wembley Stadium, with their huge pop concerts. They're very farsighted. And we did workshops with them for two weeks. We were trying out methods of setting fire to things in contained ways. And we had a fireman onstage with a hose all the way through the production. Everyone kept saying, How on earth have you been allowed to put this on? It really did use fire in a very creative way. It was very exciting to do, especially after the theatre was burned down only eight years before.

Lighting designer David Taylor told me about a scene in that production.

David Taylor: We did a reveal for [the] banquet scene that was essentially at the back wall. A little like the mural [in *The Great Game*], you had no idea that there was anything beyond. And there was a slow reveal in the dark: this steel wall split and opened, and there were a hundred candles on a steel table tilted. They were all real and alight. There was this massive living light.

Iced (1998) and the stolen seats

Warning: Some of the following might be apocryphal, but it's part of the lore.

Actor Ray Shell is the author of the novel *Iced*; his stage version of the book, directed by Felix Cross, played at the Tricycle in 1998. By all accounts, this play about a crack addict attracted a young, non-traditional audience – it was cool to see it – and the attendance records show full houses for much of the four-week run. Benedict Nightingale wrote in his *Times* review that the novel 'reportedly became one of the most shoplifted books in publishing history', but, he added, stealing theatre seats would be hard to do 'without the box-office staff noticing'.[1] However, I was told by the Tricycle's management that that's exactly what happened. With no seat assignments in the mostly unreserved house, audience members would go out to the loo and pass along tickets to their friends, swelling the house to beyond capacity.

An eyeful in Eltham

In 1999 Christopher Fox went to Eltham in southeast London, where Stephen Lawrence had been murdered six years earlier in an attack by a gang of youths. He was doing research for The Colour of Justice *in which he portrayed Jamie Acourt, one of the suspects. Fox got more than he bargained for when he visited the scene of the crime.*

Christopher Fox: When I was getting ready to play Jamie Acourt for the tour – there's a book by an investigative journalist called Brian Cathcart [*The Case of Stephen Lawrence*]. I bought that book and I was reading it, and in the front there's a map of the area where Stephen Lawrence was murdered, and you can walk around the various streets where the five boys lived. So I took the train down there one day to walk around the street just to get the feel of where they came from and the various houses where they lived.

And after taking a tour of the estate – it was quite a hot day – I sat down on this park bench in Well Hall Road, down from where Stephen Lawrence was killed, and there was a phone box next to this park, next to this bench. This car pulled up next to the phone box – it was a silver Renault Clio – a guy gets out of the car, and I see it's Jamie Acourt. It's Jamie bloody Acourt. And I'm sitting there reading this book about Stephen Lawrence, and my jaw literally drops, and we lock eyes, and he's looking at me. I'm thinking, Does he know that I'm playing him? All this stuff comes into your head. Anyway he walks around the car, gets into the phone box, makes a real quick phone call, comes out of the phone box, gets in the car and drives off. And I followed the car, I ran after the car, and he literally parked it down the road outside Gary Dobson's house, and three of the guys came out of the house, into the car and drove off.

It's not easy to see yourself portrayed onstage

Jan Chappell played the renowned human-rights lawyer Gareth Peirce in Guantanamo: 'Honor Bound to Defend Freedom' *(2004). Chappell had been to the lawyer's office and talked with her – and one night Peirce came to see the show.*

Jan Chappell: Fortunately I didn't know she was in (some people did know) because that would have been so hard. I'd met Clive Stafford Smith on a couple of occasions. And one night after a performance, he said to me, 'I've been trying to get hold of Gareth for days, but I can't. Seeing you on the stage tonight, I thought, well, I'll talk to her now.' It was really kind. Gareth did come to see it. I was introduced to her in the theatre bar afterwards, and there was a point where she called me quietly aside into the gallery at the Tricycle, and she said, 'I just want to tell you this. I thought everybody was very good, and I really believed them, everybody, except you.' I, of course, giggled and said, 'You don't think perhaps you're feeling a little subjective? I would hate to see anyone playing me onstage. I wouldn't go.' She said, 'I just didn't believe a word' . . .

I have to say – confident, arrogant, or not – I remain unfazed by it because I had had different kind of feedback, and as I say I felt sorry that she'd come at all. And do you know the next day, I was down in the country where I was living, I was walking around the garden centre and my mobile phone rings, and it was Gareth: 'I'm just phoning to say I'm so sorry if I was rude.' And I said, 'It's absolutely fine. I think it must be a horrible thing, somebody pretending to be you.' I was very touched by that.

Mama Benin is hot

Joy Richardson's Mama Benin in the 2004–5 production of Playboy of the West Indies *by Mustapha Matura was hotter than usual one night.*

Joy Richardson: There's a scene where I strike a Swan match on my arm, and it lights. We used to have a rough surface of tape stuck to the inside of my arm, which was black so that it wouldn't be highly visible. And when I go to smoke my pipe, I strike the match on my forearm . . . And when we were doing the performance, I struck it once, the match didn't light. I struck it a second time, and I thought to myself – meanwhile I'm acting the scene – I thought, if it doesn't light the third time, I'm not going to bother. I struck it a third time, and it didn't light. So I carried on acting, and then I heard the audience becoming very restless, and I'm thinking, What's going on here? I'm trying to act, and they're chattering away. And then an audience member leaned forward and said to me, 'Excuse me, but you're on fire'. The head of the match had caught light, broken off and landed in my lap. As I was seated and the table was there, I couldn't see the flames coming up from my skirt. I jumped up and had to put out this fire by beating it, and I pretended the spirits were sending me a message, by some sort of movement of, 'Thank you, gods, thank you for your warning'. Of course the audience had burst out laughing. The costume people said, 'Shall we patch the skirt?' and I said, 'No leave it'. From then on, the skirt had a hole, and they sprayed it to fireproof the skirt.

A scary night at *The Arab-Israeli Cookbook* (2005)

Marion Bailey was in The Arab-Israeli Cookbook *by Robin Soans in July 2005, the summer terrorists attacked London's transportation system, 'which made her feel slightly vulnerable'.*

Marion Bailey: I can remember one night, there was one scene in the beginning of the second half, where I had a little speech on my own onstage when I was playing an older Arab Christian woman. She was describing how at the end of her garden there was a gatepost with bullet holes in it. And out of the corner of my eye,

I could see someone stand up in the gallery at the side and peer like that, and my heart started going, and I thought, This is it; some nutter is going to take a potshot at me or something awful. Then I heard this *dadadada* – the sound of feet on the stairs – and I thought, My God, they're running down. They're going to leap onstage. And I'm thinking in my brain (and still talking), What am I going to do? I got finished, and I got off and said to the stage manager, 'There's somebody –' She said, 'Yes, I know. Front of house are dealing with it.' And all it was was some poor guy upstairs wanted to stand up to get a better view. And the *thud, thud, thud* had been front of house running up to tell him to sit down. We were all so fragile and on tenterhooks. And because of the nature of that play, we were all slightly: Supposing some loopy person gets in? You just thought what's afoot here? Is someone going to do something insane and stupid because they object to the politics of this piece? Not that it had politics, particularly.

A director for *Doubt* (2007–8)

I interviewed Paulette Randall in 2007. That very day I had been given a tip, which I asked her about.

TS: I hear you might be doing John Patrick Shanley's *Doubt*.

PR: I'm seeing Nick tonight.

TS: That's when he's going to tell you?

PR: No, the man is impossible. I will tell you exactly what's happened. He's known me since 1991, at least since then, possibly before that. He said to me, 'I've got this play that I want you to read, but it's not an offer, and there's someone else in the loop'. I said, 'OK, all right then', thinking I'd better not like it. I read this play. I love it . . . Anyway, apparently I've got to meet him and wow him and persuade him that I'm the right director for it. So I'm thinking, when I meet him, I'll ask him who this other director is, because I need to know who I'm up against. Then before I can even think, I get another message from him: 'I really want you to take this seriously, Paulette' – I know he thinks I'm a bit of a space cadet – 'because I ought to let you know that the person you're up against is me'.

Aml Ameen takes his clothes off

Roy Williams's Category B (part of the Not Black & White season, 2009) takes place in a prison. Aml Ameen's character has just been incarcerated and is ordered by the prison officers to strip. Kobna Holdbrook-Smith, who was one of the officers, told me this story about a very appreciative audience.

Kobna Holdbrook-Smith: Aml Ameen is quite famous. There was a film here called *Kidulthood* [2006]. He played one of the central characters in it. He has this enormous youth following. It was one of the first films for young urban Britons about their lifestyles. *Kidulthood* was along the same lines that *Boyz N the Hood* might have been for the States 20 years ago. He's got this enormous following from that. Not only from that. He's also been in *The Bill*. So when he would take his clothes off in *Category B*, the girls would be like, *Uhhhh (gasp)*. People couldn't believe they were actually seeing Trife (that was the character in *Kidulthood*) take his clothes off. And one night it went particularly off the scale. There were screams and whistles, and they would not stop. So of course I had to play my character with a smile for the rest of the scene. Rob Whitelock as a prison guard had to laugh his way through his lines. No, he didn't quite; he was still on it. It shifted the dynamic of the scene. We had to take it on board and turn what was a scene about showing Aml's character how tough prison was to finding him risible. Just quickly switch intentions. That's what happens. The audience gets a bit giddy. But I love that.

The Tricycle as matchmaker

Kent's claim that romances bloom at the Tricycle was confirmed by Tariq Jordan in a story that took place during previews for The Bomb – A Partial History *in 2012.*

Tariq Jordan: Because I'm a big film fan, I often watch a film when I do the show. So I'll go downstairs and watch a film in the cinema. They sometimes have a 2.30 film. The cinema space is a lovely space, and it's really quiet. Sometimes I go in there when there's not a film on and go through my lines. And I was doing that one time before a show, when we were doing the previews, and I got locked in. They put the chain on the door and had locked me in, and there's no reception in there. I tried to use my phone. There's nothing. And I thought, What happens if I don't get out in time for the show? No one knew I was there. There was a small gap in the door, so I was trying to poke my pen through to see if I could get the chain off. I did think to myself, If no film is on tonight, I'm not going to be found. Luckily a film started about 40 minutes later, so they unlocked it.

I later found out that there is a fire exit, but I didn't know about it. But the person who locked me in was my girlfriend. This was before we were going out. It kind of got us talking. That was one of the icebreakers – and a week later, I asked her out.

The Tricycle family

Rod Rhule was the Tricycle's cinema manager from 2000 through 2008. We talked in 2006 about why people enjoyed working in the administration there.

Rod Rhule: It still is quite a small organisation, in spite of its size and how much it does and how much it covers and how much press it gets. There's a certain family feel to it, which is what I think people really want. They want to feel they can talk to Nick, talk to Mary, as well as talk to Trish [McElhill] or Gill [Christie]. That's part of it, the family-naturedness of it. It's quite intimate. Most people who leave still come back. They come back to say hello. What we do, for the theatre, anyway, is that anyone who's ever worked as an actor or in admin or director, technician, goes on the first-night list. So when we've got a new play, they'll get a letter sent to them saying, 'We've got a new play. There are two complimentary tickets for you, for the first previews. If you want to collect your tickets, let us know. We'll keep two aside.' It's quite a generous thing, and it keeps everyone that has worked there involved.

And some memories from an avid fan

David Taylor was with Theatre Projects Consultants and was on the team for the theatre rebuild after the fire in 1987. He was also the light-ing designer on a number of plays, including the US tour of The Great Game: Afghanistan *in 2010. I interviewed him right before that tour. He was unabashed in his regard for the Tricycle and all the staff there, whom he called 'solid anchors that enable people to do amazing things'. Sadly, Taylor, age 48, died in January 2011 while on a job in Taipei.*

David Taylor: I've enjoyed every production experience I've ever had there, and it has never technically disappointed me. And whilst I know that we tend to suspend our critical abilities when we're involved with a show, I also feel pretty proud of everything I've done there and think that everybody involved on the productions has tried hard to do a good show. I've seen a lot of shows there. I saw *A Love Song for Ulster* [by Bill Morrison, 1993]. My wife Sara and I had a trilogy-day experience that was in my top ten theatre experiences ever. And I had nothing to do with that. I was just an audience member. I loved it. When I'm in town, I try to go to the Tricycle rather than do other things . . . because I know it's going to be a comfortable, pleasant, manageable experience.

Appendix A: Interviewees cited and their work for the Tricycle Theatre, 1980 to May 2012

Michael Abbensetts
Playwright: *Samba* (1980).

Marion Bailey
Actress: *Dance of Death* (1998), *The Arab-Israeli Cookbook* (2005).

Shirley Barrie
Cofounder and associate director (through June 1984).
Playwright (from 1980): *Jack Sheppard's Back* (1982–3); children's plays: *Now You See It* (1981), *Shusha and the Story Snatcher* (1984).

Pauline Black
Actress: *Love in Vain* (1982), *Trinidad Sisters* (1988, at the Donmar), *All or Nothing at All* (1989), *Sitting in Limbo* (1998); former board member.

Jan Chappell
Actress: *Half the Picture* (1994), *The Colour of Justice* (1999), *Guantanamo: 'Honor Bound to Defend Freedom'* (2004).

Gillian Christie
Education director (2001–12); freelance staff member (1990s); theatre administrator trainee, London Arts Board Bursary (1990–1).

Ken Chubb
Cofounder and artistic director (through June 1984).

Director (from 1980): *Samba* (1980), *Space Ache* (1980), *Gone with Hardy* (1981), *Love in Vain* (1982), *Artichoke* (1982), *Jack Sheppard's Back* (1982–3), *Beyond the 'A' Penny Steps* (1983), *Buried Treasure* (1983), *Nightshoot* (1983–4).

Michael Cochrane
Actor: *Nuremberg* (1996), *Dance of Death* (1998), *The Colour of Justice* (1999), *Bloody Sunday* (2005), *The Great Game: Afghanistan* (2009, 2010), *The Bomb – A Partial History* (2012).

Shane Connaughton
Playwright: *I Do Like to Be* (1986); actor: *The Hostage* (1986) (also wrote additional lyrics).

Kerry Lee Crabbe
Playwright: *Flann O'Brien's Hard Life* (1985, 1986), Harold Pinter's *The Dwarfs* (adaptation) (2003); writer-in-residence (1986–7, 1990); writers' workshops (1989–90).

Dona Croll
Actress: *Joe Turner's Come and Gone* (1990), *Victor and the Ladies* (1995), *The Riots* (2011).

Dermot Crowley
Actor: *Flann O'Brien's Hard Life* (1985, 1986).

Sharon Duncan-Brewster
Actress: *Blues for Mr. Charlie* (2004), *Playboy of the West Indies* (2004–5), African American season: *Fabulation* (2006), *Let There Be Love* (2008), *Not Black & White: Category B, Seize the Day, Detaining Justice* (2009).

Tim Foster
Architect; board member.

Christopher Fox
Actor: *The Colour of Justice* (1999), *Tactical Questioning* (2011), *The Riots* (2011, 2012).

Clare Fox
Coproducer, *The Amen Corner* West End transfer (1987); board member (1982–2004).

Lucy Freeman
Board member; education officer (2004–6); administration staff (2003); front-of-house staff (2000).

David Ganly
Actor: *The Cavalcaders* (2001–2), *John Bull's Other Island* (2003), *The Quare Fellow* (2004, 2005), *The Arab-Israeli Cookbook* (2005), *The Field* (2006).

Carlo Gébler
Playwright: *Dance of Death* (1998), *10 Rounds* (2002), *How Long Is Never? Darfur – A Response: Silhouette* (2006).

Terry Hanafin
Former board member; Brent councillor (1974–85).

Kobna Holdbrook-Smith
Actor: *Playboy of the West Indies* (2004–5), African American season: *Walk Hard – Talk Loud, Gem of the Ocean, Fabulation* (2005–6), *Not Black & White: Category B, Seize the Day, Detaining Justice* (2009).

Philip Honour
Assistant to the director: *The War Next Door* (2007); assistant director: *Called to Account* (2007).

Pamela Howard
Designer: *Crossing Jerusalem* (2003), *The Great Game: Afghanistan* (2009, 2010).

William Hoyland
Actor: *Half the Picture* (1994), *Nuremberg* (1996), *Srebrenica* (1996, 1997), *The Colour of Justice* (1999), *Justifying War* (2003), *Guantanamo: 'Honor Bound to Defend Freedom'* (2004), *Bloody Sunday* (2005), *Called to Account* (2007).

Zoe Ingenhaag
Associate producer/Tricycle (2008–), *The Great Game: Afghanistan* (2009, 2010), *Women, Power and Politics* (2010), *Broken Glass* (2010, 2011), *The Riots* (2011, 2012), *The Bomb – A Partial History* (2012).

Tariq Jordan
Actor: *Guantanamo: 'Honor Bound to Defend Freedom'* (2004), *The Bomb – A Partial History* (2012); front-of-house staff (Nov./Dec. 2011).

Jenny Jules

Actress: Tricycle youth theatre/front-of-house staff (1980s), *The Great White Hope* (1985), *Pecong* (1991), *Two Trains Running* (1996), *The Colour of Justice* (1999), *Wine in the Wilderness* (2000, 2001), *The Promise* (2002), African American season: *Walk Hard – Talk Loud, Gem of the Ocean, Fabulation* (2005–6), *How Long Is Never? Darfur – A Response: Many Men's Wife, Words Words Words, Give, Again?* (2006); board member.

Nicolas Kent

Artistic director/director (July 1984–May 2012).

Playwright: *Srebrenica* (1996, 1997).

Director: *Playboy of the West Indies* (1984), *The One O'Clock World* (1984), *Lonely Cowboy* (1985), *The Great White Hope* (1985), *The Hostage* (1986), *Trinidad Sisters* (1988, at the Donmar), *Pentecost* (1989, at the Lyric Studio, Hammersmith), *All or Nothing at All* (1989), *The Factory Girls* (1990), *A Free Country* (1991), *A Long Way from Home* (1991), *Once a Catholic* (1991–2), *Una Pooka* (1992, with Mark Lambert), *Trouble in Mind* (1992), *A Love Song for Ulster* (1993), *Playboy of the West Indies* (1993–4), *Half the Picture* (1994), *Ain't Misbehavin'* (1994–5, with Gillian Gregory), *Macbeth* (1995), *Nuremberg, Ex-Yu, Haiti,* and *Reel, Rwanda* (1996), *Srebrenica* (1996, 1997), *The Mai* (1997), *Dance of Death* (1998), *The Colour of Justice* (1999), *Dreyfus* (2000), *Wine in the Wilderness* (2000, 2001), *The Promise* (2002), *10 Rounds* (2002), *Justifying War* (2003), *Guantanamo: 'Honor Bound to Defend Freedom'* (2004, with Sacha Wares), *Playboy of the West Indies* (2004–5), *Bloody Sunday* (2005), African American season: *Walk Hard – Talk Loud* (2005), *How Long Is Never? Darfur – A Response: Words Words Words, Silhouette* (2006), *The War Next Door* (2007), *Called to Account* (2007), *Doubt* (2007–8), *The Great Game: Afghanistan: Durand's Line, Campaign, Now Is the Time, Black Tulips, Honey, Canopy of Stars,* monologue/duologue, verbatims (2009, 2010), *Greta Garbo Came to Donegal* (2010), *Tactical Questioning* (2011), *A Walk in the Woods* (2011), *The Riots* (2011, 2012), *The Bomb – A Partial History* (2012).

Kwame Kwei-Armah
Playwright/director: *Let There Be Love* (2008), *Not Black & White: Seize the Day* (2009); Tricycle Playwrights Group; former board member.

Mary Lauder
General manager (1985–Oct 2012).

Joseph Marcell
Actor: *Joe Turner's Come and Gone* (1990), *King Hedley II* (2002–3), African American season: *Walk Hard – Talk Loud, Gem of the Ocean* (2005–6), *Let There Be Love* (2008), *Radio Golf* (2008).

Trish McElhill
Administrative manager (1989–).

Shaz McGee
Technical director (1996–).

David Michaels
Actor: *Justifying War* (2003), *The War Next Door* (2007), *Called to Account* (2007), *Tactical Questioning* (2011).

Dearbhla Molloy
Actress: *Pentecost* (1989, at the Lyric Studio, Hammersmith), *Doubt: A Parable* (2007–8).

Andrée Molyneux
Board member (1983–2011).

Terry Mortimer
Musical director/actor: *Gotterdammerung* or *Twilight of the Göds* (actor only, 1982), *The Great White Hope* (1985), *The Hostage* (1986), *All or Nothing at All* (1989), *A Love Song for Ulster* (1993).

Cecilia Noble
Actress: *Pecong* (1991), *The Piano Lesson* (1993), *Playboy of the West Indies* (1993–4), *Iced* (1998), *Water* and *Wine in the Wilderness* (2000, 2001), *Not Black & White: Seize the Day, Detaining Justice* (2009).

Richard Norton-Taylor
Playwright: *Half the Picture* (1994), *Nuremberg* (1996), *The Colour of Justice* (1999), *Justifying War* (2003), *Bloody Sunday* (2005), *Called to Account* (2007), *The Great Game: Afghanistan:* Verbatims (2009,

2010), *Tactical Questioning* (2011), *The Bomb – A Partial History:* verbatim (2012).

Alan Parnaby
Actor: *Four Nights in Knaresborough* (1999), *Justifying War* (TV production, 2004), *Guantanamo: 'Honor Bound to Defend Freedom'* (2004), *Bloody Sunday* (2005), *Tactical Questioning* (2011), *The Riots* (2011, 2012).

Anton Phillips
Director: *The Amen Corner* (1987), *Remembrance* (1990), *Sitting in Limbo* (1998), *The Amen Corner* (1999–2000); actor: *Smile Orange* (1983), *Trinidad Sisters* (1988, at the Donmar).

Winsome Pinnock
Playwright: *Water* (2000, 2001), *One Under* (2005), *How Long Is Never? Darfur – A Response: IDP* (2006); writer-in-residence and writers' workshops (1989–90); Tricycle Playwrights Group (2001–9).

Daniel Rabin
Actor: *Chicken Soup with Barley* (2005), *The Great Game: Afghanistan* (2010), *Tactical Questioning* (2011), *The Bomb – A Partial History* (2012).

Paulette Randall
Director: *Pecong* (1991), *Pinchy Kobi and the Seven Duppies* (1992–3), *The Piano Lesson* (1993), *Victor and the Ladies* (1995), *Two Trains Running* (1996), *Up Against the Wall* (1999, and cowriter), *King Hedley II* (2002–3), *Blues for Mr. Charlie* (2004), African American season: *Gem of the Ocean* (2006), *Radio Golf* (2008), *Not Black & White: Category B* (2009).

Selva Rasalingam
Actor: *Guantanamo: 'Honor Bound to Defend Freedom'* (West End, 2004), *The Riots* (2011, 2012).

Rod Rhule
Cinema manager (2000–8).

Joy Richardson
Actress: *Playboy of the West Indies* (1984), *Lonely Cowboy* (1985), *Macbeth* (1995), *Playboy of the West Indies* (2004–5); visual artist: artwork for *Wine in the Wilderness* (2000, 2001), gallery shows.

Billy Roche

Playwright: *The Wexford Trilogy* (2000–1); playwright/actor: *The Cavalcaders* (2001–2); playwright/director: *Lay Me Down Softly* (2011).

Indhu Rubasingham

Artistic director (from May 2012).

Director: *Starstruck* (1998), African American season: *Fabulation* (2006), *How Long Is Never? Darfur – A Response: IDP, Give, Again?* (2006), *The Great Game: Afghanistan: Bugles at the Gates of Jalalabad, Miniskirts of Kabul, The Lion of Kabul, The Night Is Darkest Before the Dawn, On the Side of the Angels,* monologue/duologue (2009, 2010), *Not Black & White: Detaining Justice* (2009), *Women, Power and Politics: The Milliner and the Weaver, Handbagged, The Lioness, Bloody Wimmin, Acting Leader, The Panel, Pink, You, Me and Wii* (and festival producer, 2010); *Stones in His Pockets* (2011–2); former board member.

Ray Shell

Actor: *Ain't Misbehavin'* (1994–5), *Two Trains Running* (1996), *The Amen Corner* (1999–2000), *Wine in the Wilderness* (2000, 2001), *Blues for Mr. Charlie* (2004), *Radio Golf* (2008); playwright: *Iced* (1998).

Claire Spooner

Designer: *Justifying War* (2003), *Bloody Sunday* (2005).

David Taylor

Theatre consultant and electrical services for the Tricycle rebuild, 1987–9; lighting designer: *Gamblers* (1992), *Macbeth* (1995), *The Mai* (1997), *Dreyfus* (2000), *Water* and *Wine in the Wilderness* (2000, 2001), *The Great Game: Afghanistan* (US tour, 2010).

Heather Tobias

Actress: *Flann O'Brien's Hard Life* (1985), *The Hostage* (1986), *Boots for the Footless* (1990), *The Factory Girls* (1990), *Bloody Sunday* (2005), *The Field* (2006).

Tessa Topolski

Literary advisor (1984–2012).

Rick Warden

Actor: *The Great Game: Afghanistan* (2009, 2010), *Tactical Questioning* (2011), *The Bomb – A Partial History* (2012); visual artist: gallery show; front-of-house staff (winter 1996–7).

Charlotte Westenra

Director: *How Long Is Never? Darfur – A Response: Many Men's Wife, Bilad al-Sudan, Distant Violence* (2006); assistant director: *Bloody Sunday* (2005); co-director: *Justifying War* (2003); assistant to the director: Harold Pinter's *The Dwarfs* (2003).

Thomas Wheatley

Actor: *Half the Picture* (1994), *Nuremberg* (1996), *Srebrenica* (1996), *The Colour of Justice* (1999), *Justifying War* (2003), *Bloody Sunday* (2005), *Called to Account* (2007), *Tactical Questioning* (2011).

Claudette Williams

Actress: *The Amen Corner* (1987), *Joe Turner's Come and Gone* (1990); voice coach: *Blues for Mr. Charlie* (2004), *Gem of the Ocean* (2006).

James Woolley

Actor: *Nuremberg* (1996), *Srebrenica* (1996, 1997), *The Colour of Justice* (1999), *Dreyfus* (2000), *Justifying War* (2003), *Bloody Sunday* (2005), *Called to Account* (2007).

Appendix B: Production chronology

The following is a select chronology, gathered from a number of sources, including the theatre's promotional materials. I've listed most of the productions for the first few years when the runs were typically short. However, the expanse of work at the Tricycle is huge. Therefore from 1984 onward, I've listed only performances and plays with substantial runs. That means that I have not included productions by the Strathcona Theatre for the learning disabled, whose plays the Tricycle was proud to host in the mid-eighties and nineties. I've also left out short-run entertainments and comics as well as fund-raising productions and political events like Day for Darfur and *Torture Team*.

A note on the months: Because the start and end dates of productions vary, in some cases the month could represent just one or two days. I've calculated the runs to include previews. The names in parentheses are visiting companies/producers; coproductions with the Tricycle are indicated.

1980
Samba by Michael Abbensetts – Sept./Oct.
Rise of the Old Cloud by Mike Dorrell (Paines Plough) – Oct./Nov.
Space Ache by Snoo Wilson, with music by Nick Bicât – Nov./Dec.
Cunning Stunts Christmas Show (Cunning Stunts) – Dec./Jan.

1981
Cunning Stunts Christmas Show – Dec./Jan.
Rien ne va plus by Pip Simmons (Pip Simmons Theatre Group) – Jan.
Black Ball Game by Don Webb (Pola Jones/Crucible Theatre) – Jan./Feb.

'*Better a Live Pompey Than a Dead Cyril*', compiled by Clare McIntyre, music by Stephanie Nunn (The Women's Theatre Group) – Feb.

Bloomers cabaret, written and performed by Eve Bland, Noreen Kershaw and Eileen Pollock (Bloomers) – Mar.

Mourning Pictures by Honor Moore (Monstrous Regiment) – Mar.

What's Got Into You? by Elaine Morgan (Bag and Baggage) – Mar./Apr.

The Opera, devised and performed by the company (Cunning Stunts) – Apr.

People Show Cabaret – Apr.

Gone with Hardy by David Allen – Apr./May

Show Trial: The Artists' Enquiry into the Arts Council, devised by Ed Berman (Inter-Action Production) – May/June

Life in a Scotch Sitting Room, Vol. II, Ivor Cutler – June

Tap Dance on a Telephone Line by Donna Franceschild (Tap Shoe Theatre Company) – June/July

Exit the Maids, devised and presented by the company (Lilith) – July

Red Door Without a Bolt by Jude Alderson (Sadista Sisters) – July/Aug.

Urfaust after Goethe (Die Vaganten/LIFT) – Aug.

Bekkanko (An Ogre), adapted by Asaya Funita (Tamagawa Dance and Drama Group/LIFT) – Aug.

In Dreams by Alan Williams (Hull Truck) – Sept.

Creeps by David E. Freeman (Midway Enterprise) – Sept./Oct.

Hotel Amigo, jazz cabaret devised by Kate and Mike Westbrook – Oct.

Blood on the Dole by Jim Morris (Tricycle/Liverpool Playhouse) – Oct./Nov.

Citizen Ilyushin by Kevin Mandry (Foco Novo/Tricycle) – Nov.

Days Here So Dark by Terry Johnson (Paines Plough) – Nov./Dec.

Winter Warmer (Cunning Stunts) – Dec.

Pierrot in Five Masks and *Isabella or The Pot of Basil* (Barry Smith's Theatre of Puppets) – Dec./Jan.

1982

Barry Smith's Theatre of Puppets – Dec./Jan.

'*Would the Real Judy Garland Please . . .*' by Sam Jacobs – Jan.

Life in a Scotch Sitting Room, Vol. II, Ivor Cutler and Phyllis King – Jan.

Behind the Lines, Roger McGough and Brian Patten – Jan.

Gandhi by Guerney Campbell – Feb.

Blind Dancers by Charles Tidler (Reunion Theatre Company) – Mar.

Behind the Lines (remount) – Mar./Apr.

Love in Vain by Bob Mason – Apr./May

Queen Christina by Pam Gems – May/June

'Ever After' by Catherine Itzin and Ann Mitchell – June/July

Red Alert: This Is a God Warning, written and performed by Leo Aylen – July

Act Without Words I and *II* by Samuel Beckett (Noho Theatre Group, Kyoto) – Aug.

Sink or Swim by Tunde Ikoli and the company (Foco Novo) – Aug.

Gotterdammerung or *Twilight of the Göds,* written by the company with Bryony Lavery (National Theatre of Brent) – Sept./Oct.

Artichoke by Joanna Glass – Oct./Nov.

Stuffing It by Robin Glendinning – Nov./Dec.

Jack Sheppard's Back by Shirley Barrie, music by Ian Barnett – Dec./Jan.

1983

Jack Sheppard's Back – Dec./Jan.

The Messiah by Patrick Barlow (National Theatre of Brent) – Jan./Feb.

Private Habits, an evening with Ivor Cutler – Feb./Mar.

Mitzi Wildebeest, First Lady of the Velt, devised and performed by Elaine Loudon – Mar.

More Female Trouble, devised by Bryony Lavery, music by Caroline Noh – Mar.

Mr Puntila and His Servant Matti by Bertolt Brecht, adapted by Jeremy Brooks (Foco Novo) – Mar./Apr.

The Messiah (remount) – Apr./May

Love and Dissent by Elisabeth Bond (The Women's Theatre Group) – May

Beyond the 'A' Penny Steps by Tony Dennis – June

Theatre of the Film Noir by George F. Walker (Factory Theatre Lab, Toronto) – June/July

Smile Orange by Trevor Rhone – July/Aug.

Objects of Affection, the Elaine Loudon Group – Sept.

A Nest of Intervals, one-man show, Neil Innes – Oct.

Buried Treasure by Olwen Wymark – Oct./Nov.

The Tooth of Crime by Sam Shepard (Black Theatre Co-operative) – Nov./ Dec.

Nightshoot by Bob Mason, music by Hazel O'Connor, Neil O'Connor, and Eddie Case – Dec./Jan.

1984

Nightshoot – Dec./Jan.

Calamity by Bryony Lavery (Monstrous Regiment) – Jan./Feb.

Poppies by Noel Greig (Gay Sweatshop) – Feb.

Playboy of the West Indies by Mustapha Matura (Oxford Playhouse Company) – Feb./Mar.

Pula and *Imbumba* by Matsemela Manaka (Soyikwa African Theatre) – Mar.

Playboy of the West Indies (remount) – Apr.

Real Estate by Louise Page – May/June

C'mon Everybody!, songs and poems by Adrian Mitchell (David Jones) – June

Mistero Buffo by Dario Fo (1982 Theatre Company) – June

The Boot Dance by Edgar White (Temba Theatre Company) – July

Black Dog – Inj'emnyama, created by Barney Simon and the Company (Market Theatre, Johannesburg) – Sept.

The One O'Clock World by Leigh Jackson – Sept./Oct.

Fire-Eaters by Paul Copley (Tricycle/Croydon Warehouse) – Oct./Nov.

Two Can Play by Trevor Rhone – Nov./Dec.

Return to the Forbidden Planet by Bob Carlton – Dec./Feb.

1985

Return to the Forbidden Planet – Dec./Feb.

Carmen: The Play, Spain 1936 by Stephen Jeffreys, based on the story by Prosper Mérimée (Communicado Theatre Company/Tricycle) – Feb./Mar.

A Raisin in the Sun by Lorraine Hansberry (Black Theatre Co-operative) – Apr./May

Lonely Cowboy by Alfred Fagon – May/June

Pantomime by Derek Walcott (Temba Theatre Company/Leicester Haymarket) – June/July

Come Back to the 5 and Dime, Jimmy Dean, Jimmy Dean by Ed Graczyk (Giant Enterprises/Bolton Octagon Theatre) – July/Aug.

Flann O'Brien's Hard Life or Na Gopaleens Wake by Kerry Crabbe – Sept./Oct.

The Great White Hope by Howard Sackler – Oct./Dec.

1986

Flann O'Brien's Hard Life (remount) – Jan./Feb.

Joyriders by Christina Reid (Paines Plough) – Feb./Mar.

Blood Sweat and Tears by John Godber (Hull Truck) – Mar./Apr.

The Lower Depths: An East End Story by Tunde Ikoli (Foco Novo/Birmingham Repertory Studio Theatre) – Apr./May

Joyriders (remount) – May

Who Killed Hilda Murrell? by Chris Martin (Sheffield Crucible) – May/June

I Do Like to Be by Shane Connaughton (Irish Company/Tricycle) – July

Born in the R.S.A., created by Barney Simon and cast (Market Theatre, Johannesburg) – Aug./Sept.

The Hostage by Brendan Behan – Oct./Dec.

Tejo Vanio (Tejo the Miser) and *Zanda Zulan* (Zulan the Flag Bearer) by Asaita Thakar (Tara Arts) – Dec.

1987

The Amen Corner by James Baldwin (Carib Theatre) – Jan./Feb. + West End transfer

Thatcher's Women by Kay Adshead (Paines Plough) – Mar./Apr.

The Greatest Story Ever Told by Patrick Barlow (National Theatre of Brent) – Apr./May

Burning Point by John Cooper – May

1988

Trinidad Sisters by Mustapha Matura, after Chekhov (at the Donmar) – Feb./Mar.

1989

Pentecost by Stewart Parker (at the Lyric Studio, Hammersmith) – Jan.

All or Nothing at All – Sept./Nov.

Nativity by Nigel Williams – Nov./Dec.

1990

Boots for the Footless by Brian Behan – Jan./Feb.

Joe Turner's Come and Gone by August Wilson – Mar./Apr.

Fashion by Doug Lucie (Tricycle/Eaglehand) – May/June

Remembrance by Derek Walcott (Carib Theatre) – July/Aug.

Curl Up and Dye by Susan Pam (Market Theatre, Johannesburg/ Michael's Company) – Sept.

The Factory Girls by Frank McGuinness – Oct./Nov.

Just So by George Stiles and Anthony Drewe (Cameron Mackintosh/ Tricycle) – Nov./Jan.

1991

Just So – Nov./Jan.

A Free Country by Jean-Claude Grumberg, translated by Tom Kempinski – Jan./Mar.

Meetings by Mustapha Matura (Black Theatre Co-operative) – Mar.

The Cure at Troy by Seamus Heaney, after *Philoctetes* by Sophocles (Field Day) – Apr.

The Brother, adapted from the works of Myles na Gopaleen (and performed) by Eamon Morrissey (Dublin Comedy Theatre) – Apr./May

A Long Way from Home by Yemi Ajibade – May/June

Starbrites, created by Barney Simon, Fats Dibeco and Arthur Molepo, and Basil Jones and Adrian Kohler of Handspring Puppet Company (Market Theatre, Johannesburg/LIFT) – July/Aug.

The Brother (remount) – Aug./Sept.

Pecong by Steve Carter – Sept./Nov.

In Broad Daylight by Lesley Bruce (Tricycle/Nuffield Theatre, Southampton) – Nov./Dec.

Watching for Dolphins by John McGrath (late night) (Freeway) – Nov./ Dec.

Once a Catholic by Mary O'Malley (Tricycle/Bill Kenwright for Liverpool Playhouse) – Dec./Feb.

1992

Once a Catholic – Dec./Feb.

Viva Detroit by Derek Walcott (Black Theatre Co-operative) – Feb./Mar.

Tolstoy's *Anna Karenina*, adapted by Helen Edmundson (Shared Experience) – Mar./Apr.

Just the One, written and performed by Eamon Morrissey (Dublin Comedy Theatre) – Apr./May

Oscar by James Clutton and Damian Landi (Centrestage/Andrew Bancroft Productions) – May

Love and a Bottle by George Farquhar, adapted by Declan Hughes (Rough Magic) – June

Una Pooka by Michael Harding – July/Aug.

Gamblers by Nikolai Gogol, a new version by Chris Hannan (SQP Productions) – Sept./Oct.

Trouble in Mind by Alice Childress – Oct./Nov.

Pinchy Kobi and the Seven Duppies, devised and performed by the Posse, music by Felix Cross (The Posse) – Dec./Jan.

1993

Pinchy Kobi and the Seven Duppies – Dec./Jan.

The Ash Fire by Gavin Kostick (Pigsback) – Jan./Feb.

Tolstoy's *Anna Karenina* (remount) – Feb./Mar.

A Love Song for Ulster (*The Marriage, The Son, The Daughter*) by Bill Morrison – Mar./May

Studs by Paul Mercier (Passion Machine) – May/June

Yerma – Scenes from an Indian Village Woman's Life by Federico García Lorca, translated into Punjabi by Surjit Patar (The Company/LIFT) – June/July

At the Black Pig's Dyke by Vincent Woods (Druid Theatre/LIFT) – July

Three Hotels by Jon Robin Baitz – Aug./Sept.

The Piano Lesson by August Wilson – Sept./Nov.

'One Hell of a Do', Jon Kenny and Pat Shortt (D'Unbelievables) – Nov.

Playboy of the West Indies by Mustapha Matura (Tricycle/Nuffield Theatre, Southampton) – Dec./Jan.

1994

Playboy of the West Indies – Dec./Jan.

The Government Inspector by Nikolai Gogol, adapted by Marie Jones (DubbelJoint) – Feb./Mar.

'One Hell of a Do' (remount) – Mar./Apr.

Lady Windermere's Fan by Oscar Wilde (Rough Magic) – Apr./May

Mill on the Floss, adapted by Helen Edmundson, from the novel by George Eliot (Shared Experience/Wolsey Theatre, Ipswich) – May/June

Half the Picture: The Scott "Arms to Iraq" Inquiry, adapted and redacted by Richard Norton-Taylor, with additional material by John McGrath – June/July

Shameless!, inspired by Brecht short stories, words and new music by Paul Sand, additional material by David Pearl; *Kill Me I Love You! . . . Too,* devised by the company (Opera Circus) – July

The Day the Bronx Died by Michael Henry Brown – Sept./Oct.

Come Good Rain, written and performed by George Seremba (Tricycle/BBC World Service/Canadian High Commission) – Oct./Nov.

Matilda Liar! by Debbie Isitt (Snarling Beasties/Warwick Arts Centre) – Nov.

Far Above Rubies by Robbie Gringras; *Telling Tales* devised by Robbie Gringras, Danny Scheinmann and Rebecca Wolman (Besht Tellers) – Nov./Dec.

Ain't Misbehavin': The Fats Waller Musical Show, based on an idea by Murray Horwitz and Richard Maltby Jr – Dec./Feb.

1995

Ain't Misbehavin' – Dec./Feb. + West End transfer

A Night in November (An Afternoon in June) by Marie Jones (DubbelJoint) – Feb./Apr.

Uncle Vanya by Anton Chekhov, in a version by Frank McGuinness (Field Day) – Apr.

Victor and the Ladies by Jenny McLeod – May/June

You ANC Nothing Yet, written and performed by Pieter-Dirk Uys – June/July

The Suit, adapted by Mothobi Mutloatse from Can Themba's story (Market Theatre, Johannesburg/LIFT) – June/July

Red Roses and Petrol by Joseph O'Connor (Pigsback) – July/Aug.

You ANC Nothing Yet (remount) – Aug./Sept.

Bedfellows by Dave Anderson and David MacLennan (Wildcat) – Sept./Oct.

Macbeth by William Shakespeare – Oct./Nov.

Desire Under the Elms by Eugene O'Neill (Shared Experience/Wolsey Theatre, Ipswich) – Nov./Dec.

Tales from Home, adapted by Robbie Gringras and Rebecca Wolman (Besht Tellers) – Dec./Jan.

1996

Tales from Home – Dec./Jan.

Two Trains Running by August Wilson – Jan./Mar.

20–52 by Jeremy Weller (Grassmarket Project) – Mar.

Byrne and *The Brother*, solo pieces by Eamon Morrissey – Mar./Apr.

Nuremberg War Crimes Trial, edited by Richard Norton-Taylor, and one-act responses: *Ex-Yu* by Goran Stefanovski, *Haiti* by Keith Reddin, and *Reel, Rwanda* by Femi Osofisan – May/June

Truth Omissions, written and performed by Pieter-Dirk Uys – June

Roll with the Punches: The Songs of Randy Newman – July

3 Ms Behaving, devised by Gillian Gregory (Infamous Five) – Aug./Sept.

Nuremberg (remount); *Srebrenica*, edited by Nicolas Kent, with *Ex-Yu* – Sept./Oct.

The Gay Detective by Gerard Stembridge (Project Arts Centre) – Oct./Nov.

Sympathy for the Devil by Roy Winston (Basic Theatre/Graeae Theatre) – Dec.

Beef, No Chicken by Derek Walcott (Talawa Theatre) – Dec./Feb.

1997

Beef, No Chicken – Dec./Feb.

Kitchensink by Paul Mercier (Passion Machine) – Feb./Mar.

'I Doubt It', says Pauline, Jon Kenny and Pat Shortt (D'Unbelievables) (Southern Comedy Theatre) – Mar.

Kings by Christopher Logue, from Homer's *Iliad* (PW Productions/David Rees) – Apr.

The Mai by Marina Carr – Apr./June

Live from Boerassic Park, written and performed by Pieter-Dirk Uys – June/July

A Tainted Dawn: Images of Partition by Sudha Bhuchar and Kristine Landon-Smith (Tamasha Theatre/Birmingham Repertory Theatre) – Sept.

David Kramer and Taliep Petersen's *Kat and the Kings* (Tricycle/Renaye Kramer) – Sept./Nov.

Srebrenica (remount, prior to tour) – Nov.

Angels and Demons by Rebecca Wolman (Besht Tellers) – Nov.

Sive by John B. Keane (Tricycle/Palace Theatre Watford) – Dec./Jan.

1998

Sive – Dec./Jan.

Iced by Ray Shell (Black Theatre Co-operative/Nottingham Playhouse) – Jan./Feb.

Kat and the Kings (remount) – Feb./Mar. + West End transfer

Dance of Death, Parts 1 and 2, a new Irish version by Carlo Gébler (an adaptation of August Strindberg's play) – Mar./Apr.

Sitting in Limbo by Dawn Penso and Judy Hepburn (Carib Theatre) – Apr./May

Europeans Only: An African Audition for Europe, written and performed by Pieter-Dirk Uys – May/June

The Basset Table by Susanna Centlivre (Wild Iris/Bristol Old Vic) – June/July

Starstruck by Roy Williams – Sept./Oct.

Ugly Rumours by Tariq Ali and Howard Brenton – Oct./Nov.

The Snow Palace by Pam Gems (Sphinx Theatre) – Nov./Dec.

1999

The Colour of Justice: The Stephen Lawrence Inquiry, edited by Richard Norton-Taylor – Jan./Feb. + transfer to Theatre Royal Stratford East and Victoria Palace + autumn tour, including the National Theatre

And the Brother Too . . ., devised and performed by Eamon Morrissey, based on the writings of Flann O'Brien – Feb.

Paddy Irishman, Paddy Englishman, and Paddy . . . ? by Declan Croghan (Birmingham Repertory Theatre) – Mar.

Up Against the Wall by Felix Cross and Paulette Randall (Black Theatre Co-operative) – Mar./Apr.

The Garden of Habustan by Rebecca Wolman (Besht Tellers/Library Theatre, Manchester) – Apr./May

Catalpa, written and performed by Donal O'Kelly (Red Kettle Theatre Company/Andrews Lane Theatre, Dublin) – May/June

Collateral Damage by Tariq Ali, Howard Brenton and Andy de la Tour – May

Ubu and the Truth Commission by Jane Taylor (William Kentridge and Handspring Puppet Company); *The Story I'm About to Tell* by Lesego Rampolokeng with cast (Mehlo Players/Khulumani Support Group); *Phakama: Be Yourself* (Project Phakama) (LIFT) – June/July

True Believers by Joseph O'Connor (Fishamble) – July

Dekaffirnated, or Calling a Spade a Spade, written and performed by Pieter-Dirk Uys – July/Aug.

Stones in His Pockets by Marie Jones (Lyric Theatre, Belfast) – Aug./Sept.

Emma, adapted by Martin Millar and Doon MacKichan, from the novel by Jane Austen – Sept./Oct.

Four Nights in Knaresborough by Paul Corcoran (New Vic Workshop) – Nov./Dec.

The Amen Corner by James Baldwin (Tricycle/Nottingham Playhouse) – Dec./Feb.

2000

The Amen Corner – Dec./Feb.

David Kramer and Taliep Petersen's *Poison,* adapted by Jenny McLeod – Feb./Mar.

Stones in His Pockets (remount) – Apr./May + West End transfer

Dreyfus by Jean-Claude Grumberg, a new translation by Jack Rosenthal – May/July

Stolen by Jane Harrison (Ilbijerri Aboriginal and Torres Strait Islander Theatre Co-operative/Playbox Theatre) – July

The Gift by Roy Williams (Birmingham Repertory Theatre) – July/Aug.

An Die Musik by Pip Simmons, from an original idea by Rudy Engelander (Artsadmin/Tricycle/Hampstead Theatre) – Sept./Oct.

Water by Winsome Pinnock and *Wine in the Wilderness* by Alice Childress – Oct./Nov.

Ruby Wax: Stressed, written and performed by Ruby Wax (Phil McIntyre) – Nov./Dec.

The Wexford Trilogy: A Handful of Stars, Poor Beast in the Rain, and *Belfry* by Billy Roche (Tricycle/Oxford Stage Company) – Dec./Feb.

2001

The Wexford Trilogy – Dec./Feb.

Water and *Wine in the Wilderness* (remount) – Feb./Mar.

The Kings of the Kilburn High Road by Jimmy Murphy (Red Kettle Theatre Company) – Mar./Apr.

Suip! by Heinrich Reisenhofer and Oscar Petersen (Baxter Theatre Centre, Cape Town) – Apr./May

Boy Called Rubbish and *Squawk*, written and performed by Ellis Pearson and Bheki Mkhwane (Sue Clarence Promotions) – May

Further Than the Furthest Thing by Zinnie Harris (Royal National Theatre Studio/Tron Theatre/Tricycle) – May/June

Foreign Aids, written and performed by Pieter-Dirk Uys – June/Aug.

The Far Side by Courttia Newland (Riggs O'Hara Theatre Company) – Aug.

Under Their Influence by Wayne Buchanan (Kushite Theatre Company) – Sept.

As the Beast Sleeps by Gary Mitchell (Lyric Theatre, Belfast/Tricycle) – Sept./Oct.

Brixton Stories or the Short & Happy Life of Ossie Jones by Biyi Bandele (RSC/Tricycle) – Oct./Nov.

Stolen (remount) (Fifth Amendment) – Nov./Dec.

The Cavalcaders by Billy Roche – Dec./Feb.

2002

The Cavalcaders – Dec./Feb.

The Promise by Alexei Arbuzov, a new version by Nick Dear (based on the translation by Ariadne Nicolaeff) – Feb./Mar.

Sorrows & Rejoicings by Athol Fugard (Tricycle/Baxter Theatre Centre, Cape Town) – Mar./Apr.

The Clearing by Helen Edmundson (Shared Experience) – Apr./May

Catwalk by Malika Booker (Nitro/New Wolsey Theatre, Ipswich) – May/June

David Kramer – *Live in London* – June/July

A Night in November by Marie Jones – July

I Dreamt I Dwelt in Marble Halls by Ade Morris (Watermill Theatre)
    – July/Aug.

HyperLynx by John McGrath (Floodtide) – Sept.

10 Rounds by Carlo Gébler – Sept./Oct.

The Price by Arthur Miller – Oct./Dec.

King Hedley II by August Wilson (Tricycle/Birmingham Repertory
    Theatre) – Dec./Feb.

2003

King Hedley II – Dec./Feb.

A Night in November (remount) – Feb./Mar.

Crossing Jerusalem by Julia Pascal – Mar./Apr.

Harold Pinter's *The Dwarfs*, adapted by Kerry Lee Crabbe – Apr./May

The History of the Troubles (accordin' to my Da) by Martin Lynch and
    Grimes & McKee (Mac Productions) – June

The Price (remount) – Aug./Sept. + West End transfer

John Bull's Other Island by Bernard Shaw – Sept./Oct.

Justifying War: Scenes from the Hutton Inquiry, edited by Richard
    Norton-Taylor – Oct./Nov.

David Kramer and Taliep Petersen's *Kat and the Kings* (return) (Tricycle/
    Renaye Kramer) – Dec./Mar.

2004

Kat and the Kings – Dec./Mar.

Singer by Peter Flannery (Oxford Stage Company) – Mar./Apr.

The Quare Fellow by Brendan Behan (Oxford Stage Company/Liverpool
    Everyman and Playhouse) – Apr./May

Waiting for Godot by Samuel Beckett (John Calder's The Godot
    Company) – May

Guantanamo: 'Honor Bound to Defend Freedom' by Victoria Brittain
    and Gillian Slovo – May/June + West End transfer

Blues for Mr. Charlie by James Baldwin (New Wolsey Theatre, Ipswich/
    Talawa/Tricycle) – June/July

Mark Thomas (Karushi) – July

Marc Salem's *Mind Games* (Andrew Fell) – July/Aug.

The Shadow of a Gunman by Sean O'Casey – Sept./Nov.

Bread and Butter by C. P. Taylor (Dumbfounded Theatre/Oxford Stage Company) – Nov.

Playboy of the West Indies by Mustapha Matura (Tricycle/Nottingham Playhouse) – Dec./Jan.

2005

Playboy of the West Indies – Dec./Jan.

One Under by Winsome Pinnock – Feb./Mar.

The Fortune Club by Dolly Dhingra (Leicester Haymarket/Tricycle) – Mar./Apr.

Bloody Sunday: Scenes from the Saville Inquiry, edited by Richard Norton-Taylor – Apr./May

Robert Newman: *Apocalypso Now or From P45 to AK47: How to Grow the Economy with the Use of War* (Karushi) – May

The Quare Fellow (remount) – May/July

The Arab-Israeli Cookbook by Robin Soans (KIT Productions/Tricycle) – July/Aug.

Marc Salem's *Mind Games* (Andrew Fell) – Aug./Sept.

Bloody Sunday (remount) – Sept./Oct. + tour

Chicken Soup with Barley by Arnold Wesker (Nottingham Playhouse) – Oct./Nov.

African American season: *Walk Hard–Talk Loud* by Abram Hill – Nov./ Dec.

2006

African American season: *Gem of the Ocean* by August Wilson – Jan./Feb.

African American season: *Fabulation or The Re-Education of Undine* by Lynn Nottage – Feb./Mar.

A Whistle in the Dark by Tom Murphy (Royal Exchange Theatre, Manchester) – Mar./May

The Field by John B. Keane – May/July

Robert Newman: *No Planet B – The History of the World Backwards* (Phil McIntyre) – July

Marc Salem: *On Second Thoughts* (Andrew Fell) – July/Aug.

John Buchan's 'The 39 Steps', adapted by Patrick Barlow (Fiery Angel/ Tricycle) – Aug./Sept. + West End transfer

Fabulation (remount) – Sept./Oct.

How Long Is Never? Darfur – A Response: Many Men's Wife by Amy Evans; *Bilad al-Sudan* by Juliet Gilkes; *Words Words Words* by Jennifer Farmer; *Silhouette* by Carlo Gébler; *Distant Violence* by Michael Bhim; *IDP* by Winsome Pinnock; *Give, Again?* by Lynn Nottage – Oct.

Mark Thomas: *As Used on the Famous Nelson Mandela (The Hindujas Cont . . .)* (Phil McIntyre) – Oct./Nov.

Orestes – Blood & Light by Helen Edmundson, based on Euripides (Shared Experience/Guilford's Yvonne Arnaud Theatre) – Nov./Dec.

Spice Drum Beat – Ghoema by David Kramer (Tricycle/Renaye Kramer) – Dec./Jan.

2007

Spice Drum Beat – Ghoema – Dec./Jan.

The War Next Door by Tamsin Oglesby – Feb./Mar.

The Caretaker by Harold Pinter (Sheffield Theatres) – Mar./Apr.

Called to Account: The Indictment of Anthony Charles Lynton Blair for the Crime of Aggression Against Iraq – A Hearing, edited by Richard Norton-Taylor – Apr./June

Mark Thomas: *As Used on the Famous Nelson Mandela (The Hindujas Cont . . .)* (Phil McIntyre) – June

Small Miracle by Neil D'Souza (Mercury Theatre, Colchester) – June/July

Marc Salem's *Mind Games Extra* (Andrew Fell) – July

Evita for President, written and performed by Pieter-Dirk Uys – July/Sept.

The Pride of Parnell Street by Sebastian Barry (Fishamble) – Sept.

Moonlight & Magnolias by Ron Hutchinson – Sept./Nov.

The Table (Karbido Theatre, Poland) – Nov.

Doubt: A Parable by John Patrick Shanley – Nov./Jan.

2008

Doubt: A Parable – Nov./Jan.

Let There Be Love by Kwame Kwei-Armah – Jan./Feb.

I'll Be the Devil by Leo Butler (RSC) – Feb./Mar.

Days of Significance by Roy Williams (RSC) – Mar.

Testing the Echo by David Edgar (Out of Joint) – Apr./May

Under Milk Wood by Dylan Thomas (London Theatre Company) – May

Topless Mum by Ron Hutchinson (Tobacco Factory Productions and
    Imagineer Productions/Tricycle) – May/June
Moonlight & Magnolias (remount) – July/Aug.
Let There Be Love (remount) – Aug.
Twelfth Night by William Shakespeare (Filter/RSC/Schtanhaus) – Sept.
Radio Golf by August Wilson – Oct./Nov.
Rank by Robert Massey (Fishamble) – Nov.
Twelfth Night (remount) – Dec.
Loot by Joe Orton – Dec./Jan.

2009
Loot – Dec./Jan.
Damascus by David Greig (Michael Edwards and Carole Winter/
    Traverse Theatre) – Feb./Mar.
Deep Cut by Philip Ralph (Sherman Cymru) – Mar./Apr.
The Great Game: Afghanistan. Bugles at the Gates of Jalalabad by
    Stephen Jeffreys; *Durand's Line* by Ron Hutchinson; *Campaign*
    by Amit Gupta; *Now Is the Time* by Joy Wilkinson; *Black Tulips* by
    David Edgar; *Blood and Gifts* by J. T. Rogers (replaced by *Wood for the
    Fire* by Lee Blessing in 2010 remount); *Miniskirts of Kabul* by David
    Greig; *The Lion of Kabul* by Colin Teevan; *Honey* by Ben Ockrent;
    The Night Is Darkest Before the Dawn by Abi Morgan; *On the Side
    of the Angels* by Richard Bean; *Canopy of Stars* by Simon Stephens;
    monologues/duologues by Siba Shakib; verbatims edited by Richard
    Norton-Taylor – Apr./June
Karoo Moose by Lara Foot Newton (Baxter Theatre Centre, Cape Town)
    – June/July
Koos Sas: Last Bushman of Montagu by David Kramer (David Kramer
    Productions) – July/Aug.
Pornography by Simon Stephens (Birmingham Repertory Theatre/
    Traverse Theatre) – Aug.
Stockwell: The Inquest into the Death of Jean Charles de Menezes by
    Kieron Barry (Sophie Lifschutz with Head over Heels/Roland Egan
    Productions) – Sept.
Mark Thomas: *The Manifesto* (Phil McIntyre) – Sept./Oct.
Not Black & White: Category B by Roy Williams; *Seize the Day* by Kwame
    Kwei-Armah; *Detaining Justice* by Bola Agbaje – Oct./Dec.

2010

Greta Garbo Came to Donegal by Frank McGuinness – Jan./Feb.

The Dead School by Pat McCabe (Nomad Theatre Network/Livin' Dred)
– Feb./Mar.

Chronicles of Long Kesh by Martin Lynch (Green Shoot Productions)
– Mar./Apr.

Twelfth Night (remount) – May

Women, Power and Politics: The Milliner and the Weaver by Marie Jones;
Handbagged by Moira Buffini; *The Lioness* by Rebecca Lenkiewicz;
Bloody Wimmin by Lucy Kirkwood; *Acting Leader* by Joy Wilkinson;
The Panel by Zinnie Harris; *Playing the Game* by Bola Agbaje; *Pink* by
Sam Holcroft; *You, Me and Wii* by Sue Townsend; verbatim accounts
edited by Gillian Slovo – June/July

The Great Game: Afghanistan (remount) – July/Aug. + US tour

Tiny Kushner by Tony Kushner (Guthrie Theater/Berkeley Repertory
Theatre) – Sept.

Broken Glass by Arthur Miller – Sept./Nov.

Midsummer by David Greig and Gordon McIntyre (Traverse Theatre)
– Nov./Jan.

2011

Midsummer – Nov./Jan.

Water by Filter and David Farr (Filter/Lyric Hammersmith) – Feb./
Mar.

Brontë by Polly Teale (Shared Experience/Watermill Theatre/Oxford
Playhouse) – Apr.

Mark Thomas: *Extreme Rambling (Walking the Wall)* (Phil McIntyre)
– May

Tactical Questioning: Scenes from the Baha Mousa Inquiry, edited by
Richard Norton-Taylor – June/July

Lay Me Down Softly by Billy Roche (Wexford Arts Centre/Mosshouse)
– July/Aug.

Broken Glass (remount) – Aug./Sept. + West End transfer

The Absence of Women by Owen McCafferty (Lyric Theatre, Belfast)
– Sept./Oct.

A Walk in the Woods by Lee Blessing (Northern Stage, Vermont) – Oct./
Nov.

The Riots by Gillian Slovo – Nov./Dec.

Stones in His Pockets by Marie Jones – Dec./Feb.

2012 (through May)

Stones in His Pockets – Dec./Feb.

The Riots (at Bernie Grant Arts Centre) – Jan.

Mark Thomas (return) – Jan.

The Bomb – A Partial History: From Elsewhere: The Message . . . by Zinnie Harris; *Calculated Risk* by Ron Hutchinson; *Seven Joys* by Lee Blessing; *Option* by Amit Gupta; *Little Russians* by John Donnelly; *There Was a Man. There Was No Man.* by Colin Teevan; *Axis* by Diana Son; *Talk Talk Fight Fight* by Ryan Craig; *The Letter of Last Resort* by David Greig; *From Elsewhere: On the Watch . . .* by Zinnie Harris; verbatim edited by Richard Norton-Taylor – Feb./Apr.

Neighbourhood Watch by Alan Ayckbourn (Stephen Joseph Theatre, Scarborough/Guildford's Yvonne Arnaud Theatre) – Apr./May

A Slow Air by David Harrower (Tron Theatre) – May/June

NOTES

Foreword

1 G. K. Chesterton, *George Bernard Shaw*, London: John Lane, The Bodley Head, New York, John Lane Co., 1910, p. 253.

2 David Hare, 'Why Fabulate?' in *Obedience, Struggle & Revolt: Lectures on Theatre*, London: Faber and Faber, 2005, p. 76.

Introduction

1 Signed 'James Baldwin, May 1987' and quoted in programme, Tricycle Theatre, *All or Nothing at All*, 1989. V&A Theatre and Performance collections.

2 Michael Billington, 'Stage right', *Guardian*, 3 September 2007, www.guardian.co.uk/stage/2007/sep/04/theatre.westend (accessed 26 July 2012).

1: A brief ride through the Tricycle's history

1 Shirley Barrie, 'Origins of the Name "Wakefield Tricycle Company"', e-mail attachment to author, 21 March 2008.

2 Castle appeared in several plays at the Tricycle in Kilburn, including the Tricycle's tribunal *Bloody Sunday* (2005). Freeman starred in *Fashion* by Doug Lucie in 1990.

3 *Stage and Television Today*, 20 February 1975. V&A Theatre and Performance collections, Tricycle Theatre archive, THM/317/4/3/1.

4 Iain Mackintosh, 'Unworthy Scaffold?' in *Sightline: The Journal of Theatre Technology and Design* (October 1989), p. 7. V&A Theatre and Performance collections, Tricycle Theatre archive, THM/317/4/2/3. (Also reprinted in the *All or Nothing at All* programme, 1989.)

5 Quoted in Barney Bardsley, 'On Yer Trike', *City Limits*, 10 October 1990, Tricycle Theatre (in-house) press archives.

6 Kent told me in 2005 that his predecessor 'had four planks of policy, which was to do new work, work that reflected the ethnic minorities in the area, work for, by and with women, and work for and with children . . . and those are still the mission statement effectively.' From my interview with Kent, 'Tribunals at the Tricycle' (March 2005), HotReview.org. The policy statement has somewhat changed since then.

7 The number of seats have changed over the years.

8 Catherine Itzin, programme essay, Tricycle Theatre, *Samba*, 1980. V&A Theatre and Performance collections.

9 Quoted in 'Theatre Has Grant Slashed', *Kilburn Times*, 6 April 1984. Tricycle Theatre (in-house) press archives.

10 Quoted in Ian Cowie, 'Taking over the handlebars', *Kilburn Times*, 22 June 1984. Tricycle Theatre (in-house) press archives.

11 'Tricycle News' programme note, Tricycle Theatre, *Black Dog*, 1984. V&A Theatre and Performance collections.

12 Nicolas Kent, programme note, *Raising the Roof*, 19 July 1987. This was a benefit for the Tricycle and for the Bush, which also suffered a fire, shortly after the Tricycle's. V&A Theatre and Performance collections.

13 For the cost of the rebuild: See Joan Bakewell, 'From a small cog to a big wheel; Tricycle Theatre', *Sunday Times*, 17 September 1989, www. lexisnexis.com (accessed 20 February 2010), and Nicholas de Jongh, *Guardian*, 25 September 1989, *London Theatre Record*, Vol. IX, No. 19 (1989), p. 1275. See also Nicolas Kent quoted in Clare Armitstead, 'Repairing the Tricycle', *Plays & Players*, No. 431 (September 1989), p. 16. About the cost of the original conversion: Although the theatre's publicity material and programme for the opening production (*Samba*, 1980) indicated that building the Tricycle cost £130,000, records from 1981 said the cost turned out to be £170,000. See Company Minutes, THM/317/1/1/1, V&A Theatre and Performance collections, Tricycle Theatre archive.

14 The Tricycle Theatre's Annual Report, 2011. The theatre's annual report is available at www.tricycle.co.uk/home/about-the-tricycle-pages/about-us-tab-menu/about/.

15 The clause was still in the contract in May 2012.

16 Nicolas Kent, email to author, 1 July 2011.

2: Black theatre at the Tricycle

1 Benedict Nightingale, *New Statesman*, 26 September 1980. See also Michael Billington, *Guardian*, 19 September 1980, and Antony Thorncroft, *Financial Times*, 20 September 1980. V&A Theatre and Performance collections, Tricycle Theatre archive, THM/317/4/3/14.

2 Bob Mason, programme note, Tricycle Theatre, *Love in Vain*, 1982. V&A Theatre and Performance collections.

3 In 2012, ticket prices for Monday nights were still reduced, and there were 'pay what you can' shows on Tuesday evenings and Saturday matinees.

4 Since the early nineties, *Time Out London* has listed 'off–West End' theatres; the Tricycle is in that category.

5 'Interview: Mustapha Matura', with Nicolas Kent, by Dominic Cavendish [Renamed: Mustapha Matura and his *Playboy of the West Indies* in Black Voices, Directors, Playwrights], TheatreVOICE, recorded 29 November 2004, www.theatrevoice.com/1973/interview-mustapha-matura-at-the-20th-anniversary-revival-o/ (first accessed 10 July 2010).

6 Alastair Macaulay, *Financial Times*, 9 December 2004; Lloyd Evans, *Spectator*, 18 December 2004, *Theatre Record*, Vol. XXIV, No. 25–6 (2004), pp. 1699, 1698.

7 Programme glossary, Oxford Playhouse at the Tricycle Theatre, *Playboy of the West Indies*, 1984. V&A Theatre and Performance collections.

8 Benedict Nightingale, *Times*, 8 December 2004, *Theatre Record*, Vol. XXIV, No. 25–6 (2004), p. 1700.

9 Programme information, Tricycle Theatre, *Lonely Cowboy*, 1985. V&A Theatre and Performance collections.

10 Ibid.

11 Harriet Cruickshank, '*Starstruck* Won the Alfred Fagon 1997 New Play Award', programme note, Tricycle Theatre, *Starstruck*, 1998. V&A Theatre and Performance collections.

12 Howard Sackler, *The Great White Hope*, New York: Samuel French, 1968, p. 47.

13 Michael Coveney, *Financial Times*, 5 November 1985, *London Theatre Record*, Vol. V, No. 22 (1985), p. 1101.

14 Alex Renton, *Independent,* 28 January 1987, *London Theatre Record,* Vol. VII, No. 2 (1987), p. 67.

15 See Delia Jarrett-Macauley, *The Life of Una Marson, 1905–65,* Manchester and New York: Manchester University Press, 1998 (paperback, 2010), pp. 53–4, for a discussion of *At What a Price* by Una Marson, reported by the author to have had a 'three-night run' at the Scala Theatre on Charlotte Street in 1934, 'the first black colonial production in the West End'. This production is also discussed in Colin Chambers, *Black and Asian Theatre in Britain: A History,* Oxon and New York: Routledge, 2011, pp. 99–100.

16 Michael Billington, *Guardian,* 8 March 1990, *London Theatre Record*, Vol. X, No. 5 (1990), p. 331.

17 Michael Arditti, *Evening Standard,* 8 October 1991; Sarah Hemming, *Independent,* 4 October 1991, *Theatre Record*, Vol. XI, No. 20 (1991), pp. 1206–7.

18 Irving Wardle, *Independent on Sunday,* 6 October 1991, *Theatre Record*, Vol. XI, No. 20 (1991), p. 1206.

19 Arditti, *Evening Standard*, p. 1206.

20 *Pinchy Kobi and the Seven Duppies* publicity pamphlet, 1992. V&A Theatre and Performance collections. Nick Curtis, *Time Out,* 16 December 1992, *Theatre Record*, Vol. XII, No. 25–6 (1992), p. 1554.

21 Michael Billington, *Guardian,* 9 October 1993, *Theatre Record*, Vol. XIII, No. 20 (1993), p. 1122.

22 Jack Tinker, *Daily Mail*, 13 January 1995, *Theatre Record*, Vol. XV, No. 1–2 (1995), p. 23. (See the other reviews, pp. 23–7.)

23 Susannah Clapp, *Observer,* 27 September 1998, *Theatre Record*, Vol. XVIII, No. 19 (1998), p. 1241.

24 'Roy and Indhu', programme note, Tricycle Theatre, *Starstruck*, 1998. V&A Theatre and Performance collections.

25 Lyn Gardner, *Guardian,* 5 October 1998, *Theatre Record,* Vol. XVIII, No. 19 (1998), p. 1240.

26 Michael Billington, *Guardian*, 18 October 2000, *Theatre Record*, Vol. XX, No. 21 (2000), p. 1357; Lauren Booth, *New Statesman,* 12 March 2001, www.newstatesman.com/200103120038 (accessed 27 June 2007).

27 *One Under* played from February through March.

28 Charles Spencer, *Daily Telegraph*, 12 February 2005, *Theatre Record*, Vol. XXV, No. 3 (2005), p. 163. *One Under* is discussed by Elizabeth Sakellaridou in her chapter on Winsome Pinnock in *The Methuen Drama Guide to Contemporary British Playwrights*, Martin Middeke, Peter Paul Schnierer and Aleks Sierz (eds), London: Methuen Drama, 2011, pp. 383–402. Sakellaridou also refers to the Spencer review.

29 Quoted in Nick Curtis, 'Making a small theatre talk loud', *Evening Standard*, 22 November 2005.

30 Marcell told me about an earlier ensemble for a season of plays called Plays Umbrella, directed by Peter Gill at the Riverside in 1980.

31 See Loften Mitchell, *Voices of the Black Theatre*, Clifton, NJ: James T. White & Co., 1975, pp. 117, 147. This is in a section titled 'A Voice: Abram Hill'.

32 In the African American season section (and quote, p. 1), an edited version of my interview material with Holdbrook-Smith appeared in Kobna Holdbrook-Smith in conversation with Terry Stoller, 'What is Black Theatre? The African-American Season at the Tricycle Theatre', *New Theatre Quarterly*, Vol. 23, No. 3, Cambridge University Press, 2007, pp. 241–52. Reprinted with permission. The play synopses for *Walk Hard, Gem*, and *Fabulation* are adapted from the sidebar.

33 Steve Bloomfield, *Independent on Sunday*, 4 December 2005; Michael Billington, *Guardian*, 29 November 2005, *Theatre Record*, Vol. XXV, No. 24 (2005), pp. 1571, 1569.

34 The remount was with a new cast, with the exception of Jenny Jules as Undine and Clare Perkins as Mother/Caseworker/Inmate 1. Karl Collins played Hervé/Guy in the remount.

35 Rachel Halliburton, *Time Out London*, 27 September 2006, *Theatre Record*, Vol. XXVI, No. 19 (2006), p. 1016.

36 Kwei-Armah wrote an article prior to the opening of *Statement of Regret* at the Cottesloe about black actors leaving Britain to work in the United States. (See Kwei-Armah, 'Bringing it home', newstatesman.com, 25 October 2007.)

37 'James Purnell: You Ask The Questions', *Independent*, 28 January 2008, www.independent.co.uk/news/people/james-purnell-you-ask-the-questions-774871.html (accessed 30 January 2008).

38 Michael Coveney, *Independent*, 4 November 2009, *Theatre Record*, Vol. XXIX, No. 22 (2009), p. 1174.

39 Charles Spencer, *Daily Telegraph*, 2 December 2009, *Theatre Record*, Vol. XXIX, No. 24 (2009), p. 1279.

40 The Best Actor in a Musical Award was given to the whole cast.

41 David Kramer, programme note, Tricycle Theatre, *Kat and the Kings*, 2003. V&A Theatre and Performance collections.

42 Nick Curtis, *Evening Standard*, 3 October 1997, *Theatre Record*, Vol. XVII, No. 20 (1997), p. 1265.

43 See David Kramer, 'My memories of Taliep Petersen', *Guardian* Theatre Blog, 18 December 2006, www.guardian.co.uk/stage/theatreblog/2006/dec/18/memoriesoftalieppetersen (accessed 21 January 2011).

3: Irish theatre at the Tricycle

1 *Kilburn Times*, 27 September 1985, Tricycle Theatre (in-house) press archives.

2 Programme information, Tricycle Theatre, *Flann O'Brien's Hard Life*, 1985. V&A Theatre and Performance collections. (Note: the copy is slightly different in the flyer, but the sentiment is the same. The bracketed word is from the flyer.)

3 Michael Coveney, *Financial Times,* 1 October 1985; Helen Rose, *Time Out*, 3 October 1985; Anthony Denselow, BBC Radio London, 5 October 1985, *London Theatre Record*, Vol. V, No. 20 (1985), pp. 972–3.

4 See Eamon Morrissey, programme essay, Tricycle Theatre, *And the Brother Too . . .*, 1999. V&A Theatre and Performance collections.

5 Christina Reid, *Joyriders* in *Christina Reid Plays: 1*, London: Methuen Drama, 1997, p. 102.

6 Programme information, Paines Plough at the Tricycle Theatre, *Joyriders*, 1986. V&A Theatre and Performance collections.

7 Programme cover, Tricycle Theatre, *The Hostage*, 1986. V&A Theatre and Performance collections.

8 Mark Sanderson, *Time Out*, 15 October 1986, *London Theatre Record*, Vol. VI, No. 21 (1986), p. 1126.

9 Martin Hoyle, *Financial Times,* 14 October 1986, *London Theatre Record*, Vol. VI, No. 21 (1986), p. 1127.

10 Sanderson, *Time Out,* p. 1126.

11 *Hampstead and Highgate Express*, 28 November 1986, Tricycle Theatre (in-house) press archives.

12 Keith Nurse, *Daily Telegraph,* 15 October 1986, *London Theatre Record,* Vol. VI, No. 21 (1986), p. 1126.

13 Nicolas Kent, programme essay, Tricycle Theatre at the Lyric Studio, *Pentecost,* 1989. V&A Theatre and Performance collections.

14 See Sabine Durrant, 'Interview: Brothers in arts', *Independent,* 8 January 1990, www.lexisnexis.com (accessed 5 October 2010).

15 Charles Spencer, *Daily Telegraph,* 20 December 1991, *Theatre Record,* Vol. XI, No. 25–6 (1991), p. 1546.

16 Quoted in John O'Mahony, 'Guns N' Rosaries', *Guardian,* 7 April 1993, www.lexisnexis.com (accessed 10 October 2009).

17 Malcolm Rutherford, *Financial Times,* 20 April 1993; Nicholas de Jongh, *Evening Standard,* 19 April 1993, *Theatre Record,* Vol. XIII, No. 8 (1993), pp. 421–2. Benedict Nightingale, 'Memories of a troubled past', *Times,* 20 February 1996, www.lexisnexis.com (accessed 17 July 2008).

18 Kate Bassett, *Daily Telegraph,* 6 April 1998, *Theatre Record,* Vol. XVIII, No. 7 (1998), p. 432.

19 See Afterword to Billy Roche, *The Wexford Trilogy,* London: Nick Hern Books, 2000, p. 187.

20 Michael Billington, *Guardian,* 24 September 2002, *Theatre Record,* Vol. XXII, No. 19 (2002), p. 1238.

21 The other cast members for *The Field* were Ross Finbow, Rita Hamill, John O'Toole, Eamonn Owens, Tony Rohr, Tom Vaughan-Lawlor, Jean-Paul Van Cauwelaert and John Watts.

22 Charles Spencer, *Daily Telegraph,* 27 November 2007, *Theatre Record,* Vol. XXVII, No. 24 (2007), p. 1425.

23 Matt Wolf, 'Feted in New York, trashed in London', *Guardian* Theatre Blog, 26 November 2007, www.guardian.co.uk/stage/theatreblog/2007/ nov/26/fetedinnewyorktrashedinl (accessed 3 March 2009).

4: The verbatim and political plays

1 Most of the Nicolas Kent interview material in this introduction and in the sections on *Guantanamo* and *Bloody Sunday* was previously

published in my article 'Tribunals at the Tricycle' (Stoller, March 2005) on HotReview.org. The rest of the Kent interview material is from my subsequent interviews with him.

2 Introduction to Richard Norton-Taylor with Mark Lloyd, *Truth Is a Difficult Concept: Inside the Scott Inquiry*, London: Fourth Estate Limited, 1995, p. 13.

3 The former Foreign Office official was David Gore-Booth. The programme indicates that Sir Robin Butler, cabinet secretary, also used the phrase with regard to answering questions in Parliament. Programme information, Tricycle Theatre, *Half the Picture*, 1994. V&A Theatre and Performance collections.

4 Subsequent to our interview, Thomas Wheatley wrote a memoir, J. G. Wheatley, *At Liberty*, London, privately published, 2009, in which he discusses his work in the tribunal plays.

5 Patrick Marmion, *What's On*, 22 June 1994, *Theatre Record*, Vol. XIV, No. 12 (1994), p. 743.

6 John Peter, *Sunday Times*, 19 June 1994, *Theatre Record*, Vol. XIV, No. 12 (1994), p. 743.

7 Irving Wardle, *Independent on Sunday*, 19 June 1994, *Theatre Record*, Vol. XIV, No. 12 (1994), p. 742.

8 Our conversation was in 2006, before the Chilcot Iraq Inquiry hearings in 2009–11 and the Leveson Inquiry hearings in 2011–2, portions of which were broadcast.

9 Charles Spencer, *Daily Telegraph*, 11 May 1996, *Theatre Record*, Vol. XVI, No. 10 (1996), p. 600.

10 Both men were able to elude arrest for many years. Karadzic was finally arrested in 2008 and Mladic in 2011.

11 See 'The Background to Srebrenica' and 'Characters' in Nicolas Kent, *Srebrenica*, London: Oberon Books, 2005, p. 10, p. 21.

12 Jane Edwardes, *Time Out*, 16 October 1996; John Peter, *Sunday Times*, 20 October 1996, *Theatre Record*, Vol. XVI, No. 21 (1996), pp. 1322–3.

13 Charles Spencer, *Daily Telegraph*, 15 January 1999, *Theatre Record*, Vol. XIX, No. 1–2 (1999), p. 43.

14 See Michael Billington, *Guardian*, 14 January 1999, *Theatre Record*, Vol. XIX, No. 1–2 (1999), p. 40.

15 'Conclusion and Summary', Chapter Forty-Six, 46.1, 'The Stephen Lawrence Inquiry', www.archive.official-documents.co.uk/document/cm42/4262/sli-46.htm (accessed 26 May 2010).

16 See Richard Eyre and Nicholas Wright, *Changing Stages: A View of British Theatre in the Twentieth Century*, London: Bloomsbury, 2000, pp. 395–6. See Michael Billington, *State of the Nation: British Theatre Since 1945*, London: Faber and Faber, 2007, pp. 385–6.

17 See 'Radio 4 Today Programme, May 29th 2003, Andrew Gilligan Piece', BBC/1/0004, the Hutton Inquiry website, www.the-hutton-inquiry.org.uk (accessed 2 June 2010). (This broadcast is discussed in the play.)

18 'In the Matter of Applications by ITN, BSkyB, Channel 4, Channel 5, ITV and IRN Radio: Ruling by Lord Hutton, 5 August 2003', p. 1 (3), p. 6 (25), the Hutton Inquiry website, www.the-hutton-inquiry.org.uk/content/rulings/ruling01.htm (accessed 29 May 2010).

19 Richard Norton-Taylor (ed.), *Justifying War: Scenes from the Hutton Inquiry*, London: Oberon Books, 2003, p. 19.

20 Kent says: 'We started those large programme booklets ages ago. When we do a big inquiry, I've always insisted that the programme is a good accompaniment to seeing the play. And people know that, and they seem willing to buy the whole programme book, and they take it home and read it.'

21 Norton-Taylor, *Justifying War*, pp. 49, 54. Norton-Taylor also appeared at the inquiry and was questioned about how he came up with Dr Kelly's identity for the *Guardian*. His testimony is not in the play.

22 Charles Spencer, *Daily Telegraph*, 6 November 2003; Paul Taylor, *Independent*, 6 November 2003; Michael Coveney, *Daily Mail*, 5 November 2003, *Theatre Record*, Vol. XXIII, No. 22 (2003), pp. 1480–2.

23 Taylor, *Independent*, p. 1481.

24 'Summary of Conclusions', Report by Lord Hutton, The Hutton Inquiry, Chapter 12, 467, 3, i–iv, www.the-hutton-inquiry.org.uk/content/report/chapter12.htm#a90 (accessed 5 July 2012).

25 Quoted in Matt Foot, 'Women on the Front Line: Keeping Torture at Bay', *Socialist Review*, June 2004, www.socialistreview.org.uk/article.php?articlenumber=8926 (accessed 18 September 2006).

26 The subtitle refers to a sign outside Camp X-Ray.

27 My synopsis is adapted from my review, 'Injustice Is Served' (Stoller, September 2004), on HotReview.org.

28 The play doesn't relate how Ruhel Ahmed got to Guantánamo. Michael Winterbottom made a film about the Tipton Three titled *The Road to Guantanamo* (2006).

29 Nicholas de Jongh, *Evening Standard*, 25 May 2004, *Theatre Record*, Vol. XXIV, No. 11 (2004), p. 683.

30 Alastair Macaulay, *Financial Times*, 26 May 2004; Charles Spencer, *Daily Telegraph*, 25 May 2004, *Theatre Record*, Vol. XXIV, No. 11 (2004), pp. 683–5.

31 Benedict Nightingale, *Times*, 25 May 2004, *Theatre Record*, Vol. XXIV, No. 11 (2004), pp. 685–6.

32 Quoted in Fiona Maddocks, 'All anyone is asking for is a fair trial', *Evening Standard*, 18 June 2004, www.lexisnexis.com (accessed 21 March 2010).

33 See www.bordc.org/grp.

34 'Prime Minister's Statement', 29 January 1998, House of Commons Official Report, Parliamentary Debates (Hansard), reprinted in 'Inquiry Background', Bloody Sunday Inquiry website, www.bloody-sunday-inquiry. org/inquiry-background/ (accessed 22 June 2010). The Widgery Report found that the soldiers had been shot at before they opened fire and that there was a 'strong suspicion' that some of the deceased had fired weapons or handled bombs that day. (Per 'Prime Minister's Statement', which is also reprinted in the *Bloody Sunday* programme.)

35 Programme glossary, Tricycle Theatre, *Bloody Sunday*, 2005.

36 Richard Norton-Taylor (ed.), *Bloody Sunday: Scenes from the Saville Inquiry*, London: Oberon Books, 2005, p. 63.

37 Ibid., p. 31.

38 Ibid., p. 72.

39 Although, as the programme notes, BBC TV had co-commissioned the play, they decided not to televise the production, per Nicolas Kent.

40 Report of the Bloody Sunday Inquiry, Vol. 1, Chapter 5, 'The Overall Assessment', 5.5, www.webarchive.nationalarchives.gov. uk/20101103103930/http://report.bloody-sunday-inquiry.org/volume01/ chapter005/ (accessed 5 July 2012).

41 The prime minister (Mr David Cameron), 'Saville Inquiry', House of Commons, 15 June 2010. www.publications.parliament.uk/pa/cm201011/ cmhansrd/cm100615/debtext/100615–0004.htm#10061522000002 (accessed 8 July 2012).

42　Nicolas Kent and Richard Norton-Taylor, programme note, Tricycle Theatre, *Called to Account*, 2007. They also write that two of the witnesses gave evidence in conference calls. [I previously wrote about *Called to Account* in 'Crimes of the PM', a review for HotReview.org (Stoller, May 2007).]

43　Richard Norton-Taylor (ed.), *Called to Account: The Indictment of Anthony Charles Lynton Blair for the Crime of Aggression Against Iraq – A Hearing*, London: Oberon Books, 2007, p. 10.

44　Ibid., p. 52.

45　Ibid., p. 32.

46　Charles Spencer, *Daily Telegraph*, 24 April 2007; Jane Edwardes, *Time Out London*, 2 May 2007, *Theatre Record*, Vol. XXVII, No. 9 (2007), pp. 490, 493.

47　Richard Norton-Taylor (ed.), *Tactical Questioning: Scenes from the Baha Mousa Inquiry*, London: Oberon Books, 2011, pp. 15–6.

48　Ibid., p. 17.

49　Mercer has since left the army, and is now a member of the clergy.

50　Norton-Taylor, *Tactical Questioning*, p. 69.

51　Ibid., p. 79.

52　'Statement by Chairman', transcript, p. 23, www.bahamousainquiry. org/report/index (accessed 17 May 2012). See Part XVIII for the recommendations.

53　Programme note, Tricycle Theatre, *The Riots*, 2011.

54　See 'Rioters Get a Voice' in 'Mailbag', *Inside Time*, October 2011, www.insidetime.org/mailbag.asp?a=566&c=rioters_get_a_voice (accessed 17 May 2012).

55　Gillian Slovo, *The Riots*, London: Oberon Books, 2011, p. 14.

56　Kate Bassett in 'West End Review: New Plays Special', Reviews and Roundtables, 26 November 2011, TheatreVOICE, www.theatrevoice. com/7351 (accessed 13 December 2011).

57　Slovo, *The Riots*, p. 42.

58　Ibid., p. 50.

59　'Manchester Riots: Doughnut Thief Jailed for 16 Months', BBC News Manchester, 18 August 2011, www.bbc.co.uk/news/ uk-england-manchester-14573000 (accessed 18 May 2012).

60 J. T. Rogers withdrew his play about the US arming the mujahideen from *The Great Game* remount and tour. An expanded version of *Blood and Gifts* was produced at the National Theatre in autumn 2010 and opened at Lincoln Center in New York City in autumn 2011. *Wood for the Fire* by Lee Blessing, which replaced *Blood and Gifts* at the Tricycle in 2010, also dealt with America arming the mujahideen, but the emphasis was on Pakistan's role as a go-between.

61 Nicolas Kent, programme note, Tricycle Theatre, *The Great Game*, 2009. Kent wrote that the Darfur project and the *Love Song for Ulster* trilogy served as his 'template'.

62 The title refers to Britain and Russia going after power in Central Asia in the nineteenth century. I previously synopsised *Great Game* in 'Designing *The Great Game*: A Conversation with Pamela Howard' (Stoller, July 2009) on HotReview. Except where otherwise indicated, Pamela Howard's interview material is from that interview.

63 The 2009 cast was: Sagar Arya, Daniel Betts, Paul Bhattacharjee, Sheena Bhattessa, Lolita Chakrabarti, Michael Cochrane, Nabil Elouahabi, Vincent Ebrahim, Tom McKay, Danny Rahim, Jemma Redgrave, Jemima Rooper, Hugh Skinner, Ramon Tikaram, Rick Warden. The 2010 cast was: Daniel Betts, Sheena Bhattessa, Michael Cochrane, Karl Davies, Vincent Ebrahim, Nabil Elouahabi, Shereen Martineau, Tom McKay, Daniel Rabin, Danny Rahim, Raad Rawi, Jemma Redgrave, Cloudia Swann, Rick Warden.

64 Pamela Howard, e-mail to author, 3 July 2009.

65 Ron Hutchinson, *Durand's Line* in *The Great Game: Afghanistan*, London: Oberon Books, 2009, p. 39.

66 See www.liberty-human-rights.org.uk/about/human-rights-awards/index.php (accessed 25 May 2012).

67 Michael Billington, *Guardian*, 25 April 2009, *Theatre Record*, Vol. XXIX, No. 9 (2009), p. 455.

68 Kate Bassett, *Independent on Sunday*, 3 May 2009; Christopher Hart, *Sunday Times,* 3 May 2009, *Theatre Record*, Vol. XXIX, No. 9 (2009), pp. 458–9.

69 Charles Spencer, *Daily Telegraph*, 23 February 2012; Matt Trueman, *Time Out London*, 23 February 2012, *Theatre Record*, Vol. XXXII, No. 4 (2012), pp. 167–8.

70 See Nicolas Kent, programme essay, Tricycle Theatre, *The Bomb*, 2012.

71 The 11 actors were: Nathalie Armin, Paul Bhattacharjee, Simon Chandler, Michael Cochrane, Tariq Jordan, Belinda Lang, Shereen Martin, Daniel Rabin, Simon Rouse, Rick Warden, David Yip. Kent directed all the plays except for *Option* by Amit Gupta and *Axis* by Diana Son, which were both directed by Tara Robinson.

5: Dressing-room stories and encores

1 Benedict Nightingale, *Times*, 23 January 1998, *Theatre Record*, Vol. XVIII, No. 1–2 (1998), p. 62.

BIBLIOGRAPHY

Interviews (by the author, tape recorded)

Abbensetts, Michael, London, 19 July 2010.
Bailey, Marion, London, 20 September 2007.
Barrie, Shirley, telephone, 25 March 2008; 7 December 2010.
Black, Pauline, telephone, 29 April 2008.
Chappell, Jan, London, 22 July 2010.
Christie, Gillian, London, 2 October 2006.
Chubb, Ken, telephone, 25 March 2008; 7 December 2010.
Connaughton, Shane, telephone, 31 July 2008.
Crabbe, Kerry Lee, London, 23 January 2007.
Croll, Dona, telephone, 9 January 2012.
Crowley, Dermot, telephone, 17 April 2008.
Duncan-Brewster, Sharon, London, 20 April 2009.
Foster, Tim, London, 22 January 2007.
Fox, Christopher, London, 24 June 2011.
Fox, Clare, London, 10 July 2007.
Freeman, Lucy, London, 14 June 2006.
Ganly, David, telephone, 21 August 2008.
Gébler, Carlo, telephone, 26 June 2007.
Hanafin, Terry, telephone, 2 February 2011.
Holdbrook-Smith, Kobna, London, 17 June 2006; 29 April 2010.
Honour, Philip, telephone, 18 October 2007.
Howard, Pamela, New York City, 25 May 2009.
Hoyland, William, London, 15 June 2006.
Ingenhaag, Zoe, London, 5 March 2012.
Jordan, Tariq, telephone, 21 October 2007; London, 7 March 2012.
Jules, Jenny, London, 9 July 2007.
Keely, Caroline, London, 17 January 2008.
Kent, Nicolas, London, 12 January 2005, 17 January 2006; telephone,
    11 September 2006; London, 15 January 2008, 18 June 2008; New York City,
    11 December 2010; London, 7 March 2012.
Kwei-Armah, Kwame, telephone, 24 February 2008.
Lauder, Mary, London, 18 June 2006; 9 July 2007.

Lloyd, Errol, London, 6 October 2006.
Marcell, Joseph, telephone, 11 November 2007.
McElhill, Trish, London, 12 June 2006.
McGee, Shaz, London, 16 June 2006.
Michaels, David, London, 25 June 2011.
Molloy, Dearbhla, New York City, 24 February 2009.
Molyneux, Andrée, London, 16 January 2008.
Mortimer, Terry, telephone, 13 July 2010.
Noble, Cecilia, London, 7 December 2009.
Norton-Taylor, Richard, London, 17 January 2008.
O'Hanlon, Sarah, London, 16 January 2008.
Parnaby, Alan, telephone, 14 July 2011; 6 February 2012.
Phillips, Anton, London, 13 June 2006.
Pinnock, Winsome, London, 4 July 2007.
Rabin, Daniel, telephone, 22 March 2012.
Randall, Paulette, London, 10 July 2007.
Rasalingam, Selva, telephone, 26 January 2012.
Rhule, Rod, London, 13 June 2006.
Richardson, Joy, London, 23 July 2010.
Roche, Billy, telephone, 14 November 2009.
Rubasingham, Indhu, London, 22 January 2007.
Ryder, Marlene, London, 18 June 2006.
Shell, Ray, London, 14 June 2006.
Spooner, Claire, London, 12 June 2006.
Taylor, David, New York City, 3 August 2010.
Tobias, Heather, London, 3 October 2006.
Topolski, Tessa, London, 9 July 2007; 18 September 2007.
Warden, Rick, New York City, 15 December 2010; London, 23 June 2011, 6 March 2012.
Westenra, Charlotte, London, 20 June 2006.
Wheatley, Thomas, London, 6 October 2006.
Williams, Claudette, London, 4 October 2006.
Woolley, James, London, 22 September 2007.

Correspondence (to the author)

Cochrane, Michael, 19 August 2006.
Cook, Martin, 10 July 2011 (e-mail).
Tobias, Heather, 22 November 2006.

Playscripts

Abbensetts, Michael, *Samba*, London: Eyre Methuen, 1980.

Agbaje, Bola, *Detaining Justice* in *Not Black & White*, London: Methuen Drama, 2009, pp. 185–269.

Antrobus, John, *Why Bournemouth?* in *Playscript 7: 'Why Bournemouth?' & Other Plays*, London: Calder and Boyars, 1970, pp. 9–48.

Baldwin, James, *The Amen Corner*, New York: Vintage International, 1998.

— *Blues for Mister Charlie*, New York: Samuel French, 1964.

Bean, Richard, *On the Side of the Angels* in *The Great Game: Afghanistan*, London: Oberon Books, 2009, pp. 213–27.

Behan, Brendan, *The Hostage*, London: Methuen Drama, 1958, 1959, 1962, 2000.

— *The Quare Fellow* in John P. Harrington (ed.), *Modern Irish Drama*, New York and London: W. W. Norton & Co., 1991, pp. 255–310.

Behan, Brian, *Boots for the Footless*, prompt script, 1990, V&A Theatre and Performance collections; playscript, 1990, British Library, MPS 4361.

Blessing, Lee, *Seven Joys* in *The Bomb—A Partial History*, London: Oberon Books, 2012, pp. 51–75.

— *Wood for the Fire* in *The Great Game: Afghanistan*, London: Oberon Books, 2010, pp. 105–25.

Brittain, Victoria and Gillian Slovo, *Guantanamo: 'Honor Bound to Defend Freedom'*, London: Oberon Books, 2004.

Carter, Steve, *Pecong*, New York: Broadway Play Publishing, 1993.

Childress, Alice, *Wine in the Wilderness* in James V. Hatch (ed.), *Black Theater, U.S.A.: Forty-Five Plays by Black Americans, 1847–1974*, New York: Free Press, 1974, pp. 738–55.

Connaughton, Shane, *I Do Like to Be*, 1977, British Library, MPS 665.

Crabbe, Kerry, *Flann O'Brien's Hard Life*, 1985, British Library, MPS 2956.

Craig, Ryan, *Talk Talk Fight Fight* in *The Bomb—A Partial History*, London: Oberon Books, 2012, pp. 173–98.

Donnelly, John, *Little Russians* in *The Bomb—A Partial History*, London: Oberon Books, 2012, pp. 103–32.

Edgar, David, *Black Tulips* in *The Great Game: Afghanistan*, London: Oberon Books, 2009, pp. 82–100.

Fagon, Alfred, *Lonely Cowboy* in *Black Plays*, selected and introduced by Yvonne Brewster, London and New York: Methuen, 1987, pp. 31–67.

Gébler, Carlo, *Dance of Death, Parts I & II*, Belfast: Lagan Press, 2000.

— *10 Rounds*, Belfast: Lagan Press, 2002.

Greig, David, *The Letter of Last Resort* in *The Bomb—A Partial History*, London: Oberon Books, 2012, pp. 199–228.

— *Miniskirts of Kabul* in *The Great Game: Afghanistan*, London: Oberon Books, 2009, pp. 123–45.

Gupta, Amit, *Campaign* in *The Great Game: Afghanistan*, London: Oberon Books, 2009, pp. 49–61.

— *Option* in *The Bomb—A Partial History*, London: Oberon Books, 2012, pp. 77–101.

Harris, Zinnie, *From Elsewhere: The Message . . .* in *The Bomb—A Partial History*, London: Oberon Books, 2012, pp. 15–29.

— *From Elsewhere: On the Watch . . .* in *The Bomb—A Partial History*, London: Oberon Books, 2012, pp. 229–39.

Hill, Abram, *Walk Hard* in James V. Hatch (ed.), *Black Theater, U.S.A.: Forty-Five Plays by Black Americans, 1847–1974*, New York: Free Press, 1974, pp. 439–71.

How Long Is Never? Darfur—A Response, London: Josef Weinberger, 2007.

Hutchinson, Ron, *Calculated Risk* in *The Bomb—A Partial History*, London: Oberon Books, 2012, pp. 31–50.

— *Durand's Line* in *The Great Game: Afghanistan*, London: Oberon Books, 2009, pp. 31–48.

Jeffreys, Stephen, *Bugles at the Gates of Jalalabad* in *The Great Game: Afghanistan*, London: Oberon Books, 2009, pp. 15–29.

Jones, Marie, *Stones in His Pockets* & *A Night in November*, London: Nick Hern Books, 2000.

Keane, John B., *The Field* in Ben Barnes (ed.), *Three Plays,* new rev. texts, Cork: Mercier Press, 1990, pp. 91–167.

Kent, Nicolas, *Srebrenica*, London: Oberon Books, 2005.

Kramer, David and Taliep Petersen, *Kat and the Kings*, 1997, British Library, MPS 7861.

Kwei-Armah, Kwame, *Let There Be Love* in *Kwame Kwei-Armah Plays: 1*, London: Methuen Drama, 2009, pp. 257–330.

— *Seize the Day* in *Not Black & White*, London: Methuen Drama, 2009, pp. 103–83.

Mason, Bob, *Love in Vain*, prompt script, 1982, V&A Theatre and Performance collections; playscript, 1982, British Library, MPS 1539.

Matura, Mustapha, *Playboy of the West Indies*, New York: Broadway Play Publishing, 1988.

McGuinness, Frank, *The Factory Girls*, 2nd rev. ed., London: Wolfhound Press, 1988.

Mitchell, Gary, *As the Beast Sleeps*, London: Nick Hern Books, 2001.

Morgan, Abi, *The Night Is Darkest Before the Dawn* in *The Great Game: Afghanistan*, London: Oberon Books, 2009, pp. 191–212.

Morrison, Bill, *A Love Song for Ulster: An Irish Trilogy*, London: Nick Hern Books, 1994.

Murphy, Tom, *A Whistle in the Dark*, London: Methuen Drama, 2001.

Norton-Taylor, Richard (ed.), *Bloody Sunday: Scenes from the Saville Inquiry*, London: Oberon Books, 2005.

— *Called to Account: The Indictment of Anthony Charles Lynton Blair for the Crime of Aggression Against Iraq—A Hearing*, London: Oberon Books, 2007.

— *The Colour of Justice*, London: Oberon Books, 1999.

— *Justifying War: Scenes from the Hutton Inquiry*, London: Oberon Books, 2003.

— *Nuremberg—The War Crimes Trial*, London: Nick Hern Books, 1997.

— *Tactical Questioning: Scenes from the Baha Mousa Inquiry*, London: Oberon Books, 2011.

— and John McGrath, *Half the Picture* in Richard Norton-Taylor with Mark Lloyd, *Truth Is a Difficult Concept: Inside the Scott Inquiry*, London: Fourth Estate, 1995, pp. 213–74.

Nottage, Lynn, *Fabulation or, the Re-Education of Undine*, New York: Dramatists Play Service, 2005.

Ockrent, Ben, *Honey* in *The Great Game: Afghanistan*, London: Oberon Books, 2009, pp. 169–90.

O'Malley, Mary, *Once a Catholic*, Oxon: Amber Lane Press, 1978, 2004.

Parker, Stewart, *Pentecost* in *Stewart Parker Plays: 2*, London: Methuen Drama, 2000, pp. 169–245.

Phillips, Caryl, *All or Nothing at All*, 1989, British Library, MPS 4279.

Pinnock, Winsome, *One Under*, London: Faber and Faber, 2005.

— *Water*, rehearsal script, 2001, V&A Theatre and Performance collections; playscript, 2000, British Library, MPS 9296.

Reid, Christina, *Joyriders* in *Christina Reid Plays: 1*, London: Methuen Drama, 1997, pp. 99–176.

Rhone, Trevor, *Smile Orange*, prompt script, 1983, V&A Theatre and Performance collections.

Roche, Billy, *The Cavalcaders*, London: Nick Hern Books, 1994.

— *The Wexford Trilogy*, London: Nick Hern Books, 2000.

Rogers, J. T., *Blood and Gifts* in *The Great Game: Afghanistan*, London: Oberon Books, 2009, pp. 101–21.

Sackler, Howard, *The Great White Hope*, New York: Samuel French, 1968.

Shanley, John Patrick, *Doubt: A Parable*, New York: Theatre Communications Group, 2005.

Shaw, Bernard, *John Bull's Other Island* in John P. Harrington (ed.), *Modern Irish Drama*, New York and London: W. W. Norton & Co., 1991, pp. 119–203.

Slovo, Gillian, *The Riots*, London: Oberon Books, 2011.

Son, Diana, *Axis* in *The Bomb—A Partial History*, London: Oberon Books, 2012, pp. 157–71.

Stephens, Simon, *Canopy of Stars* in *The Great Game: Afghanistan*, London: Oberon Books, 2009, pp. 229–49.

Teevan, Colin, *The Lion of Kabul* in *The Great Game: Afghanistan*, London: Oberon Books, 2009, pp. 147–65.

— *There Was a Man, There Was No Man* in *The Bomb—A Partial History*, London: Oberon Books, 2012, pp. 133–56.

Walcott, Derek, *Remembrance* in *Remembrance & Pantomime: Two Plays*, New York: Farrar, Straus and Giroux, 1980, pp. 1–87.

Williams, Roy, *Category B* in *Not Black & White*, London: Methuen Drama, 2009, pp. 1–102.

— *Starstruck* in *Roy Williams Plays: 1*, London: Methuen Drama, 2002, pp. 73–159.

Wilson, August, *Gem of the Ocean*, New York: Theatre Communications Group, 2003, 2006.

— *King Hedley II*, New York: Theatre Communications Group, 2005.

— *Joe Turner's Come and Gone*, New York: Plume, Penguin Books, 1988.

— *The Piano Lesson*, New York: Plume, Penguin Books, 1990.

— *Radio Golf*, New York: Theatre Communications Group, 2007.

Audio recordings

Ain't Misbehavin': The Fats Waller Musical Show, London Cast Recording, First Night Records, 1995 [on CD].

Kramer, David and Taliep Petersen, *Kat and the Kings*, First Night Records, 1998 [on CD].

Video recordings: V&A Theatre and Performance collections

The Colour of Justice, Tricycle Theatre, 1999.

John Bull's Other Island, Tricycle Theatre, 2003.

The Marriage; The Son; The Daughter (*A Love for Ulster* trilogy), Tricycle Theatre, 1993.

A Night in November, Tricycle Theatre, 2002.
Water and *Wine in the Wilderness*, Tricycle Theatre, 2001.

Video recordings: Tricycle Theatre (in-house) collection

Half the Picture, copy of TV production, 1996; *Justifying War*, 2003; *Nuremberg*, 1996; *Srebrenica*, 1996.

Archives consulted

Brent Archives, Willesden Green Library Centre: Tricycle Theatre materials: LHC1/ENT/2; clippings (Entertainments); Tricycle Theatre programmes, 2010/2.
Tricycle Theatre (in-house) archives: press clippings, programmes, attendance records.
V&A Theatre and Performance collections: Tricycle Theatre Archives, 1972–2004, THM/317 and Tricycle Theatre programmes.

Secondary sources consulted

Journals

Plays and Players, 1968–83.
Theatre Quarterly, 1971–3.

Select books and articles consulted

Ansorge, Peter, *Disrupting the Spectacle: Five Years of Experimental and Fringe Theatre in Britain*, London: Pitman, 1975.
Billington, Michael, *State of the Nation: British Theatre Since 1945*, London: Faber and Faber, 2007.
Bradwell, Mike, *The Reluctant Escapologist: Adventures in Alternative Theatre*, London: Nick Hern Books, 2010.
— (ed.), *The Bush Theatre Book*, London: Methuen Drama, 1997.
Colloms, Marianne and Dick Weindling, *Images of London: Kilburn and Cricklewood*, Stroud, Gloucestershire: Tempus, 2001, 2003.

Craig, Sandy (ed.), *Dreams and Deconstructions: Alternative Theatre in Britain*, Ambergate, Derbyshire: Amber Lane Press, 1980.

Elsom, John, *Post-War British Theatre*, London, Boston and Henley: Routledge & Kegan Paul, 1976, 1979.

Ewans, Martin, *Afghanistan: A Short History of Its People and Politics*, New York: HarperCollins, 2002.

Forsyth, Alison and Chris Megson (eds), *Get Real: Documentary Theatre Past and Present*, Basingstoke, Hampshire: Palgrave Macmillan, 2009.

Griffiths, Trevor R., *The Theatre Guide: A Comprehensive A-Z of the World's Best Plays and Playwrights,* 3rd edn, London: A&C Black, 2003.

Hammond, Will and Dan Steward (eds), *Verbatim Verbatim*, London: Oberon Books, 2008.

Itzin, Catherine, *Stages in the Revolution: Political Theatre in Britain Since 1968*, London: Eyre Methuen, 1980.

— (ed.), *British Alternative Theatre Directory: 1981*, Eastbourne, East Sussex: John Offord, 1981.

Lawrence, Doreen, *And Still I Rise: A Mother's Search for Justice*, London: Faber and Faber, 2006.

Lonergan, Patrick, 'Speaking Out', *Irish Theatre*, 5(23) (2005), pp. 26–34.

O'Brien, Flann, *The Various Lives of Keats and Chapman and The Brother*, London: Scribner/TownHouse, 2003.

Rashid, Ahmed, *Taliban: Militant Islam, Oil and Fundamentalism in Central Asia*, 2nd edn, New York and London: Yale University Press, 2000, 2010.

Rees, Roland, *Fringe First: Pioneers of Fringe Theatre on Record*, London: Oberon Books, 1992.

Reinelt, Janelle, 'Toward a Poetics of Theatre and Public Events: In the Case of Stephen Lawrence', *TDR/The Drama Review*, 50(3) (2006), pp. 69–87.

Shellard, Dominic, *British Theatre Since the War*, New Haven and London: Yale University Press, 1999.

Trussler, Simon, *Cambridge Illustrated History: British Theatre*, Cambridge: Cambridge University Press, 1994.

Wandor, Michelene, *Post-War British Drama: Looking Back in Gender*, London and New York: Routledge, 2001.

INDEX

Page numbers for figures are in *italics*.